THE DOME

PRINCETON MONOGRAPHS
IN ART AND ARCHAEOLOGY
XXV

BARR FERREE FOUNDATION

PUBLISHED FOR THE
DEPARTMENT OF ART AND ARCHAEOLOGY
PRINCETON UNIVERSITY

THE DOME

A STUDY IN THE HISTORY OF IDEAS

BY E. BALDWIN SMITH

PRINCETON, NEW JERSEY

PRINCETON UNIVERSITY PRESS

PUBLISHED BY PRINCETON UNIVERSITY PRESS,
41 WILLIAM STREET, PRINCETON, NEW JERSEY 08540
IN THE UNITED KINGDOM: PRINCETON UNIVERSITY PRESS, GUILDFORD, SURREY

First Princeton Paperback printing, 1971

LCC 75-160543
ISBN 0-691-00304-1
ISBN 0-691-03875-9 (pbk.)

Clothbound editions of Princeton University Press books are printed on
acid-free paper, and binding materials are chosen for strength and durability.
Paperbacks, while satisfactory for personal collections, are not usually
suitable for library rebinding.

PRINTED IN THE UNITED STATES OF AMERICA
BY PRINCETON UNIVERSITY PRESS, PRINCETON, NEW JERSEY

Merely because this is the first monograph to be published with funds of the Barr Ferree Foundation is not the reason that the author takes so much pleasure in dedicating this book to the memory of Barr Ferree. The real incentive comes from having known him and his great interest in the history of architecture.

This cultivated and learned gentleman devoted much of his life to an appreciation of the arts and a systematic study of the Gothic cathedrals which he particularly admired. Born in 1862, he graduated in 1884 from the University of Pennsylvania where for some years he served as a special lecturer on architectural subjects in its new School of Architecture. Before entering business he became known as a lecturer and, as a result of his addresses delivered at the Brooklyn Institute of Arts and Sciences, he was made President of its department of Architecture and the Fine Arts. In the course of years his articles and interest in cataloguing "the buildings of architectural merit everywhere in the world" resulted in his being the first American writer to be elected to honorary membership in the Royal Institute of British Architects.

All his life, even after he became a successful businessman, he continued to study the arts and compiled an extensive catalogue of the French cathedrals. At the same time he gathered a fine and rare collection of books on mediaeval churches and towns in France, which now forms the nucleus and chief ornament of the Barr Ferree Library at Princeton. During the First World War he gave eloquent expression to his wrath when his beloved cathedrals were attacked and seriously injured. In New York he organized the Pennsylvania Society, now the largest of the state societies in the United States, and from its foundation in 1899 until his death in 1924 he was its Secretary and Director. Because of the patriotic work of the Society and his personal efforts during the war, he was decorated in 1922 with the Grand Cross of the Legion of Honor.

His death, a sudden one, occurred October 14, 1924. In accordance with his wish, however, his estate was converted into a Foundation for the publication of books "on architecture and related topics in the Fine Arts." Thus, the stimulation of intelligent cultivation of the Fine Arts, toward which the sustained effort of his life was directed, now lives on, working through the avenues whereby a University influences its students and the public. The dedication of his books and property to the cause of the Fine Arts in America has become what he wanted—

a lasting memorial of the ultimate indestructibility of his intellectual purpose and spiritual conviction.

PREFACE

THE admission that this book falls short of what it was intended to be is merely a statement of fact and not an apology. There was a time when the author optimistically believed that he could present the major aspects of domical ideology and evolution in one study. That, however, was before the rapidly expanding complexities of the subject and the difficulties of organizing the material in a written form where the ideas would not be reburied under a mass of accumulated evidence had become inescapable factors. Once it had become evident that the dome was not just a utilitarian form of vaulting, which had originated for structural and environmental reasons in some one country, but was primarily a house concept, which had acquired in numerous cultures its shape and imaginative values upon an ancestral shelter long before it was translated for ideological reasons into more permanent and monumental form by means of wood carpentry and masonry, the whole problem of the dome opened up into a comprehensible but infinitely complex chapter in the history of ideas.

After the broad outlines of this evolution from the primitive house had been traced in the various ancient and retarded cultures of Europe, Asia, Africa, and the Americas there arose the disquieting question of to what extent one scholar had the time and equipment to reconstruct the whole development of domical beliefs. The matter of time was settled conclusively when Karl Lehmann's "The Dome of Heaven" showed that no one could expect to enjoy indefinitely a monopoly of domical ideas. The other question remains to be tested now that the scaffolding has been removed and *The Dome* in skeleton form has to stand alone. Since so many of the conclusions are contrary to prevailing opinions, a partial study of the dome, which at least precipitates the major issues, has the advantage of testing out the basic method of approach before it is applied to such controversial aspects of domical evolution as the origin of the Iranian dome and the still more delicate question of whether even ancient Greece did not have its own tradition of a symbolic, wooden dome.

It is difficult to imagine how certain portions of this study could have been written if it had not been for the assistance and cooperation of Glanville Downey, whose wide knowledge of Byzantine literature and Greek architectural usage has made it possible to base much of the essential evidence on the texts. Another contributing factor of great importance, since it necessitated rewriting much of the manuscript, was the publication of André Grabar's *Martyrium*. Had the author's indebtedness been limited to the *Martyrium* the references in the text might have been an adequate acknowledgement. It was when Grabar read his last chapter and encouraged him to publish it, even though it advanced an explanation for the Syrian bema which was quite different from the one Grabar had published, that the author became indebted to the man himself and came to appreciate the generosity of his fine scholarship. The fact that A. M. Friend has listened patiently to the mutterings of a dome-obsessed mind, has read the manuscript and endeavored to protect the author from the dangers of Byzantine liturgies, does not, of course, make him responsible for the unorthodox approach to some of the problems. The author is indebted to Mrs. Estelle Brown for her help in preparing the manuscript and to Miss Rosalie Green for her scholarly care in checking the references.

E. BALDWIN SMITH

Princeton University
April 1949

CONTENTS

CONTENTS

THE DOME

I · DOMICAL ORIGINS

How the dome took shape, where it originated, and why it became the outstanding feature of Byzantine and Islamic architecture are questions which have not been satisfactorily answered either by the *Orient oder Rom* controversy or by the misconceptions implicit in the prevailing theories regarding the origin and purpose of the domical shape.

Ever since the nineteenth century it has been generally believed that the dome, from its inception, was a functional means of vaulting which originated for environmental reasons either in the brick architecture of the Orient or in the masonry construction of the Romans. This effort to trace the dome back to a single place of origin has disregarded the Syro-Palestinian region as a country which should have played an important role in the development and spread of a Christian domical tradition, because the early explorers, such as De Vogüé and Howard Butler, found so few extant domes among the Syrian ruins and because more modern excavators have uncovered no traces of masonry domes on central-type churches before the sixth century.

Even if it were true that the dome had started only as a utilitarian form of roofing and had a neat unilateral development as it spread from Mesopotamia, Persia, or some Hellenistic center in the Roman Empire, it would still be necessary to explain, first, why men had come to build such curvilinear shapes; second, why they came to associate the dome in pagan, Christian and Islamic periods with tombs, memoriae, aediculae, tabernacles, ciboria, baldachins, martyria, baptisteries, churches, fire temples, mosques, and audience halls; third, why the East Christians during the fifth and sixth centuries began to manifest so much interest in the dome as a form of church architecture; and fourth, why the Islamic builders elected to make the dome the dominant feature of their tombs and mosques. All of these questions can be answered in whole or in part by a study of the domical ideology which prevailed in the late antique and Early Christian world and by the existing evidence for the use of the wooden dome in Syria and Palestine.

Between 1935 and 1939 the Princeton Excavations at Antioch-on-the-Orontes uncovered the plans of two important Early Christian churches of the central type—the fourth century martyrium at Kaoussie (Fig. 170), a suburb of Antioch, and the fifth century martyrium at Seleucia Pieria (Fig. 182), the port of Antioch. At the same time the excavators of Gerasa disclosed other churches of the central type. Since it has become apparent that in the cities of Syria and Palestine the churches were far from being all of the basilican type, there arise the questions of how these central-type martyria and churches were roofed and what part they played in the growth of a domical, Christian architecture in the Near East. As long as the dome is thought of only as one kind of functional roofing, it is of relatively little importance whether these Syrian and Palestinian cult houses had pyramidal, conical, or domical roofs of wood or of "light volcanic scoriae," and there is little justification for devoting a whole monograph to a study of the dome and a hypothetical restoration of two Antiochene churches.

3

Actually, however, the dome was of great symbolical interest to the Christians. It was a shape which, regardless of the materials used for its construction, had an antique sepulchral association with memorials to the dead and a long and highly complicated history in various parts of the antique world. Not only is it possible to show that the dome was ideologically an essential feature of the central-type martyrium, but it is also possible to demonstrate why the two Antiochene churches, and other similar Syro-Palestinian churches, must have been roofed with great wooden domes of conoid shape, sheathed in gilded metal, which had a symbolical content in the Christian thought of the period. It is also becoming increasingly evident that the sacred buildings of the Holy Land, with their mosaics, frescoes and illuminated gospels, had a powerful and lasting influence upon all forms of Christian art. Consequently it is difficult to believe that the popularity of the dome on the religious architecture of Byzantium, Armenia, and northern Mesopotamia was not influenced by the revered churches of Palestine.

The necessity of reexamining the prevailing conclusions regarding the origins of Byzantine architecture, and the value of relating the development of domical architecture in the Near East to the history of ideas, are indicated by the fact that the results of a study of domical ideas so closely parallel the conclusions of André Grabar in his *Martyrium*. Although Grabar has not attempted to deal with the problems of the dome in tracing the growing popularity of the martyrium-type church, the dome was peculiarly associated with the martyrium because of its traditional mortuary symbolism. Therefore, because of this relationship and the bearing which some of the domical evidence has upon the pattern of development outlined by Grabar, it is desirable to integrate the two approaches.

It is Grabar's conclusion that the mortuary implications of the Cult of Relics, the prestige of the martyrium churches of Syria and Palestine, and the spread of Syrian symbolism regarding the meaning of the House of God exerted a widespread influence throughout the Near East, including Mesopotamia and Armenia, both in popularizing the central-type martyria and in transforming them into churches of the regular cult.[1] This spread of the martyrium concept, he says, coincided with the dissemination of the *Areopagitica* throughout the Greek world. By the sixth century, then, when the Syrian churchmen were insisting upon the idea of the church as a mystic temple, a replica of the comprehensible universe, it becomes more apparent why the dome, which the Christians had taken over from pagan mausolea and commemorative monuments, should have become popular, because for centuries the dome had been a symbolic form of varied but related meanings. In explaining the growing popularity of the martyrium-type church, Grabar derives all the basic forms of martyria from the pagan tombs, memorials, and heröa of Rome and does not, because of the magnitude of his investigation, attempt to deal with the other sources of domical ideology which were involved in the development of domical architecture. It is to be hoped,

---

[1] A. Grabar, *Martyrium, recherches sur le culte des reliques et l'art chrétien antique*, Paris, 1946.

4

therefore, that a partial history of domical concepts and the evidence for the early use of the wooden dome will show that Syria and Palestine had a native domical tradition which not only readily combined with the Roman and Hellenistic traditions of a mortuary dome, but also account for certain specific types of free-standing domes and help to explain why the dome, as the manifestation of an idea, became so important in Byzantine and Islamic architecture.

Behind the concepts involved in domical development was the natural and persistent primitive instinct to think in terms of customary memory images and to attribute actual being and inner power to inanimate objects, such as the roof and other parts of the house. To the naïve eye of men uninterested in construction, the dome, it must be realized, was first of all a *shape* and then an *idea*. As a shape (which antedated the beginnings of masonry construction), it was the memorable feature of an ancient, ancestral house. It is still a shape visualized and described by such terms as *hemisphere, beehive, onion, melon,* and *bulbous*. In ancient times it was thought of as a *tholos, pine cone, omphalos, helmet, tegurium, kubba, kalubé, maphalia, vihâra, parasol, amalaka tree, cosmic egg,* and *heavenly bowl*. While the modern terms are purely descriptive, the ancient imagery both preserved some memory of the origin of the domical shape and conveyed something of the ancestral beliefs and supernatural meanings associated with its form.

A key to the origin of the domical shape as a house concept is furnished by the derivation of our modern word "dome" from the Greek and Latin *domus*. In Middle and Late Latin *doma* meant "house," "roof," and only at times "cupola," while during the Middle Ages and the Renaissance it was used all over Europe to designate a revered house, a *Domus Dei*. This persistent association with the idea of an important house, which will be seen going back to the first beginnings of domical architecture, survived in the Italian *duomo*, the German, Icelandic, and Danish *Dom*, meaning "cathedral," and as late as 1656 in the English *dome* meaning "Town-House, Guild-Hall, State-House, and Meeting-house in a city."[2] For centuries, apparently, dome was applied to any outstanding and important house, sacred or otherwise, which might or might not have had a cupola roof. During the seventeenth century, however, the original meaning began to fade into poetic usage and by 1660 *dosme* in France had acquired the specific meaning of a cupola vault, which in the course of the eighteenth century became standard usage for dome in English. This gradual limitation of meaning was partly the result of the growing scientific need for technical terms, but largely because the eighteenth century, in its admiration of such churches as S. Peter's in Rome, S. Paul's in London, Les Invalides and the Pantheon in Paris, as well as scores of other domical structures, still considered the monumental dome as the designating feature of all truly impressive houses of God, and hence synonymous with *domus*. What is revealing in this derivation is that even in English the idea of a "dome" began as a house concept, just as in ancient Italy, Syria, India and Islam words for

---

[2] *New English Dictionary*, Oxford, 1897; T. Blount, *Glossographia . . .* , London, 1656, "dome."

5

house, tent, or primitive shelter, such as *tegurium, kalubé, vihâra,* and *kubba,* came to designate a dome or domical structure.

It is impossible within the limits of a study of the domical tradition in Syria and Palestine to trace all the beginnings of domical shapes and domical ideas in the different countries of antiquity and to note their parallels in the retarded primitive cultures of Africa, Asia and the Americas. Instead, a series of already carefully investigated postulates, which can at least be checked against the evidence for the origin of the domical ideas of Syria, is advanced.

A. The domical shape must be distinguished from domical vaulting because the dome, both as idea and as method of roofing, originated in pliable materials upon a primitive shelter and was later preserved, venerated, and translated into more permanent materials, largely for symbolic and traditional reasons.

1. At the primitive level the most prevalent and usually the earliest type of constructed shelter, whether a tent, pit house, earth lodge, or thatched cabin, was more or less circular in plan and covered by necessity with a curved roof. Therefore, in many parts of the ancient world the domical shape became habitually associated in men's memories with a central type of structure which was venerated as a tribal and ancestral shelter, a cosmic symbol, a house of appearances and a ritualistic abode.

2. Hence many widely separate cultures, whose architecture evolved from primitive methods of construction, had some tradition of an ancient and revered shelter which was distinguished by a curved roof, usually more or less domical in appearance, but sometimes hoop-shaped or conical.

B. This domical shape, as an ancient and revered house form, was preserved in many cultures and gradually translated into more permanent materials as a family or royal tomb, a cult house and abode of the Great One, or as a utilitarian granary, sweat house and kiln.

1. Because of the animistic habits of thought which continued to attach inner meaning and magical power to the memorable shape of the ancestral round shelter, most early civilizations had deeply rooted domical ideologies which resulted in the veneration of the domical shape as a mortuary, sacred, royal and celestial abode of the Great One long after the ordinary domestic architecture had become rectangular with flat or gabled roofs.

2. This tendency was strengthened by the primitive habit of visualizing both the cosmos and divinities in the shape of the ancestral house.

C. Therefore, there is no historical justification for the assumption that the domical vault originated for purely structural and environmental reasons in either brick or stone. Instead, all the evidence shows that early vault forms, like the dome and the tunnel vault, were traditional roof shapes originating in pliable materials and later imitated in masonry for ideological reasons.

1. Hence, in tracing the evolution of the dome in any particular region, a distinction must be made between the cultural level when the domical idea took shape and acquired symbolic values and the historical period when there was a social

organization with the incentive, technical equipment, and craftsmen to translate an ancestral dwelling into a tholos tomb, to turn a royal tent into a domical audience hall of brick and to erect monumental hemispheres, or conoid domes, upon temples, martyria, palaces, churches, baptisteries and mosques.

2. Moreover, the dome, like any other curvilinear form such as the horseshoe arch, could not have originated in cut stone, because rock is shapeless and the image has to exist in the mind of the stonecutter. Stone architecture the world over, from India to Stonehenge, began as an imitative and sculptural effort on the part of organized society to reproduce venerated forms which had formerly been constructed in more pliable materials.

D. There were various domical traditions in both the West and the East.

1. It was the mortuary, divine, royal and celestial meanings of these domical traditions with their symbolic ideologies which led to the popularity and monumental use of the domical shape in India and the late Roman Empire, then in the Christian and Sassanian East, and later in the Islamic Empire.

2. Because the conception and meanings of the domical shape were primarily derived from primitive habitations, many cultures had domical ideologies before they had domical vaults of masonry. Even after some cultures developed or acquired a monumental architecture with temples, palaces and churches of stone and brick, they religiously preserved the shape, and often the ancient construction, of ancestral and ritualistic shelters for their inner sanctuaries, tabernacles, aediculae, ciboria and baldachins.

E. At the same time that the dome was taking on utilitarian values as a vault upon granaries, baths (sweat houses) and kilns—which in the beginning were special adaptations and survivals of the primitive round house—the domical shape, regardless of its construction, acquired persistent symbolic values.

1. It was the mortuary, divine, royal and celestial meanings of these domical ideologies which, in different civilizations and at different periods, furnished the incentive to translate the idea of an ancient *tentorium, kalubé, maphalia, tegurium, vihâra,* and *kubba* into a monumental structure of wood, brick, stone, or concrete.

2. The process, however, was never wholly independent and indigenous in any civilization. The formation of domical architecture in the Roman Empire, India, the Christian and Sassanian East, and the Islamic Empire was the result of an intricate fusion of various domical traditions and a multilateral dispersion of structural methods of building domical shapes.

3. By the late Roman Empire, when the dome was acquiring so much distinction as a symbol of celestial greatness and imperial immortality, its ideology was further enriched by the popular ideas already associated with similar shapes, such as the *tholos, mundus, heroön, sacred baetyl, omphalos, divine helmet, umbrella, cosmic egg* and *pine cone,* also by the interests of the Orphic cults in a celestial cosmogony and a heavenly salvation, and by the introduction of ancient Indian beliefs regarding the cosmic significance of the dome.

7

4. By the fourth century the widespread popularity of these ideas and the belief that the domical shape was a heavenly shelter, going back to an ancient and ancestral past when the gods and men lived together in an idyllic paradise on earth, gave the dome, especially in Syria and Palestine, its growing appeal to the Christians with their Cult of the Dead, their veneration for the martyred dead, and their desire for some tangible proof of a heavenly Domus.

F. In those regions with an established domical tradition, where timber was at first plentiful or easily imported, wood carpentry, as in India and Syria, was an early and natural method of reproducing the symbolic shapes on an imposing and monumental architectural scale. Hence, in many widely separate cultures the wooden dome was an early form in the evolution of domical architecture.

As a result of this evolution there were both historical significance and symbolic content involved in the different kinds of domical shapes which were prevalent in the late antique and Islamic periods. The most primitive and natural shape, derived directly from a round hut made of pliable materials tied together at the top and covered with leaves, skins or thatch, was the pointed and slightly bulbous dome which is so common today among the backward tribes of Nubia and Africa (Fig. 93). This type of dome, resembling a truncated pine cone or beehive, is preserved in the tholos tombs of the Mediterranean (Fig. 63), the rock-cut tombs of Etruria and Sicily (Figs. 64, 65), in the Syrian qubâb huts (Fig. 88), on the tomb of Bizzos (Fig. 61) and on many of the early Islamic mosques (Figs. 38-43). To distinguish this shape of dome from the geometric cone we will call it conoid, because of its recognized likeness to the actual pine cone.[3]

Other types of domical shapes, flatter and unpointed, were derived from the tent and preserved as tabernacles, ciboria and baldachins (Figs. 144-151). These tent forms, however, could be puffed-up and bulbous owing to the light framework of the roof, as is shown by the celestial baldachin above the great altar of Zeus at Pergamum (Fig. 106) and the Parthian dome among the reliefs of the arch of Septimius Severus at Rome (Fig. 228). There were also in Syria and other parts of the Roman Empire sacred rustic shelters whose ritualistic and domical coverings sometimes had an outward curving flange at the bottom of the dome as the thatch was bent out to form an overhang (Figs. 111-117). In other examples the curve of their light domical roof was broken by the horizontal bindings which held the thatch in place (Fig. 10).

The hemispherical shape, which is today so commonly associated with the dome, undoubtedly acquired its geometric curve largely from the theoretical interests of the Greek mathematicians and the practical considerations of Roman mechanics.[4]

---

[3] See pp. 74-75.

[4] While the Hellenistic and Roman mathematicians and engineers undoubtedly developed the scientific aspects of arcuated construction, the geometric forms of arches and vaults were already known. The Assyrians probably knew the hemispherical form because on the reliefs of Ashurnasirpal's palace at Nimrud (H. R. Hall, *Babylonian and Assyrian Sculpture in the British Museum*, 1928, pl. XVI) there is pictured such a shape. This representation, however, does not strengthen the out-of-date theory that the masonry dome originated in the brick architecture of Mesopotamia. In-

This Roman standardization of the domical shape, which made it easier to construct accurately in brick, stone and concrete, became the customary form of the antique domical vault. In erecting the hemispherical vault on a monumental scale on baths, tombs and temple walls, the Romans found it necessary, in order to withstand the outward thrust, to conceal it on the exterior either partially, by loading the walls up to the haunch of the dome, or entirely, by carrying up the supporting walls around it and then covering it with a protecting roof of tile (Fig. 73). Hence, in the Roman tradition most domes of masonry were largely concealed on the exterior. In some regions, such as Armenia, where there may have been originally a wooden domical tradition in wood which was later translated into stone, there may have also been climatic reasons for protecting the dome under a conical or polygonal roof.

In those regions, such as Syria, where there was a persistent tradition of wooden domes and strong ideational reasons for making the dome the dominant feature on the exterior, there was a marked tendency to exaggerate its conoid and bulbous appearance. In addition to the conoid, hemispherical and bulbous domes there were also melon domes (Figs. 16, 152, 153, 188), which were common in the Near East by the Early Christian period, whose corrugations on the exterior were due to their original construction in wood, although their peculiar shape was later imitated in brick and stone. The probable symbolism of the melon dome and its relation to the lotus rosette of Egypt and the lotus domes of India will be discussed later.[5]

stead, it sustains the assumption that domical forms took shape in pliable materials and were translated into wood carpentry before being reproduced in brick and stone masonry. The dome in question is a protective covering on the tower of an Assyrian battering ram. Ob-

viously it could not have been constructed of masonry on this portable war-machine, but must have been made of wood and, perhaps, sheathed with metal.

[5] See p. 122.

9

II · THE USE OF THE WOODEN DOME
IN THE NEAR EAST

BEFORE discussing the historical evidence for the early use of the wooden dome in the Near East, some consideration should be given to the theoretical advantages of the wooden dome and to the question of why a domical style of architecture should have developed apparently so rapidly in Asia Minor, Byzantium and Syria—regions which suffered such severe and recurrent earthquakes. If the dome was only a practical form of masonry vaulting, why was it adopted in regions where the heavy masonry dome was more difficult and dangerous to construct than gabled and flat roofs?

Because of its disruptive thrusts the masonry dome was in constant danger of collapsing if supporting walls, piers or buttressing were disturbed. When built large and imposing, it required massive supports and buttressing up to its haunch, which made it impossible or at least very dangerous to make its domical shape fully visible upon the exterior. The wooden dome, on the contrary, was light and could safely be raised up large, free standing and of wide span on relatively thin walls and high clerestories. Once constructed, its rigid framework exerted relatively little thrust. Furthermore, in wood carpentry the builders could easily and safely reproduce on a large scale the curved profiles of those conoid and bulbous shapes which were impractical in masonry but which had become customary and symbolically significant upon the traditional ritualistic shelters. Once completed, the wooden dome could be protected and made resplendent, like the celestial symbol that it was, by a gilded metal sheathing.

And yet, in spite of the advantages of the wooden dome, we find in some countries which started with the tradition of wood carpentry and where the masonry domes were in danger of being destroyed by the recurrent earthquakes an evident desire or necessity to translate the domical shape into masonry. In those regions where timber was becoming scarce through deforestation and limited transportation facilities it is easily understood why the wooden dome was abandoned. At the same time there was in the antique world the conviction, regardless of fact, that masonry construction was in itself enduring and a mark of superior greatness. Roman interest in the mechanics of vaulting, and imperial ideas of a state architecture of solid and enduring masonry, had perfected domical construction and introduced it into various parts of the empire. The masonry dome had come to be a mark of royal and divine power. Since all large churches were built with the approval and assistance of the State, the Church was strongly influenced by imperial building methods, and the masonry dome of stone, brick and concrete became more and more common. At the same time the wooden dome continued, in Syria at least, to be so characteristic of the church architecture that it was taken over by the Arabs as the distinctive feature of their mosques.

Individual scholars have recognized and discussed the use of the wooden dome in the ancient and Early Christian periods and its later importance in the domical architectures of India, Russia and the Islamic world.[1] Nevertheless, the significance of the wooden dome in the early evolution of domical styles has been largely disregarded, partly, it would appear, because it has left so little archaeological evidence, but largely because historians of architecture have been schooled to the belief that the wooden dome was a derivative form of construction, imitating masonry vaults. As long as the dome was considered to have been only a kind of vaulting essentially peculiar to the exotic art of the Orient, as it was known in the nineteenth century, and the wooden roofs upon the circular and polygonal buildings of Greece and the Hellenistic world were thought to have been always conical rather than domical, scholars were unable to reverse their reasoning and assume that domical traditions of wood were not only earlier than those of masonry but were also developed independently in different parts of both Europe and Asia. The Etruscans certainly knew the wooden dome, as did the later Roman builders, and in the Saar basin of the Germanic North it can be shown that the domical shape was used upon houses, tombs, temples and city towers and was not translated into masonry form until after the Romans came to dominate the country. It is also possible that domical houses and temples of wood carpentry were common from an early period along the borders of the Black and Caspian Seas from the Danube to Armenia and the Caucasus before contacts with the Byzantine and Sassanian Empires introduced the organized labor and technical means of reproducing the traditional domical shapes in more permanent masonry. It is only in India, however, that the importance of wood carpentry in the development of domical architecture has been fully recognized:[2] in a study entitled "Origin and Mutation in Indian and Eastern Architecture," William Simpson outlined the stages by which arcuated and domical forms developed from primitive habitations of bamboo and thatch and were later translated into cut stone.[3] In fact, Simpson laid down the premise that wood carpentry was "one of the necessary steps between the first origin and its full development in stone."

In 1913, when Birnbaum endeavored to demonstrate from literary sources that

---

[1] H. Thiersch ("Antike Bauten für Musik," *Zeitschrift für Geschichte der Architektur,* II, 1908/9, 33ff.) restored the tholos of Epidauros with a wooden dome whose construction recalled the carpentry domes "en parasol" reproduced in a number of rock-cut Etruscan tombs (J. Martha, *L'Art étrusque,* 1889, 156, fig. 124; G. Dennis, *The Cities and Cemeteries of Etruria,* 1878, I, 239, 274, 448; K. Lehmann, "The Dome of Heaven," *Art Bulletin,* XXVII, 1945, 20 n. 176). Other references to the use of the wooden dome in Greece: P. Cavvadias, "La Tholos d'Épidaure et le peinture Pausias," *Mélanges Nicole,* 1905, 611; H. Pomtow, "Die Grosse Tholos zu Delphi," *Klio,* XII, 1912, 216ff.

[2] A. K. Coomaraswamy (*History of Indian and Indonesian Art,* 1927, 49) wrote, "Practically, it can hardly be doubted that, as in other countries, the form of the god's house is derived from that of human dwellings and tombs, the main source leading back to the domed thatched hut and the barrel vaulted types of the Todas"; and in tracing the origin of the domical vihâra and fire temple, A. Foucher (*L'Art gréco-bouddhique du Ghandhâra,* I, 1905, 128) pointed out that the domical forms went back to the primitive round hut and were constructed in wood long before they were translated into stone.

[3] W. Simpson, *R.I.B.A. Transactions,* VII, 225ff.

the octagonal churches of Antioch, Nazianzus and Nyssa had wooden roofs, he disregarded the literal meanings of the texts and insisted that their wooden roofs were either conical or pyramidal in shape because, as he wrote, a *wooden dome is a paradox*.[4] Strzygowski, although he repeatedly pointed out the possible influences of wooden prototypes upon the stone architecture of Armenia and suggested certain wooden derivations for the Asiatic adjustment of the dome to a square plan, always came back to his undemonstrated conviction that the dome itself originated in the brick architecture of Mesopotamia and Iran.[5] As early as 1921, however, Herzfeld insisted that the Early Christian churches of Syria had wooden domes which were taken over by the Arabs for their mosques.[6] Later, K. A. C. Creswell in his *Early Muslim Architecture* undertook to trace the Islamic wooden dome back to its probable prototypes in Syria.[7] Having shown that the early Arab domes of wood must have been built by Syrian workmen and presumably represented the continuation of a Syrian tradition, Creswell apparently disregarded the logic of his own arguments, considering the evidence as "somewhat ambiguous and unsatisfactory," and invariably came back to the traditional conclusion that the Syrian and Palestinian churches of the central type must have had wooden roofs of conical rather than domical shape.

By 1935, however, C. Watzinger, without discussing the evidence, fully accepted the existence of the wooden dome as the prevailing type of roof upon the circular, polygonal and cruciform churches of Syria and Palestine.[8] Somewhat later, the experienced archaeologist D. Krencker, after careful study, restored the great octagon of S. Simeon Stylites at Kal'at Sim'ân with a pointed and bulbous dome of wooden construction.[9] In 1943 W. Born, in an article on the history of the bulbous dome, made no attempt to trace the wooden dome back to its early origins and was reluctant to admit that its bulbous form could have antedated the Islamic period in the architecture of Syria.[10] At the same time he advanced the conclusion, which seems to require further explanation, that the bulbous dome must have evolved "in the stratum of wood architecture which extended through India, the Near East and Russia" and even suggested that Syria must have led in the development. Even though he says that the wooden dome in Islamic architecture was at an early date translated into stone, he does not intimate that it may have had a long previous history in widely separate regions.

In 1945 K. Lehmann, in his study of the celestial symbolism of the dome, cited

[4] A. Birnbaum, "Die Oktogone von Antiochia, Nazianz und Nyssa," *Repertorium für Kunstwissenschaft*, XXXVI, 1913, 181-209.

[5] J. Strzygowski, *Altai-Iran*, 1917; *Die Baukunst der Armenier und Europa*, 1918; *Die altslavische Kunst*, 1929; *Origin of Christian Church Art*, 1923, 8.

[6] E. Herzfeld, "Mschattâ, Hîra und Bâdiya," *Jahrbuch der preussischen Kunstsammlungen*, XLII, 1921, 120-121.

[7] K. A. C. Creswell, *Early Muslim Architec-*

ture, 1932-40, I, 83-87.

[8] C. Watzinger, *Denkmäler Palästinas*, 1933-35, II, 131.

[9] D. Krencker, *Die Wallfahrtskirche des Simeon Stylites in Kal'at Sim'ân* (Abhandlungen der preussischen Akademie der Wissenschaften, Phil. hist. Klasse, 1938, no. 4), 1939.

[10] W. Born, "The Origin and Distribution of the Bulbous Dome," *Journal of the American Society of Architectural Historians*, III, 1943, 32ff.

much of the evidence for the importance of the wooden dome in Etruscan and Roman architecture and suggested that it may have been used in ancient Greece.[11] The following year Herzfeld wrote: "In Syria wood was throughout antiquity the specific material for ceilings" and said that the great Syrian domes of Bosra, Jerusalem and Damascus, all of wood, were constructed as double cupolas with an elaborate system of girders and ribs which was the result of experience acquired in shipbuilding.[12]

Before the central-type churches of Antioch can be restored and properly related to the history of the domical tradition in Syria from pagan times down to its adoption by Islam, it is necessary to review the evidence for the use of the wooden dome. At the same time it is essential to note to what extent the dome was primarily the distinguishing feature of the mortuary shelter and the martyrium. With the growth of the ritual of the dead and the architectural elaboration of the simple provisions for the *mensa martyrium* into a commemorative monument and church, the symbolism of the primitive shelter and house of the dead was extended to the whole church: the dome gradually became the manifest symbol of the martyrium. In Syria this association of the dome with the martyrium and its transformation from a symbolic shape into a monumental form of architecture was first brought about by wood carpentry, which made it possible to construct in the architecture itself a sepulchral ciborium, a royal baldachin, a divine form and celestial symbol over an altar, throne, tomb, pulpit and baptismal font.

Early archaeologists and many later students of Early Christian architecture minimized the importance of the dome in Syria and Palestine because they found so few remains of masonry vaults on churches of the central type, and they disregarded the possibilities of domical construction in wood because so much of Syria and Palestine was thought to have been barren and timberless. Even the acknowledged use of great timbered roofs on both the pagan and Christian temples and the knowledge that fine timber was plentiful in the Lebanese mountains, while forests are known to have existed north of Hebron and in the region of Lake Tiberius, did not outweigh the existing testimony of stone roofs in the Hauran and the unquestioned conviction that the dome was primarily a form of vaulting. The existence of forests and the use of timber as late as the sixth century are clearly verified by the account of Procopius. In describing the new church of the Virgin at Jerusalem, which may have been domical, he tells how the builders, in order to find large enough timbers for the roof, "searched through all the woods and forests and every place where they had heard that very tall trees grew and found a certain dense forest produced cedars of extraordinary height."[13]

Ever since recent excavations have made it clear that the central churches of Antioch, Bosra and Gerasa could not have had masonry domes, many excavators and scholars have somewhat casually assumed, because they did not realize how much

[11] K. Lehmann, "The Dome of Heaven," *Art Bulletin*, XXVII, 1945, 1-27.
[12] Herzfeld, "Damascus: Studies in Architecture. III," *Ars Islamica*, XI/XII, 67.
[13] Procopius, *Buildings*, v, vi.

content the Christians attached to specific architectural forms, that their wooden roofs must have been either pyramidal or conical. Nevertheless, the evidence for the use of the wooden dome in Syria and the Near East is very specific and surprisingly large considering how few records attempt to describe the appearance and construction of churches and the fact that excavations can never reveal more than very indirect indications as to the use of carpentry domes upon the ruined churches. Once the use of the wooden dome is recognized and the mystic importance of the domical shape is understood, it becomes necessary to reexamine not only the prevailing theories regarding the origin and dissemination of domical beliefs but also the plans of many Syrian churches which may have had domical, rather than gabled, wooden roofs.

1. MARNEION, GAZA (c. 130 a.d.)

The Marneion was one of the most renowned pagan temples and the earliest known building in the Syro-Palestinian region which presumably had a wooden dome.[14] Since Karl Lehmann has already shown that the dome in Roman, Persian and Christian architecture had a clearly recognized celestial symbolism,[15] it is significant that this temple was dedicated to Marnas, a sky god, who was probably a Palestinian adaptation of the Cretan Zeus, the ruler of the universe.[16] The temple and its final destruction by fire in 402 a.d. are reliably described in the *Life of Porphyry* by Mark the Deacon, who knew the Bishop of Gaza between 382 and 392 a.d.[17] In his description of the temple, Mark is very specific in saying that it "was round, being supported by two colonnades, one within the other, and in the center was a dome (κιβώριον), puffed-up and rising on high."[18] According to this account, then, its dome was free standing ("rising on high"), bulbous ("swollen"), and perhaps pointed like a pine cone. That it was built of wood can only be inferred from the account which tells of a burning beam falling from the roof upon the tribune who was supervising the efforts to save this "most renowned center of a dying heathen world."

Although most historians of the period have accepted the fact that the Marneion had a wooden dome, "puffed-up," which resembled a pine cone, some scholars have

[14] F. Cabrol and H. Leclercq, *Dictionnaire d'archéologie chrétienne et de liturgie*, VI, cols. 695ff.; Pauly-Wissowa, *Realencyclopädie*, XIV, cols. 1899ff.

[15] Lehmann, *op.cit.*, 1-27.

[16] A. B. Cook, *Zeus: a Study in Ancient Religion*, 1914-40, III, 549ff.

[17] G. F. Hill, *The Life of Porphyry, Bishop of Gaza, by Mark the Deacon*, 1913, 75-87, 140; Cabrol, *Dictionnaire*, XIV, cols. 1464ff.; Creswell, *Early Muslim Architecture*, I, 83f.; G. Dehio and G. von Bezold, *Die kirchliche Baukunst des Abendlandes*, I, 1887, 36; H. Grégoire and M.-A. Kugener, *Marc le Diacre*, 1930; J. N. and B. Sepp, *Die Felsenkuppel*, 1882, 46; K. B. Stark, *Gaza und die philis-*

täische Küste, 1852, 599-600; Strzygowski, *Kleinasien*, 1903, 101; Watzinger, *Denk. Paläs.*, II, 87.

[18] Creswell (*op.cit.*, I, 84) points out that there was no opening in the top of the dome as Dehio, Stark, Sepp and Strzygowski inferred from the Latin translation. Although Mark is the first writer to use the term *kiborion* for the dome of a building, the domical meaning of the word is clearly indicated by Athenaeus (*Deipnosoph*, I, iii, 72) who describes it as cuplike, by its use for a domical covering over either a tomb or altar (J. Braun, *Der christliche Altar*, 1924, II, 192), and by its later Byzantine use for a domical vault.

disregarded the text and insisted that its wooden roof was conical.[19] While admitting that *kiborion* meant dome, Creswell resorted to argument in a circle when he insisted that it must have been conical "on the analogy of the Anastasis."[20]

Following the destruction of the Marneion in 402 A.D. there was a dispute at Gaza as to whether its round plan should be reproduced as a Christian church. In the end, when the Empress Eudoxia decided that the new church should be cruciform, "the Holy Man (Bishop Porphyry) engaged Rufinus, an architect of Antioch, a faithful and expert person" to build the new edifice, which was finished in 407 and dedicated to Holy Easter, the day of the Resurrection. The new church was undoubtedly a martyrium, as the dedication would imply, for by this time there was a recognized symbolic relation between the cruciform plan and a commemorative building,[21] but it was a martyrium, like so many Palestinian churches, intended to commemorate a holy event rather than to enshrine any actual relics.[22]

Although little is known about the church, other than it was cruciform and called the Eudoxiana, the fact that it was cruciform is a strong indication that it had a domical crossing, as did the other fourth and fifth century cruciform martyria, such as the Holy Apostles at Constantinople, S. Babylas at Kaoussie-Antioch, the one built by S. Gregory at Nyssa, S. John at Ephesus and the church of S. Simeon Stylites at Kal'at Sim'ân. Since one purpose of this study is to show that the cruciform plan carried with it the concept of a monumental, sepulchral ciborium, or celestial dome, at the center of the cross, it is significant that the Eudoxiana was built by an Antiochene architect who knew, and perhaps actually built, the cruciform martyrium at Kaoussie-Antioch about 381 A.D.[23]

Over and above this general argument that by the fifth century the dome was symbolically associated with a cruciform type of martyrium, there are other indications to show that the Eudoxiana was domical. Finding it difficult to believe that Gaza had two cruciform churches and did not continue to preserve its first Christian sanctuary, Leclercq suggested that the Eudoxiana was actually the cruciform church of S. Sergius which Choricius of Gaza saw in the sixth century and described as domical.[24] The case for this presumption seems to be somewhat stronger than Leclercq stated it, because he only drew attention to the possibility that the four columns of Carystos marble seen by Choricius in the church of S. Sergius may have been part of the thirty-two of this particular marble which the Empress Eudoxia is known to have presented to Bishop Porphyry for the construction of his church.[25] Since the only cruciform

[19] G. T. Rivoira, *Moslem Architecture*, 1918, 123.

[20] Creswell, *op.cit.*, I, 84.

[21] Grabar, *Martyrium*, I, 152-157.

[22] *Ibid.*, 314-334.

[23] See p. 109.

[24] See p. 39.

[25] Cabrol, *Dict.*, XIV, cols. 1496, 1499; it was not unusual for a church built with imperial assistance to be known for a time by the name of the royal donor: at Alexandria, where another famous domical temple of the pagan world, the Serapeion, was destroyed at about the same time as the Marneion, the church which replaced it was a martyrium containing the relics of John the Baptist (Grégoire and Kugener, *Marc le Diacre.*, 137) and was known by the name of the Emperor Arcadius (Sozomenus, VII, 15; A. M. de Zogheb, *Études sur l'ancienne Alexandrie*, 1910, 35). Further-

church mentioned by Choricius is the domical church of S. Sergius and since the later mosaics at Ma'in show the city of Gaza as characterized by a cruciform church, we must assume that both cruciform sanctuaries were the first church of Gaza.[26] If this is a reasonable deduction, then it is merely unfortunate that the Ma'in mosaic is so schematic that it only shows the three gabled arms of a cruciform plan and, because of the restricted space, did not undertake to depict a domical crossing. While this identification of S. Sergius with the Eudoxiana is still problematic, it does prove that the Christian builders at Gaza carried on a domical tradition which went back to pagan times.

2. THE HOLY SEPULCHRE, JERUSALEM (326-335 A.D.)

The memorial tomb of Christ erected by order of Constantine was the most revered sepulchral monument of Christendom. It is, therefore, of supreme importance to the history of architecture to know whether or not this sacred martyrium had a gilded wooden dome. If domical, this omphalos of the Christian faith, built in the center of the New Jerusalem, would have established the type for subsequent martyria and carried over into Christian symbolism the antique ideas of the domical shape as an ancestral abode which was given to man by God, as a celestial form, a divine heroön, a ritualistic sanctuary, a royal baldachin and a cosmic house. Unfortunately, very little is known about the appearance and construction of the Constantinian rotunda, which was burnt by the Persians in 614 A.D. and then underwent a long succession of restorations and three rebuildings, one by Modestus between 616 and 618 A.D., a second by the Byzantine Emperor Constantine Monomachus in 1048 after the destruction of the building by the Fatimite Caliph in 1009, and the third by the Latin crusaders in the twelfth century. There has been no agreement as to whether the original martyrium had a domical or conical roof constructed of masonry or wood: Heisenberg and Leclercq believed that it had a massive, hemispherical dome of masonry; Grabar, while favoring a masonry dome, entertains the possibility that it may have been wooden;[27] Crowfoot and Watzinger are of the opinion that its dome was wood;[28] Creswell arrived at the conclusion that it had a conical roof of wood, and Vincent endeavored to prove that its original dome of masonry was changed in the seventh century to a truncated cone of carpentry construction, open at the top. A few scholars, it should be noted, have found evidence in the accounts of Eusebius and Aetheria to show that the circular rotunda could not have been erected until after the fourth century.[29] For the purpose of this study it is possible to disregard their theories,

more, if we accept the evidence of the mosaics at Gerasa (Figs. 30, 31) the martyrium of S. John the Baptist at Alexandria was domical.

[26] R. de Vaux, "Une Mosaïque byzantine à Ma'in," *Revue biblique*, XLVII, 1938, pl. XIV/2.

[27] Grabar, *Martyrium*, I, 257.

[28] J. W. Crowfoot, *Early Churches in Palestine*, 1941, 105, "The later dome over the Anastasis was built of timber and so probably

was the Constantinian dome"; Watzinger, *Denk. Paläs.*, II, 131.

[29] H. G. Evers ("Zu den Konstantinsbauten am Heiligen Grabe in Jerusalem," *Zeitschrift f. ägypt. Sprache u. Altertumsk.*, LXXV, 1935, 53-60) without advancing any new evidence suggests that the Holy Sepulchre was an open semicircular exedra; Ejner Dyggve ("Gravkirchen i Jerusalem," *Studier fra Sprog-og*

because, even if there were valid reasons, which there do not seem to be, for questioning the Constantinian origin of the rotunda, the arguments why an imperial type of mausoleum was built and why it must have had a gilded dome of wood apply with equal validity to a successor of Constantine.

Quite apart from the ideological reasons why a mausoleum erected by Constantine as an *aeterna memoria* of Christ, the Divine Imperator, must have been domical, even the structural history of the Holy Sepulchre, as we know it, provides some indication of the shape and carpentry construction of its roof. Considering the Christian reverence for tradition and the immediate restoration of the holy monument by the Modestus between 616 and 618 A.D., it is reasonable to assume that he restored the Holy Sepulchre to the sacred form and character which it had before the Persians burnt it in 614, instead of altering its symbolic dome to a truncated cone of wood, as suggested by Vincent, Duckworth and Creswell. That Modestus rebuilt the roof in wood carpentry is made clear by the account of Eutychius (876-940 A.D.), who tells how the Patriarch Thomas between 807 and 820 A.D. rebuilt the roof "bit by bit," sending to Cyprus for cedars and pines in order to introduce new timbers in place of those erected by Modestus.[30] It is equally clear from this account of Eutychius that the wooden roof, carefully replaced by the Patriarch Thomas, was constructed with two domical shells, which must have resembled the two wooden domes on the Qubbat-aṣ-Sakhra (Fig. 37). Regarding the construction of these domes Eutychius relates how Thomas "covered the dome with plaster inside and out and then built another dome, leaving between the two a space sufficient for a man to walk around." Evidently this ninth century wooden roof, which Eutychius and others after him so specifically designate as a "dome," or *qoubah*, must have been domical, because there was no structural reason for building a conical roof with an inner and outer shell. In fact, as late as 1106/7, the Russian Daniel described the church as "not closed by a vault of stone" but covered with a cupola constructed of wood.[31]

Oldtidsforskning, Publication of the Philological-Historical Society, Copenhagen, no. 186, 1941) endeavors to prove that the tomb was in a large semicircular exedra which was the apse of an unroofed basilica; E. Weigand ("Zwei neue Hypothesen über die Konstantinischen Bauten am heiligen Grabe in Jerusalem," *Byzantinische Zeitschrift*, XL, 78-88) refutes both theories that the Constantinian structure was not a rotunda. In order to assume that the rotunda was built after the fourth century it is necessary to disregard the evidence of S. Cyril of Jerusalem, who was a ward of Bishop Makarius and present at the dedication in 335 A.D. In his Catechetical Lectures, written in 347/8, in which he instructed a group of neophytes on the mysteries of the Resurrection, he said, "The piety of actual Rulers has clothed with silver and gold this

holy church *in which we are united*" (II, 6) and then goes on to attribute "the building of this Holy Church" to Constantine; and earlier in the lesson (II, 1), where he was preparing his audience for the simplicity and significance of the actual cave in which Christ was buried, it must be assumed that he pointed to the grave monument and the enclosing mausoleum as he asked the rhetorical questions: "Is it a tomb made by the hand of man? Is it elevated above the ground [as here] like the royal mausolea?" (Vincent and Abel, *Jerusalem*, II, 208ff.).

[30] Eutychius, *Corpus Scriptor. Christian. Oriental.*, series III; Pococke ed., II, 422-425; C. S. Clermont-Ganneau, *Récueil d'archéologie orientale*, II, 1898, 334-335; H. Vincent and F.-M. Abel, *Jérusalem*, II, 1914-26, 242-247.

[31] Vincent and Abel, *op.cit.*, II, 258. The

The evidence, therefore, is clear, as far as it goes, that if the Constantinian building was *burnt* by the Persians and immediately replaced with a timber roof, constructed by Modestus, then the original roof of the Holy Sepulchre, as recognized by Creswell, must have been made of wood.[32] Furthermore, if Modestus reproduced the original roof and his roof was repaired in the ninth century by Thomas, then the wooden roof of the Constantinian building was domical. Hence, by accepting Creswell's arguments that the present dome of Qubbat-aṣ-Sakhra (Fig. 37), which is known to have had a double dome of wooden planks in 903 A.D., reproduces, as it should, the original Islamic dome of 685-705 A.D., one arrives at the conclusion that the Arab dome of the early seventh century over the Sakhra—which Eutychius says was a dome taken from a Christian church at Baalbek—and the ninth century dome on the Anastasis both continued a native tradition of domical construction in wood which was followed in the original Holy Sepulchre and went back to pagan structures like the Marneion.[33]

Why, then, have highly competent scholars disregarded this evidence and concluded that the Holy Sepulchre, at least since the seventh century, was covered with a truncated cone?[34] Is it that they have been too skeptical about the early use of the wooden dome and the existence of a domical tradition in Palestine and Syria? Or is it that they have not realized the tremendous symbolic importance of the dome in the late antique period and hence have attached too much significance to some of the seals of the Latin kings of Jerusalem and the fact that the roof of the Anastasis was not domical after the twelfth century? It is true that a few Crusader seals depict the Holy Sepulchre with a truncated cone, open at the top, and that scholars have generally assumed that all the representations of the twelfth century were intended to show the building as having had a conical and hypaethral roof of wood. Actually, however, a chronological comparison of the different types of Latin seals of the twelfth century, as is illustrated in Figures 218-227, make it evident that the Holy Sepulchre had its Byzantine dome until about 1169.[35] On the basis of the graphic evidence, which it is

---

translation by Mme. Khitrowo (*Itineraires russes en Orient*, Geneva, 1889, 13) reads, "la coupole de l'église n'est pas fermée par une voûte de pierre, mais se compose de poutres en bois en guise de charpente, de sorte que l'église est découverte par le haut. Le Saint Sépulcre est [placé] sous cette coupole découverte."

[32] Creswell, *op.cit.*, I, 84.

[33] The Marneion could not have been the only antique temple of Syria which was domical. There were many square fire temples, usually restored with open interiors, which were presumably covered with similar gilded domes of wood, or great domical baldachins (Fig. 123) like the one over the Great Altar of Zeus at Pergamum (Fig. 106) or like the bulbous dome on the square Parthian fire temple (Fig. 228) which is carved on the arch

of Septimius Severus (H. P. L'Orange, "Domus aurea . . . der Sonnenpalast," *Serta Eitremiana*, 1942, 74, Abb. 1). Grabar has suggested (*Martyrium*, I, 249) that the Syrian temple of the Janiculum at Rome may have been a domical structure because at the center of its polygonal plan there was, as in a Christian martyrium, either a symbolic tomb or altar (P. Gauckler, *Le Sanctuaire syrien du Janicule*, 1912; *idem*, "Le Couple héliopolitain . . . ," *Mélanges d'archéologie et d'histoire*, XXIX, 1909, 239ff.).

[34] Vincent and Abel, *op.cit.*, 220; H. T. F. Duckworth, *The Church of the Holy Sepulchre*, 1922, 161; Creswell, *op.cit.*, 87.

[35] Ever since De Vogüé (*Les Églises de la Terre Sainte*, 1860, 453) made use of the Latin seals in his study of the churches of Jerusalem and said, "During the Middle Ages the trun-

cated cone with its beams showing characterized the rotunda at Jerusalem," architectural historians and numismatists have assumed that all the representations of the Holy Sepulchre on the lead seals of the Crusaders were intended to represent a conical roof. It is necessary to question this conclusion when the different types of seals depicting the Holy Sepulchre are arranged in chronological order and the variations in the treatment of the roof are noted. The only series which unquestionably depicts the building with a truncated cone of straight timbers converging on the opening at the top is that of the Canons of the Holy Sepulchre (Figs. 222, 223). What is most significant is that the earliest example in the series is dated 1172 (G. Schlumberger, F. Chalandon and A. Blanchet, *Sigillographie de l'orient latin*, 1943, 134, nos. 163-167, pls. v/9, xx/2).

In contrast, the royal seals start out at the beginning of the century by showing the Holy Sepulchre with a conoid dome (Fig. 218), like the one on the *Templum Domini*. Following the capture of the city in 1099 and the establishment of the Kingdom of Jerusalem, the new rulers began to renovate and enlarge the Holy Sepulchre; at the same time they converted the Aksa mosque (Fig. 43) into a part of the palace and transformed the Dome of the Rock (Figs. 37, 38), which the Arabs had built in imitation of the Holy Sepulchre, into a church known as the *Templum Domini*. When the royal seal was designed during the reign of Baldwin I (1110-1118) the two great historic and domical buildings of Jerusalem were presented on either side of the Tower of David, which guarded the western and principal entrance of the city. Since the Sepulchre lay immediately to the left of the Porta David, while the Templum was on the eastern side of the city, it was natural for the design to have the Anastasis on the left, balancing the Templum, which was crowned with a cross in place of the Arab crescent. Therefore, it is important to note that the seal of Baldwin I, the first of the series (Fig. 218), shows the Holy Sepulchre with a conoid dome similar to the one on the Templum (*ibid.*, no. 1, pl. xvi/1).

The method of representation, while not entirely true to fact because at this time the Anastasis had an oculus in the top of its dome, proves that the building was still symbolically thought of as a domical structure. One of the difficulties in interpreting the architectural

evidence of these seals has been the disregard of a chronological development, for Vincent (*Jérusalem*, ii, fig. 386) attributes a seal of Baldwin III to Baldwin I. The strongest proof that the designers were at first consciously presenting the Holy Sepulchre as domical, and not conical, is the seal of Baldwin II (Fig. 221) which shows that he had taken over the royal design of a tower flanked by two domical buildings for the seal of his city of Ramah (*ibid.*, no. 126, pl. xix/3), with the difference that one dome is surmounted by a crescent and the other by a cross. The domical intent of the die-makers is again illustrated by another seal of Ramah, belonging to Baldwin III of Mirabel and dating between 1168 and 1174, on which the domical buildings flanking the tower are surmounted by flying banners (*ibid.*, no. 127, pl. xviii/4).

The subsequent seals of Baldwin II (1118-1131) and Baldwin III (1144-1162) modify the design and present the Holy Sepulchre more accurately (Fig. 219) with a hypaethral opening, so exaggerated in many cases that it looks like a crescent (*ibid.*, no. 5, pl. xvi/2). Although this change, intended to distinguish the Anastasis from the Templum, gave rise to some stylized simplifications which in some cases make the roof look like a truncated cone surmounted by a crescent, the series as a whole shows that the intent was to present the roof as a dome with an oculus (Fig. 220). This intent is evident in the way that the single, curved lines, intended to depict the gores of the dome, are clearly different from the straight, double lines of the timbered cone on the seals of the Canons (Figs. 222, 223). Furthermore, the curious variations and even misunderstandings of the roof on the later seals all indicate the persistence of a domical tradition: on the seal (Fig. 220) of Amaury I (1162-1175) the Holy Sepulchre looks like a domical structure surmounted by a crescent (*ibid.*, no. 12, pl. xvi/3); on the later seal (Fig. 225) of Baldwin V (1183-1185) the Holy Sepulchre, now moved to the right of the tower, appears to have an onion-shaped dome surmounted with a crescent (*ibid.*, no. 17, pl. xvi/5); its domical shape (Fig. 226) on a seal of Guy de Lusignan (1186) is still very apparent (*ibid.*, no. 18, pl. i/2); and on the seal of Jean de Brienne (1210-1237), executed after the loss of Jerusalem (Fig. 227), the traditional intent of presenting the dome with an hypaethral opening is more evident (*ibid.*, no. 26, pl. i/3). What is most significant in this whole series

true has not been fully published and studied, there are indications that the Crusaders, after having built the new domical choir of the Calvary church and joined it to the rotunda of the Anastasis, removed the outer shell and left the Holy Sepulchre proper with a truncated cone.

Whatever may have happened to the domical roof under the Crusaders, the fact that the church was covered with a truncated cone after the twelfth century is no proof that the Holy Sepulchre in the Byzantine period, and back to the time of Modestus, was conical. The case for the conical roof, as presented by Vincent and Abel, is not only based upon the Latin seals and the account of Ladoire in 1719,[36] but it implies a modern and Western disregard of all that the dome had come to symbolize in the Early Christian and Byzantine architecture of the Near East. The fact that there were periodic rebuildings of the roof of the building does not lessen the presumption that it continued to be distinguished by its heavenly dome until the Westerners shifted the emphasis to the dome over the choir. After the fire of 916 the wooden cupola, which Thomas had restored in the previous century, was repaired between 969 and 983. Then, following the systematic destruction of both the Anastasis and the Martyrium in 1009, the Byzantines undertook to rebuild the Holy Sepulchre, but not the Martyrium, in 1048. Even though they did not have time to complete the rebuilding before the arrival of the Turks and then of the Crusaders, we may be sure that they restored this venerated monument with a wooden roof in their own domical tradition. Their introduction of an oculus is testified to by Saewulf in 1102/3, which was after the Crusaders had captured the city but before they had had time to establish a kingdom and start rebuilding. He wrote: *Et opertum ne dum pluit, pluvia cadere possit super sanctum sepulchrum, quia ecclesia desuper patet discooperto.*[37] This opening in the roof was later referred to by William of Tyre between 1160 and 1180,[38] but

---

of royal stamps are the seals of Amaury I (Fig. 224), dating from 1169 and 1172, which present the Holy Sepulchre in the same manner as it appears on the seals of the Canons of the Holy Sepulchre with an unquestionable truncated cone of rigid timbers (*ibid.*, nos. 9, 10, 11; De Vogüé, *Les Églises de la Terre Sainte*, 454). One is immediately struck by the fact that these particular seals of Amaury I are of the same period as the seals of the Canons, while the seal of Amaury I dating from 1168 shows the Anastasis in the traditional manner with an oculus in its dome. From the evidence, then, it may be assumed that some change was made in the shape of the roof around 1169. Although it is clear from the various pilgrim accounts that nearly all the work on the new Crusader choir, the church of Calvary in the plan of Cambrai (Fig. 6), was completed in 1149 when it was consecrated (C. Enlart, *Les Monuments des croisés dans le royaume de*

Jérusalem, 1928, II, 138-140; Vincent and Abel, *op.cit.*, II, 266-279), De Vogüé (*op.cit.*, 217-220) advances the evidence from the *Cartulaire du Saint-Sepulchre* and the complaint of the Republic of Genoa regarding the removal of their inscribed charter from the wall of the Holy Sepulchre in 1169 to show that it must have been in 1169 that the old rotunda was combined with the new choir. Hence it seems probable that it was at this time, when the two parts were united, that the Crusaders shifted the domical emphasis to their own massive cupola of masonry, and for some reason removed the outer, domical shell from the roof of the Anastasis, leaving it with a truncated cone.

[36] Vincent and Abel, *op.cit.*, fig. 140; Ladoire, *Voyages* . . . , Paris, 1720, 93-95.

[37] Vincent and Abel, *op.cit.*, 257.

[38] *Ibid.*, 259.

there are no indications in any of these accounts that the hypaethral roof was not domical in shape. In fact the Russian pilgrim, Daniel, in 1106/7 specifically describes the roof as a wooden cupola.[39] Furthermore, the plan of Cambrai (Fig. 6), which is thought to depict the city of Jerusalem around 1150 but may date somewhat later because of the presence on it of the bell tower alongside the Holy Sepulchre, not only shows both the Anastasis and the Crusaders' choir with domes, but also strengthens the evidence of the Latin seals that it was about 1169 that the Anastasis was left with only a truncated cone. While the subsequent drawings prove rather conclusively the conical form of the roof after the twelfth century, they also prove that the dome continued to be associated with the monument, even though the emphasis was shifted to the masonry dome, capped by a lantern, on the Crusaders' church. Both a Greek manuscript (Fig. 5) of the early fifteenth century and the drawing of Bernard de Breitenbach at the end of the century still emphasize the bulbous and domical character of the structure, regardless of whether it was the dome of the choir or the traditional roof of the Anastasis which is depicted.[40]

[39] *Ibid.*, 258.

[40] The plan of Jerusalem (Fig. 6) in the library at Cambrai (no. 437) shows the "Anastasis" with a gored dome, capped with a round finial, or perhaps with a stylized oculus, alongside the Crusaders' choir, which has a plain dome (R. Röhricht, "Karten und Pläne zur Palästinakunde aus dem 7. bis 16. Jahrhundert," *Zeitschrift des deutschen Palästina-Vereins*, XIV, 1891, 137-141, Taf. 4; Vincent and Abel, *Jérusalem*, II, 756, figs. 317, 387). Although dated by the writing around 1150, this plan of Cambrai may be somewhat later if Enlart (*Les Monuments des croisés dans le royaume de Jérusalem*, II, 140) is correct in believing that the bell tower, represented in the plan, was not constructed until sometime between 1160 and 1180. The significance of the drawing is not so much a question of its accuracy, but the fact that at this time the Holy Sepulchre, like the Templum which was formerly the Dome of the Rock, was thought of as domical and hence depicted with a melon dome, such as was used to characterize the Holy Sepulchre in the Codex Rossanensis (Fig. 16). Another, much more schematic, representation of the building on the plan of Stuttgart, which is dated about 1180, shows the church called "Calvaria" with an onion-shaped dome (Röhricht, *Zeit. d. deut. Palästina-Vereins*, XV, 1892, 38, Taf. 4).

Because of the traditional association of the dome with the Holy Sepulchre, the drawings give no clear indication of when the Anastasis was left with only a truncated cone, although a representation of the end of the fourteenth century in the Bibliothèque Nationale (MS fr. 64) at Paris clearly shows the Anastasis with a truncated cone and the Crusaders' church with a hemispherical dome, capped by a small domical lantern (Enlart, *op.cit.*, II, 152, fig. 282). This drawing is apparently exceptional, because the domical association of the building was still so strong that a Greek manuscript of the beginning of the fifteenth century (Fig. 5), which includes the Crusaders' bell tower and dome, presents the Anastasis after the Byzantine tradition with a bulbous dome and a lantern over the oculus (Vincent and Abel, *op.cit.*, II, fig. 136). Even in the drawing of Bernard de Breitenbach at the end of the fourteenth century, where the emphasis has been shifted to the Crusaders' dome, the building still has a large bulbous dome and a lantern over the oculus (*ibid.*, II, 285, fig. 135). Again this shift of emphasis is seen in the engraving of about 1485, made by Erhard Rewick of Utrecht, where it is the Crusaders' dome with a lantern that is depicted (Enlart, *op.cit.*, 153, fig. 289). The key to all these mediaeval discrepancies in the representations of the Holy Sepulchre is the traditional ideological association of the dome with the monument of Christ, as is best illustrated by the drawing of 1436 in the British Museum (MS Egerton 1070) where the Anastasis has a melon dome with a small oculus and the Crusaders' dome is depicted in great detail with the steps up the exterior of the stone cupola and with an elaborate lantern (P. Durrier, *Florilegium Melchior de Vogüé*, 1909, 197-207).

Later in the history of the monument the casualness of the Western interest in the shape of the roof is illustrated at the end of the seventeenth century by De Bruyn, who calls it a "dome," but describes it as a truncated cone and so shows it in his drawing of the exterior; and yet at the same time his drawing of the interior (Fig. 4), which is done in careful perspective, gives it the appearance of having been domical. Twenty-five years after Ladoire described and drew the interior as conical, Pococke, in 1745, shows the interior as domical in the same way that De Bruyn did and writes, "The roof was of cypress, and the King of Spain, giving a new one, what remained of the old roof was preserved as reliques. . . . There is a hole in the top of the dome to give light, as in the Pantheon at Rome."[41] By 1810 the roof, which had been seriously damaged in the fire of 1808, was rebuilt with a dome that was replaced between 1863 and 1869 by the present metal roof consisting of two domical shells pierced by an oculus. It is, therefore, impossible to see how the history of the Holy Sepulchre, which the Arabs consistently described as a domical building, furnishes any evidence in support of the belief that there was a conical roof on either the seventh century or the Byzantine structure.

Regarding the construction and appearance of the original and presumably Constantinian building, authorities for the most part have accepted Père Vincent's restoration (Fig. 1) and assumed that it had a gigantic masonry dome supported upon a circular colonnade in two stories. Quite apart from the historical evidence for the use of a wooden dome, and without considering the question of either the gallery or the shape of the actual tomb, this restoration, in its relation of solids to voids (Fig. 3), shows why a rotunda of this kind must have always had a wooden roof, as it did after the rebuilding by Modestus. Structurally a masonry dome of seventy-two feet in span, such as is shown in the restoration, could not have been supported on light columnar supports and without massive and much heavier buttressing up to its haunch. Since all the evidence for the Holy Sepulchre combines with the other evidence for the Syrian use of the wooden dome to prove that the rotunda had a wooden roof, it is only a question of establishing its shape.

[41] A drawing of 1586 (G. Zuallardo, *Il Devotissimo viaggio di Gerusalemme*, 1595; R. Krautheimer, "Santo Stefano Rotondo a Roma e la chiesa de San Sepolcro a Gerusalemme," *Rivista di archaeologia cristiana*, XII, 1935, 88, fig. 7) depicts in a crude fashion a wooden roof with an oculus which gives the impression of a cone on the interior and a dome on the exterior; the Callot drawings in the account of Bernardino Amico (*Trattato alle Piante & Imaginj delle Sacri Edifizi di Terra Sante*, 1620, Florenze), written in 1596 and first published in 1609, show what is called the "cupola del S. Sepulchro" with a truncated cone (pls. 23, 24); the account of J. Goujon (*Histoire et voyage de la Terre-Sainte*, Lyon, 1671, 129-135) says that the Holy Sepulchre has two domes, the one over the tomb being made of cedars and covered with lead, and the other over the Crusaders' choir being made of stone, and the crude drawing shows the roof of the Anastasis as a truncated cone; in 1681 (Dr. O. Dapper, *Asia, Beschreibung des ganzen Syrien und Palestins . . .* , 1681, 345) the roof is depicted as a wooden, truncated cone; C. de Bruyn (*Voyage au Levant*, 1700, 260, 288, exterior, pl. 114, interior, pl. 144) writes, "Au milieu de l'Église & directement sous le Dome (qui est ouvert par le haut, mais ensorte pour tant qu'il est garni d'un treillis de fer entrelacé en façon de lozanges, par ou la lumière vient, comme à la Rotonde qui est à Rome); R. Pococke, *A Description of the East*, II, 1745, 15-16, pl. 4.

One reason several competent scholars have favored a conical rather than a domical roof for the original Holy Sepulchre is that they have attached too much importance to the few representations which show the Holy Sepulchre with a conical roof (Fig. 9). The representations of the tomb of Christ, and especially those of Western origin, which are nearly always in connection with the scene of the Holy Women at the Sepulchre, are unreliable as evidence of the actual appearance of the Anastasis because the intent of the Christian artist was not to show a specific building that few had seen, but to present a traditional and ideal tegurium whose implications of salvation would be readily comprehensible. This habit of the mediaeval imagination of dealing primarily with the symbolic content of architectural forms resulted, as Krautheimer has shown in the Western imitations of the Holy Sepulchre,[42] in never copying a building *in toto* but, instead, presenting it figuratively as a divine type.

Because of this subjective interest in the meaning of the forms, the memorial of Christ was represented in a great variety of ways. Sometimes it was shown as a simple round hut covered with either a domical (Fig. 7) or conical roof, for the Christian, like the antique man, was fully accustomed to think of a shepherd's hut, an ancestral dwelling like the *Domus Romulus*, as an ideal eternal house in the celestial garden of an afterlife. Symbolic imagery of this kind, as will be seen, was taken over by the Christians with the result that various forms of ritualistic shelters, like a mortuary ciborium over either a tomb or altar, were frequently called a *tegurium*, *tigurium*, *tugurium* and *tiburium*. As late as the seventh century Arculph described the tomb of Christ as *in medio spatio huius interiores rotundae domus rotundum inest in una eademaque petra excisum tegurium*. Because of this predominant interest in the meaning of the architectural forms, the representations of the sepulchral dwelling of Christ vary according to local types and iconographic purpose. On the Trivulzio book cover (Fig. 9), for example, it is not a two-storied mausoleum which is depicted. Instead, the representation is made up of two quite separate iconographic scenes which the artist combined in superimposed registers. In the upper register the symbolic tomb is a traditional tegurium with the tree of the garden growing beside it and the guarding soldiers asleep on the ground, while in the lower register is the subsequent event of the angel receiving the Holy Women at the door of the empty Sepulchre. Later in the West, partly as a result of this fortuitous combination and also because of the influence of existing pagan heroä and mausolea, the Holy Sepulchre was actually visualized in more monumental terms as a two-storied structure (Fig. 8). In the end it is likely that this new conception of the Sepulchre actually influenced the rebuilding of the inner tomb.[43]

[42] R. Krautheimer, "Introduction to an 'Iconography of Mediaeval Architecture,' " *Journal of the Warburg and Courtauld Institutes*, v, 1942, 1-33.

[43] E. Baldwin Smith, "A Source of Mediaeval Style in France," *Art Studies*, II, 1924, 90; Grabar (*Martyrium*, I, 277-282) is of the opin-

ion that the western ivories preserve the appearance of the tomb. The representations have been compiled by N. C. Brooks, "The Sepulchre of Christ in Art and Liturgy, with Special Reference to the Liturgic Drama," *University of Illinois Studies in Language and Literature*, VII, 1921, 6-110.

The purely symbolic intent of these representations is best shown in the mosaics of S. Apollinare Nuovo (Fig. 12) where the tomb is a traditional classical and mortuary tholos, a memorial, or heroön. Even in the East, where one might expect more fidelity to fact, the forms of the tomb are more ideological than naturalistic: on the Madaba mosaic (Fig. 11) it is only a domelike omphalos rising out of the center of the Holy City,[44] and on the Rabula Gospels (Fig. 10) it is a Syrian rustic shelter, a kind of native and ritualistic kalubé. At about the same period, in the scene of the Entry into Jerusalem on the Rossano Gospels (Fig. 16), the city is dominated by a structure whose melon dome, regardless of the sequence of events, was intended to represent the Holy Sepulchre.

Quite apart from the various ways in which the tomb of Christ was presented in the ideational art of this period, the Holy Sepulchre had to be domical because at the time when Constantine undertook to honor the King of Heaven the domical mausoleum was an established type of imperial tomb or memorial, which had a profound symbolic significance in relation to the Cult of the Caesars. On the eternal memorial of an immortal kosmokrator the dome, surmounted by the celestial eagle (Figs. 17-21), had a heavenly implication which appealed to all those who by the fourth century had come to visualize the Saviour in all the conventional terms of a divine imperator.[45] Therefore, the domical tomb, as a glorified tegurium and cosmic dwelling which occurs so frequently during the Constantinian period on the coinage as an *aeterna memoria* and from the time of Diocletian became the standard mausoleum of Western and Early Byzantine emperors, was the only form under which Constantine could recognize a heavenly master.[46]

[44] Grabar, *Martyrium*, I, 235.
[45] A. Alföldi, "Insignien und Tracht der Römischen Kaiser," *Römische Mitteilungen*, L, 1935, 1-158.
[46] The importance of the domical mausoleum during the Constantinian period is shown by its appearance on the imperial coins. While there are several types of memorial, or tomb, they are all characterized by a dome surmounted by a celestial eagle. The simplest type (Fig. 17) has a plain, masonry cylinder pierced by a rectangular doorway (J. Maurice, *Numismatique constantinienne*, 1908-12, I, pls. XVII/12, XIX/10); it usually occurs on coins dedicated to Romulus, but a variant with an arcuated doorway occurs on coins of Valerius Romulus (*ibid.*, pl. VII/14), of Divus Maximianus (H. Cohen, *Description historique des monnaies frappées sous l'empire romain*, 1880-92, VI, 533), and on others (Fig. 18) struck in honor of Constantius Chlorus (Maurice, *op.cit.*, II, pl. VII/5; F. Gnecci, *I Medaglioni romani*, 1912, II, pl. 128/2). The second type has columns, six on a coin of Maxentius (Fig. 20) and four on others (Fig. 19) (Maurice,

op.cit., I, pls. XVII/10, 11 and XIX/1, 2, 9; Cohen, *op.cit.*, VII, 102, 183; *Collection R. Jameson*, II, 1913, pl. XV/339). The third type (Fig. 21), on coins struck by Maxentius, has its drum decorated with statues in projecting gabled niches and suggests the appearance of Theodoric's mausoleum at Ravenna (J. Liegle, "Architekturbilder auf antiken Münzen," *Die Antike*, XII, 1936, 221, Abb. 25/d; Voetter, *Münzen . . . Diocletianus bis Romulus*, figs. 44, 48). It is to be noted that the mausoleum with one door open undoubtedly indicates that no body was actually buried in the memorial.

Although the domical tomb had great antiquity in various parts of the Mediterranean world, it had become by the late antique period essentially a Roman form of mausoleum. There is no evidence, however, that it became an imperial type of monument until after Diocletian erected his domical tomb temple next to his royal dwelling and made of it a kind of omphalos in the center of his city of Spalato. This idea of constructing a heavenly and eternal memorial in the center

According to Grabar it was with a conscious and profound symbolic intent of establishing a monumental parallel between himself and Christ that Constantine had constructed an eternal memorial, or heroön, for the King of Heaven at Jerusalem and another for himself at Constantinople. Like Diocletian's domical tomb, erected next to his palace, which was a kind of omphalos in the center of his city and, hence, in the middle of his empire, Constantine built at Jerusalem, the center of the spiritual universe, an *aeterna memoria* (the Holy Sepulchre) in connection with a spiritual "residence" (the "Royal Church") for the founder of the heavenly kingdom; and then at Constantinople, the center of his own earthly kingdom, he erected for himself a similar domical tomb adjacent to the martyrium church of the Holy Apostles.[47] Although successive generations of Christians, with varying degrees of condemnation, held the belief that Constantine built the church of the Holy Apostles and had the desire to be compared to the King of Heaven, even to memorializing himself in his mausoleum as the Thirteenth Apostle, the parallel breaks down when it is realized that there are no longer any secure grounds for believing that Constantine, rather than his son Constantius, built the church of the Holy Apostles and probably the imperial mausoleum in connection with it.[48] While it may still seem unlikely that Constantine would have neglected to build a mausoleum for himself, the historical evidence indicates that Constantius was the builder of the church and tomb. Nevertheless, the combination of a symbolic, domical and imperial tomb with a *Domus Dei*, whether it started with Diocletian's palace at Spalato, Constantine's construction of the Holy

of his earthly domain was carried on by Constantine, or more probably by Constantius, when his domical mausoleum was built in the center of Constantinople and next to the church of the Holy Apostles. That the actual construction of the church and tomb was carried to completion by his son, Constantius, does not lessen the presumption that the plan was prepared by Constantine. This imperial tradition was continued by the Gothic Emperor Theodoric at Ravenna and the Frankish Emperor Charlemagne when they built their sepulchral memorials near their palaces. The popularity of the domical tomb at Rome and throughout the late Empire was a strong contributing factor in the development of domical architecture and in associating the domical shape with a divine and heavenly hereafter. At Rome there were the so-called tomb of Helena on the Labicana, the Torre de' Sciavi, the hypogeum near Monte dell' Incastro all' Inviolatella, the mausoleum of Santa Costanza and that of Monte del Grano. Also at Rome was the domical heroön of Romulus and later the tomb of Honorius attached to the transept of S. Peter. Outside of Rome there was a domical and presumably

imperial mausoleum at Milan, which may have been erected by Valentinian II, and at Saloniki the rotunda of San Giorgio was originally a royal tomb, perhaps constructed by Theodosius I (H. Koethe, "Das Konstantinsmausoleum und verwandte Denkmäler," *Jahrbuch der deutschen archaeolische Institut*, XLVIII, 1933, 185-203; Koethe, "Zum Mausoleum der weströmischen Dynastie bei Alt-Sankt-Peter," *Röm. Mitt.*, XLVI, 1931, 9-26; C. Cecchelli, "Mausolei imperiali e reale de basso impero e dell' alta medioevo," *Saggi sull' architettura etrusca e romana*, Rome, 1940, 142ff.; G. de Angelus d'Ossat, "La Forma e la costruzione delle cupole nell' archittetura romana," *Saggi sull' architettura etrusca e romana*, 1940, 223ff.; Rivoira, *Architecttura romana*, 1921).

[47] Grabar, *Martyrium*, I, 229-239.

[48] I am indebted to G. Downey for the reinterpretation of the parts which Constantine and Constantius played in the building of the tomb and church, because he permitted me to read the manuscript which he has prepared as part of the study of the Holy Apostles being written by the scholars at Dumbarton Oaks.

Sepulchre at Jerusalem, or Constantius's erection of a mausoleum adjacent to the church of the Holy Apostles, had a lasting influence upon imperial sepulchral architecture. At Rome the round and domical tomb of Honorius was built adjacent to the church of S. Peter; at Ravenna the cruciform and domical tomb of Galla Placidia (Fig. 73) was near to the church of Santa Croce; the tomb of Theodoric, based on an imperial type, was close to his palace, and, in Carolingian times, the domical tomb of Charlemagne was next to his palace at Aachen.

The only essential difference between this imperial mortuary tradition and the Holy Sepulchre was in the shape and construction of the dome. Instead of having been built in the Roman manner as a geometrical hemisphere of masonry, which would have required concealing much of its domical shape on the exterior by buttressing, the dome of the Anastasis was a free-standing and gilded form of wood carpentry which rose on high to make manifest the heavenly character of the abode of Christ. It was constructed of wood in the Syrian manner and by Syrian workmen, as the name of its architect, Zenobius, would suggest. That it was slightly puffed-up and pointed, having the form of a truncated pine cone like the domes on the pagan Marneion, the church of S. Stephen at Gaza, and the Arab mosques, is indicated by some graphic evidence and by the fact that the conoid shape had long been a manifestation of divine presence in Syria. Later, in Chapter IV, will be considered the other beliefs which were combined with these traditional conceptions of a domical structure as a kingly tomb and ideal dwelling in the afterlife to give added content to the shape of the Holy Sepulchre.

The appearance of its light, soaring dome of wood is probably preserved in the scene of the Resurrection painted on the reliquary from Jerusalem in the Museo Sacro of the Vatican (Fig. 14), which cannot be dated later than the seventh century.[49] The box "is the only certain piece of Palestinian painting of the Early Christian period which we possess" and, according to C. R. Morey, "affords us the best indication we have of the appearance of the Holy Sepulchre in the sixth century."[50] The shape of the dome suspended above the ciborium is slightly puffed-up and pointed, while its evident symbolism is shown by the stars painted on its under surface[51] and by the trees in the background.[52]

[49] C. R. Morey, "The Painted Panel from the Sancta Sanctorum," *Festschrift zum sechzigsten Geburtstag von Paul Clemen*, 1926, 151-156, fig. 13; P. Lauer, "Le Trésor du Sancta Sanctorum," *Mon. Piot.*, XV, 1906, 97ff., pl. XIV/2; H. Grisar, *Die römische Kapelle Sancta Sanctorum und ihr Schatz*, 1908, 113, fig. 59; O. Wulff, *Altchristliche und byzantinische Kunst*, I, 1918, 312, fig. 290; Grabar, *Martyrium*, I, 259.

[50] Lauer dated the box by the inscription as late as the tenth century. C. R. Morey obtained the opinions of Monsignor Mercati, Pio Franchi de' Cavalieri and Professor Mercati,

who arrived at the "unanimous conclusion that the script cannot be of so late a date, is earlier than the eighth century and so far as existing criteria indicate might date as early as the sixth" (Morey, *op.cit.*, 151). Grisar attributed the box to the ninth or tenth centuries; Diehl favored a late date; Wulff and Dalton were both inclined to the sixth century; Vincent (*Jérusalem*, II, 177, fig. 108) published the scene as a representation of the Constantinian Holy Sepulchre on a tenth century miniature from the Lateran.

[51] For celestial symbolism, see p. 91.

[52] In the Resurrection scenes on the Sancta

Sanctorum panel (Fig. 14), the Trivulzio ivory (Fig. 9), the Munich ivory (Fig. 8) and the Rabula Gospels (Fig. 10), the combination of a tree with a circular and domical sanctuary, or mortuary tholos, was a traditional form of pagan symbolism appropriated by the Christians. The association of a sacred tree with a domical tholos, rustic shrine and ancestral tegurium was a common theme in both Hellenistic and Roman art, sometimes used to depict the ancient abode of a god in his sacred woods, but more often to show the antique veneration for the mythical golden age when men, gods and animals lived together in a sylvan and earthly paradise. The subject was also a popular motif in sacred, divine and funerary gardens (P. Grimal, *Les Jardins romains*, 1943, 61) of Hellenistic origin. A representation of an early Hellenistic funerary garden is preserved on an inlaid cover of a pyxis (Fig. 25) found in a tomb at Tresilico in the Italian province of Reggio Calabria, which antedates the first century B.C. and was, as were other objects in this and similar graves, presumably of Alexandrian origin (E. Galli, "Riflessi di pittura allesandrina in Calabria," *Rivista del R. Istituto d'archeologia e storia dell' arte*, VI, 1937, 32-46, tav. 1). Here on this sepulchral pyxis are all the elements of an ideal paradise—the round, domical dwelling for the soul, the sacred trees of the garden, the romantically ruined columns, the statuary and the narrow bridge over which the soul had to pass. In using this scene I am indebted to Miss Berta Segall, who tells me that the scene, although completely Hellenized, reflects an underlying Egyptian tradition of the Isle of the Blessed which was a Nilotic conception of the future life, connected with the Isis cult that influenced Roman representations of funerary gardens and late antique ideas of the afterlife. Since this study went to press, Miss Segall has heard rumors that the cover may be a forgery.

While it is difficult to disentangle the various antique beliefs which combined to give the domical tholos a mortuary significance and to make its association with a sacred tree the symbol of a future paradise, it is easy to see how the Christians came to take over this prevalent, classical combination of a domical shrine, an ancestral and divine tegurium, with a sacred tree, for their own ideological representation of a heavenly paradise. In Roman art the subject began to appear in Pompeiian painting and on the stucco ceilings of Roman tombs: in the *Domus Vesonius Primus* (Fig. 145) a great tree has its branches mingled with the supports of a domical baldachin which covers an open-air altar in an idyllic and sacred garden of love and happiness (M. Rostowzew, "Die hellenistisch-römische Architekturlandschaft," *Röm. Mitt.*, XXVI, 1911, 44, fig. 24); the domical shrine, or heroön, of Melicertes at Corinth appears on the coins (Fig. 22) with a tree on either side of the rotunda dedicated to this particular hero cult (T. L. Donaldson, *Architettura numismatica*, 1859, 61; F. Robert, *Thymélè*, 1939, 156ff.); and a Renaissance sketch (Fig. 24) by Fra Giocondo (H. de Geymüller, "Trois albums de dessins de Fra Giocondo," *Mélanges d'arch. et d'hist.*, XI, 1891, 136, pl. 1; R. Jaeger, "Die Bronzetüren von Bethlehem," *Jahrb. d. deut. arch. Inst.*, XLV, 1930, 110, Abb. 22), shows a domical shrine as a monumental version of a sylvan tegurium in combination with a dead tree, figures of Pan, a maenad and two female divinities, all indicating the romantic interest in an idyllic past and a kind of lost paradise.

In Early Christian art the representation of the Holy Sepulchre as a traditional domical tomb, tholos, kalubé, or tegurium, in combination with a tree, shows not only that the domical shelter had a symbolic significance which the Christians had appropriated from Roman and Hellenistic art, but also that there were mystic implications in the domical shape as the sacred dwelling of a divinity who once lived on earth among men, and as the ideal abode of the soul in a *paradisus*, or heavenly garden. This conception of the tomb of Christ as a funerary symbol in a celestial garden is also indicated by the references of early Western pilgrims to the atrium in front of the Anastasis as a *hortus* and *paradisus*. In adapting the antique symbolism of the domical shelter and its rustic setting to their own use, the Christians did not limit the symbolism to the sepulchral abode of Christ, for the tomb of Lazarus is depicted on an early piece of gold-glass (Fig. 23) as a domical tegurium with a tree behind it (G. Ferretto, *Note storico-bibliografiche di archeologia cristiana*, 1942, 236, fig. 40). As early as the end of the third or the beginning of the fourth century the paradise to which the soul of Jonah is transported is depicted in a tomb at Cagliari in Sardinia (Fig. 70) by means of a domical tegurium and two trees, one the olive tree of peace and happiness, and the other the palm as a symbol of Jerusalem (see p. 54; G. B. de

As far as the actual domical character of the Holy Sepulchre is concerned, this scene is equally significant whether the reliquary was executed, as Professor Morey has argued, in the sixth century before the Anastasis was burnt by the Persians in 614 A.D. or was painted shortly after Modestus restored the monument in 616-618. Grisar's argument for a later date in the ninth or tenth century was based upon the fact that the panel shows a rectangular altar stone in front of the ciborium. This Grisar considers to be the rectangular altar that Modestus had cut out of one of the pieces of the round millstone at the door of the Sepulchre after it had been broken in two by the Persians in order to remove the band of gold that decorated it. Since the inscriptions inside the box cannot be dated later than the seventh century,[53] and there is no reason to believe that Modestus made any change in the shape and construction of the dome built for Constantine, it does not alter the domical evidence to assume that the panel may have been executed shortly after 618 A.D., although Professor Morey has presented a strong case for a sixth century date. The emphasis given to the dome, decorated with yellow dots as stars, suspended like the canopy of heaven above the tomb of Christ suggests that the reliquary was made to contain one of the pieces of True Cross which had been recovered from the ruins of the holy site and that the novel presentation of the Resurrection was to commemorate the restoration of the Holy Sepulchre.

The Palestinian origin of the box and the reliability of its representation of the rotunda are further strengthened by the similarity of its scene of the Holy Women at the Tomb to the same scene on two ampullae, one in the Dumbarton Oaks Collection (Fig. 158) and another in the Detroit Institute of Arts.[54] On these two phials from the Holy Land the rotunda is also depicted as a circular building with interior columns and round-headed, clerestory windows; the only difference being that the designer of the ampullae, because of the small, circular space at his disposal, left off the celestial dome which is so prominent on the box.

In either event the building on the reliquary box, whether it preserves the appearance of the Constantinian or the early seventh century memorial of Christ, strongly supports the other evidence of its having had a dome of wood. The radial and segmental lines on the dome, which appear in a good photograph of the box, suggest a

Rossi, "Cubicoli sepolcrali cristiani adorni di pitture," *Bolletino di archeologia cristiana*, series 5, III, 1892, 130-144, pl. VI). The significance of sacred trees in relation to the martyria of the Holy Land has been discussed by Grabar (*Martyrium*, I, 71-75) and will again be considered on p. 66.

[53] In front of the tomb of Christ was the millstone which had been adorned with a band of gold and jewels as is shown on the Rabula Gospels (Fig. 10). In 614 A.D. the gold excited the cupidity of the Persians, who broke the stone into two pieces. When the monument was re-

stored the fragments were squared and used as altars, one in the vestibule and the other in the presbyterium, according to Arculph. Grisar's arguments for the late date of the reliquary box lay great emphasis upon the white, rectangular altar stone seen in front of the ciborium (Fig. 14). Morey dismisses this argument as "not a serious one," because "the existence of an altar at the entrance of the Sepulchre proper is attested by the Breviarius de Hierosolyma and the Itinerarium Antonini, both of the sixth century" (p. 152).

[54] See p. 99.

domical construction in wooden gores such as is described in Choricius' account of the dome at Gaza (p. 39) and are so frequently shown on representations of Palestinian domes (Figs. 15, 16, 168). Also its slightly puffed-up shape, its soaring character and size are all indications that it was made of wood and "not surely a vault of stone" as has been insisted.[55]

Two other bits of evidence, slight in themselves, support the contention that the original dome of the Constantinian monument had the conoid shape which was characteristic of the domical tradition in Syria. In the section "De Sepulchris" of the *Agrimensorum Romanorum* the drawing of a typical sepulchral monument (Fig. 13) has a dome puffed-up, free standing, and pointed.[56] Although the *Agrimensorum Romanorum* is derived from early Roman sources, the drawings are a later addition, possibly of the sixth or seventh century, at a time when the Holy Sepulchre with its free-standing and pointed dome of wood would have been pictured as the ideal type of memorial tomb rather than the traditional imperial Roman mausoleum with a hemispherical dome of masonry. Furthermore, a ninth century Greek manuscript (Ambr. 49-50) which Grabar says was strongly influenced by the archaic and Oriental traditions, probably of Palestine, presents Jerusalem by a schematic and symbolic drawing of the Holy Sepulchre (Fig. 15) as a tholos with a conoid dome within the walls of a massive edifice.[57] Therefore, when all this evidence is combined and taken in conjunction with the shape of the wooden dome on the church of S. Stephen at Gaza and the tomb of Bizzos (Fig. 61), which may have been influenced by the Martyrium of Christ, the form and construction of the dome on the Holy Sepulchre become consistent with the whole tradition of the dome in Syria and Palestine.

3. DOMUS AUREA, ANTIOCH (327 and 526-588 A.D.)

The other important early central church (Fig. 26), presumably begun by Constantine but finished by Constantius, was the "Great Church," or *Domus aurea*, at Antioch. Little is known of the Constantinian building before its rebuilding after the fire of 526 except that it was a large domical octagon with interior colonnades of great magnificence and that its interior was raised "to an enormous height."[58] It was dedicated to Christ-Concord and according to Eusebius was a "unique" building of particular beauty in order to be worthy of Antioch, which was the "head of all the peoples [of the Orient]."[59] That it was domical and situated on the island in the "New City" as a part of the imperial palace of Antioch has been fairly well established

[55] Grabar, *Martyrium*, I, 259.

[56] Wolfenbüttel, cod. 36.23 Aug. fol., *Agrimensorum Romanorum*, fol. 77ᵛ; C. Thulin (*Die Handschriften des Corpus Agrimensorum Romanorum*, Preuss. Ak., 1911) says that the manuscript shows a strong Byzantine influence and that the actual archetype does not antedate 450 A.D.

[57] Grabar, *op.cit.*, I, 237, fig. 19; Grabar, *Les Miniatures du Grégoire de Nazianze de l'Ambrosienne*, I, 1943, pl. XLVIII/3 and LII/1. As

late as the fifteenth century Symeon of Thessalonica in *De sacro Templo* (133-Migne, *P.G.*, CLV, col. 341) says that κιβώριον symbolizes the tomb of Christ.

[58] Cabrol, *Dict.*, I, "Antioche," cols. 2372ff.; Eusebius, *Vita Constantini*, III, 50; Malalas, *Chronographia*, ed. Bonn, 1831, 318, 324, 325; Malalas records that it was founded by Constantine but was completed by Constantius.

[59] Grabar, *Martyrium*, I, 220-227.

by the fifth century topographical mosaic at Yakto, a village near Antioch. It is presented as a polygonal building (Fig. 29) having a cupola and apsidal vault, with a man standing beside it looking up in prayer and veneration.[60]

By derivation, location and symbolism this domical church of Christ, according to Grabar, was a martyrium like the Holy Sepulchre, a traditional funereal, triumphal and memorial heroön of the imperial cult, located like Diocletian's mausoleum at Spalato in the center of his city and next to his palace and intended to make another symbolical parallel between Constantine and Christ.[61] Here in this temple, with the title of *Concordia poenitentiae*, was worshipped Christ, the heavenly ruler and conqueror, who accorded to his universe the gift of Concordia, just as the Emperor, after his triumph of 325, brought about a union of the Roman universe in the unique religion of Christ. As a traditional imperial memorial, which became known as the *Domus aurea* because of its gilded and celestial covering, it was a domical, central structure, but its religious purpose as a church of Christ necessitated an apse at the west side. Beyond the fact that it was domical and presumably built of wood covered with gilded lead like the structure which replaced it, nothing more is known about the roof of the original "Great Church."

When the Golden House was destroyed by fire in 526, Malalas says, "The Great Church of Antioch, which had been built by the Emperor Constantine the Great, when the disaster occurred and everything else fell to the ground, stood for two days after the frightful visitation of God occurred, and it *caught fire* and was destroyed to the ground."[62] Later, in 588, Evagrius, an eye-witness, described the effect of the second great earthquake which wrecked Antioch. "Many buildings," he wrote, "were destroyed when the very foundations were thrown up, so that everything about the most holy church fell to the ground, only the *hemisphere* being saved, which had been constructed of wood from Daphne by Ephraemius after it had suffered in the earthquake under Justinus."[63] "It was tilted," he goes on to relate, "toward the north by the earthquake which followed [under Justinian in 528] so that it received bracing timbers. These fell through the violence of the shock [in 588] when the hemisphere settled back and was restored to its right place as though it was set there by a rule." Evagrius' account leaves no doubt that the sixth century dome was made of wood, for no masonry dome could have been tilted, braced with timbers and then settled back into place.

[60] Doro Levi, *Antioch Mosaic Pavements*, 1947, 332, pl. LXXX/c; the theory of Eltester, that the inscription, PIAVA, signifies the Porta Tauriana and thereby locates the church inside the entrance gate of the palace area, is considered unsound by Levi but has been developed by Grabar (*Martyrium*, I, 215-227) into a convincing argument for the location and purpose of the church as part of the palace on the island.

[61] Grabar, *op.cit.*, 223-225.

[62] Malalas, *op.cit.*, 419, 21, as translated by G. Downey.

[63] Evagrius, VI, 8, translated by G. Downey; the "Ephraim," whom Strzygowski (*Kleinasien*, 95) called the master-builder who erected the wooden cupola, was Ephraemius, the *comes Orientalis* who became Patriarch of Antioch in 527 (Downey, "Ephraemius, Patriarch of Antioch," *Church History*, VII, 1938, 364-370).

4. MARTYRIUM, NAZIANZUS (before 374 A.D.)

Gregory of Nazianzus, when describing the "living memorial" of his father, writes, "It surrounds itself with eight regular equilaterals, and is raised aloft by the beauty of the two stories of pillars and porticoes, while the statues placed upon them are true to life; its vault [οὐρανῷ, *heaven*] flashes down upon us from above, and it dazzles our eyes with the abundant sources of light."[64] Although there is nothing in the account to prove that this martyrium of eight sides (Fig. 28) had a wooden dome, as Watzinger says it had,[65] it is very evident from Gregory's use of words that Birnbaum was wrong in thinking that the church had a polygonal roof with a hypaethral opening.[66] Regardless of whether the roof was constructed of wood or masonry, the use of the word "heaven" and the emphasis upon its being a dazzling source of light show, as Keil recognized,[67] that it was a cupola, because the Christians with their cosmic symbolism always thought of the dome as a celestial shape.

Further confirmation of the domical form of this memorial is furnished by a scholion of uncertain date, which compares the martyrium to an octagonal sanctuary at Alexandria, presumably the martyrium of S. John the Baptist, and to "the Theotokos naos at Tyre."[68] While nothing is known about the church of the Virgin at Tyre, which must have been later than the fourth century, except that it was customary in the Near East to erect domical martyria in honor of the Virgin, there is every reason to believe that the famous martyrium of the Baptist at Alexandria was domical. Not only did it replace the pagan Serapeion, when that renowned domical temple was destroyed by the Christians at the beginning of the fifth century, but it depicted as domical in the sixth century mosaics at Gerasa (Figs. 30, 31).

5. MARTYRIUM, NYSSA (c. 379-394 A.D.)

The martyrium which Gregory had built around 380 at Nyssa in Cappadocia consisted of a central apsidal octagon with four exedras (Fig. 27), making it, according to Grabar,[69] a cruciform structure like the martyrium of Antioch-Kaoussie (Fig. 170) and the church of S. Simeon Stylites at Kal'at Sim'ân (Fig. 32). The letter of Gregory to Amphilochius sometime between 379 and 394 furnishes important and conclusive evidence regarding the shape and construction of domical martyria in the fourth century. In describing the martyrium which he was undertaking to build at Nyssa he writes, "Above the eight apses the octagon will rise. The pine cone which rises from this will be cone-shaped (κωνοειδής), the vortex reducing the shape of the roof from a plane to a point."[70] This specific statement that the roof of the martyrium was like

---

[64] Migne, *P.G.*, xxxv; "On the death of his Father," *Nicene and Post-Nicene Fathers*, vii, chap. 39, 267.

[65] Watzinger, *Denk. Paläs.*, ii, 133.

[66] A. Birnbaum, "Die Oktagone von Antiochia, Nazianz und Nyssa," *Rep. f. Kunstwiss.*, xxxvi, 1913, 207.

[67] Keil in Strzygowski, *Kleinasien*, 94 n. 4.

[68] See Chap. ii n. 25 and Chap. iv n. 41.

[69] Grabar, *Martyrium*, i, 152ff., 157.

[70] Migne, *P.G.*, xlvi, 1093ff.; Birnbaum, *op. cit.*, 181-209; Keil (*Kleinasien*, 77ff., fig. 63) interprets Gregory as saying that it was a geometrically conical roof, and his plan (Fig. 27), based upon Gregory's description, is structurally inexplicable in its location of the columns.

a pine cone, when taken in combination with the description of the Marneion, the account of the wooden dome on the church of S. Stephen at Gaza, the conoid dome on the tomb of Bizzos, the persistence in the Christian East of the conoid shelter as a ritualistic kalubé and cosmic house, and the later Arab adoption of the wooden conoid dome, is proof that the "pine-cone" shape and the idea of a domical martyrium were already traditional by the last quarter of the fourth century.

It is also significant for the history of domical architecture that Gregory goes on to say he would prefer to build this martyrium with a wooden dome if it were possible. After asking Amphilochius to send him the required workmen, he writes, "It is especially necessary to give attention to the point that some of them shall know how to build domes (εἴλησις) without centering, for I have learned that when this is done it is steadier than if it rests on supports; the *scarcity of wood*, indeed, leads to this plan, namely that the whole structure shall be roofed with stones, because there is no wood suitable for roofing in this region." This is confirmation of the assumption that domes of swollen and pine-cone shape were commonly built of wood and were sufficiently customary so that the conoid shape, because of the scarcity of wood, was to be reproduced in stone. It is difficult to visualize what Gregory meant by domes built without centering being steadier than those resting on supports unless he is thinking of stone squinches, or pendentives, rather than wooden supports at the corners where the dome had to be fitted onto the octagon.

6. MARTYRIA OF CONSTANTINOPLE (fourth and fifth centuries)

It has been customary to think of the Byzantine dome as a masonry vault which began to be common upon the churches largely because of Justinian's interest in a monumental state architecture of stone and brick. Now it is becoming evident that the real incentive to build domical structures came from the ascendancy of the Cult of Martyrs and the gradual adoption by both the State and the Church of a martyrium type of sanctuary with its central plan of commemorative and mortuary implications and its symbolic dome. It is most unlikely that this apparently sudden popularity of the dome, which we have known only in its masonry form, could have been solely the result of either a veneration for the martyrium churches of Palestine or of the introduction of domical construction from Asia Minor. Back of it must have been a customary pattern of ideas which had already associated the domical shape with buildings for the commemoration and glorification of the dead. Long before Justinian undertook to rebuild such famous churches as the Holy Apostles and S. Sophia, there were in Constantinople, as there were in Syria and Palestine, earlier martyria with wooden domes which had already established the domical tradition for the churches which Justinian and his successors rebuilt with masonry domes. The specific evidence for the existence of these fourth and fifth century wooden domes is neither reliable nor conclusive for any particular church, but the collective evidence proves that the Christian chroniclers of Constantinople knew and accepted the tradition of the wooden dome.

32

Regarding the original fourth century church of the Holy Apostles, which was a cruciform martyrium probably planned by Constantine but actually built by his successor Constantius, the *Patria* says that it had a wooden dome. Two passages state that it was ξυλόστεγος, i.e. that it had a "wooden roof,"[71] but a third passage says that the original church was ξυλότρουλος, i.e. had a "wooden dome."[72] Since the *Patria* was compiled in the tenth or eleventh century from sources going back for the most part only to the eighth and ninth centuries, it must be admitted that these references, when taken by themselves, are not highly reliable. In fact, Heisenberg, with the customary attitude of his generation toward the wooden dome, assumed that a mistake had been made and that the writer of the *Patria*, who was acquainted with the domical appearance of Justinian's church of the Holy Apostles, merely imagined that the wooden roof of the original church was domical.[73] If one views all evidence with the presupposition that wooden domes were improbable, it may also be argued that Glycas made the same mistake when he wrote that the original church of S. Sophia was ξυλότρουλος because his source, *The Anonymous Description of the Building of St. Sophia*, refers only to a wooden roof.[74]

[71] *Scriptores originum Constantinopolitanarum*, ed. T. Preger, Leipzig, 1901-1907, II, 9-13; 214, 5-8. I am indebted for these references to G. Downey of Dumbarton Oaks, Washington, D.C., who is preparing a documentary study of the church of the Holy Apostles.

[72] *Ibid.*, 286, 18. Although this passage, by itself, cannot be taken as evidence that the original Holy Apostles had a wooden dome, the presumption is strengthened by Downey's interpretation of the word DOMATION which is used in the *Vita Constantini* to differentiate the "little roof" over the crossing of the Holy Apostles from the DOMA or regular roof over the rest of the church. Downey's translation of the account in the *Vita*, attributed to Eusebius (IV, 58) reads as follows: "And above, over this [ceiling], on the roof-top itself, bronze instead of tiles provided protection for the building, furnishing safety for the rains. And much gold lit this up, so that it shot forth dazzling light, by means of the reflection of the sun's rays, to those who beheld it from afar. And he encircled the little roof [DOMATION] round about with pierced grilles, executed in gilded bronze."

In his forthcoming note on this passage Downey goes on to say: "Heisenberg, in his translation of the passage, follows the notes in the Migne text and takes *domation* as the equivalent of *doma*, referring to the roof as a whole. However, he does not seem to have taken into account the possibility that the writer of this passage used the two forms in order to make clear that he had some distinction in mind. . . . The context of the passage in the *Vita Constantini* would suggest, in fact, that *domation* might be employed here to mean a lantern or wooden structure. The reference to the 'pierced grilles' or 'lattices' which follows immediately of course suggests windows at the base of a dome, such as are shown in the representations of domes in the painted box from the Sancta Sanctorum [Fig. 14] . . . and the unpublished Monza ampulla in the Dumbarton Oaks Collection [Fig. 158]. . . . Descriptively, a lantern or outer casing of a dome would be regarded as a special or symbolic kind of 'little roof,' a 'little house,' and hence could be designated by the diminutive of the word meaning roof or house."

If I may add to Downey's interpretation what I hope will become evident in this study, in the Early Christian period a domical "little house," figuratively a tegurium or kalubé, had very specific symbolic meanings as the dwelling of the Good Shepherd (Fig. 70), a tomb, a heavenly home in paradise (Figs. 94, 99) and the celestial covering of a *Domus aurea* of God. Hence there is every reason to accept Downey's suggestion that *domation*, in this context, must mean a gilded dome with a clerestory over what was the martyrium proper.

[73] A. Heisenberg, *Grabeskirche und Apostelkirche, zwei Basiliken Konstantins*, 1908, II, 102-103. Heisenberg takes ξυλότρουλος, which is copied by Michael Glycas in his account of the church of the Holy Apostles (498f., 21ff., ed. Bonn, 1836) to be a false interpretation of ξυλόστεγος.

[74] Michael Glycas, 495, 15, ed. Bonn; "Anon-

At a period more nearly contemporary with the rebuilding of the martyrium church of S. Anastasia in the ninth century by Basil I, the *Patria* says that the original church, attributed to Maurice, had a wooden dome.[75] It can, therefore, be argued that there was no misunderstanding or confusion in the use of ξυλόστεγος and ξυλότρουλος because it was well understood that any reference to a wooden roof on a martyrium carried with it the implication of a symbolic domical shape. The collective weight of the evidence would seem to justify this conclusion because the *Scriptores originum Constantinopolitanarum* says that "St. Mark near Taurus was a great church with a wooden dome (μεγάλη ξυλότρουλος) built by Theodosius the Great [379-395 A.D.]. And when it collapsed the Emperor Romanus the Elder [920-944 A.D.] rebuilt it."[76] It is most unlikely that all these references to a wooden dome were the result of a misunderstanding. Instead, they should be accepted as evidence that the wooden dome was not exceptional but for the first two centuries after the Peace of the Church was associated in men's minds with a martyrium. As Grabar has remarked in discussing these Constantinopolitan references to a wooden dome, they make one "think of the analogous coverings of the ancient martyria of Syria."[77]

7. S. SIMEON STYLITES, KAL'AT SIM'ÂN (460-490 A.D.)

The great cruciform church of S. Simeon Stylites at Kal'at Sim'ân (Fig. 32) was undoubtedly built by workmen from Antioch. It was both a church of the eucharistic cult and a martyrium, built around not the tomb but the column of the saint. As the goal of a celebrated pilgrimage this column, according to Grabar,[78] was a major relic of the saint, comparable to the tomb of a martyr. In fact, the suggestion has been made, but not fully supported by archaeological investigation, that it was originally, like the martyria of S. John at Ephesus and the church at Korykos, a relic sanctuary to which the cruciform arms were added later.[79] Ever since the church was published by De Vogüé and restudied by Howard Butler, it has seemed curious that the octagonal crossing, the important focal point and martyrium form, should have been uncovered, making it necessary for the assembled visitors to listen to long sermons of the Stylite from his columnar pulpitum under the intense Syrian sun.[80]

---

ymous Description of the Building of St. Sophia," *Scr. orig. Const.*, ed. Preger, 75, 1.

[75] *Scr. orig. Const.*, II, 234, 2; Grabar, *Martyrium*, I, 376.

[76] *Ibid.*, II, 277, 10.

[77] Grabar, *Martyrium*, I, 376. Grabar (82) also cites the terracotta tabernacle, or reliquary, from Bawit which consisted of a square chamber surmounted by a cupola with an imitation of either "wood or metal coffers" (J. Maspéro and E. Drioton, *Fouilles exécutés à Bawît* [Mémoires de l'Institut français d'archéologie orientaledu Caire, 59], 1932, plates unpublished).

[78] Grabar, *Martyrium*, I, 365.

[79] M. Écochard ("Le sanctuaire de Qal'at Sem'ân: Notes archéologiques," *Bulletin d'études orientales de l'Institut français de Damas*, VI, 1936, 61ff.) has presented the evidence for the difference in date of construction for the various parts of the building and suggested that it was originally an octagon comparable to the Constantinian *Dominicum aureum* at Antioch.

[80] C. J. M. de Vogüé, *Syrie centrale, architecture civile et religieuse*, 1865-77, I, pls. 139-150; H. C. Butler, *Architecture and Other Arts* (Part II of the Publication of an American Archaeological Expedition to Syria in 1899-1900), 1903, 184.

This central octagon, where the saint dwelt and preached as one directly inspired from heaven, was 27 m. in diameter and had walls only .80 m. thick. If covered, then it must have had a light wooden roof. Inasmuch, however, as Evagrius, a Syrian of Antioch, writing about 560 A.D., described the octagon as αὐλὴ ὑπαίθριος, scholars concluded that it was an open court with only the sky above it. Even after Krencker had restudied the remains and found conclusive evidence that the octagon had been covered with a timber roof, he assumed that the original roof must have been destroyed at the time when Evagrius wrote.[81] In view, however, of the Christian respect for tradition and the importance attached to a symbolic covering both for a martyrium and for the public appearance of either a Divine or Great One, it is most unlikely that the elevated pulpitum and sacred dwelling place of the Stylite was allowed to remain without its architectural ciborium in the sixth century. Since sepulchral domes and royal baldachins at this time were heavenly symbols decorated with stars, it seems more likely that Evagrius took for granted the actual dome with its celestial implications and, hence, was referring to the ideational meaning of the covering when he wrote of the "court under the sky."

Certainly Krencker has proved that it was once covered, for he not only found pieces of the stone cornice of the octagon with notches for the roofing timbers, but he also discovered recognizable fragments of horseshoe-arched niche squinches supported on corbels at the angles of the cornice (Fig. 35). These he quite rightly assumed would only have been necessary to fit the continuous round base of a wooden dome onto the octagonal walls, since a polygonal wooden roof could have rested directly upon the cornice. Because the clerestory windows and the squinches at Kal'at Sim'ân were horseshoe-shaped, as were the niches of the church of El Hadra and of the martyrium at Resafa, and because the horseshoe profile occurs so frequently in the church apses of northern Syria, suggesting that it must have originated in an earlier architecture of wood and pliable materials, Krencker restored the octagon with a wooden dome. This dome he made with two shells, the outer one slightly bulbous like the "puffed-up" and pointed dome described by Mark the Deacon on the pagan Marneion at Gaza, the pine-cone dome constructed by Gregory on the martyrium at Nyssa and the wooden dome on the Qubbat-aṣ-Sakhra (Fig. 37). Later it will be seen that this shape had a special religious significance in the region around Antioch and Emesa (Homs).

If the great church of the saint at Kal'at Sim'ân had a wooden dome over the crossing, it should follow that the cruciform church of S. Simeon the Younger at Mont Admirable (Fig. 173) near Antioch, which also had an octagonal center, was covered with a similar dome.[82]

[81] D. Krencker, *Die Wallfahrtskirche des Simeon Stylites in Kal'at Sim'ân* (Abh. d. preuss. Akad. d. Wiss., Phil. hist. Klasse, 1938, no. 4), 1939; Krencker, "War das Oktagon der Wallfahrtskirche des Simeon Stylites in Kal'at Sim'ân überdekt?", *Röm. Mitt.*, XLIX, 1934, 62-89.

[82] See p. 111.

8. SION CHURCH, JERUSALEM (456-460 A.D.)

The Sion Church, which according to the liturgy of S. James was "the mother of all churches" and the most illustrious of the holy places glorified by the manifestation of Christ, was a five-aisled basilica whose liturgical provisions and murals had a far-reaching influence upon Christian art and Syrian iconography.[83] Among its special chambers or oratories it had in the upper story of the east end, to the south of the apse, two domical sanctuaries. One of these chapels, according to an Armenian text of the seventh century, was the "Chamber of Mysteries," the *Coenaculum*, which was covered with a wooden cupola.[84] It was around the lower zone of this cupola that was depicted the sacred Last Supper of the Saviour, which was supposed to have taken place in the *Coenaculum* when Christ and his Apostles withdrew to it in order to perform the mystical repast that was both a communion performed by Christ and also his martyr's feast. Therefore, this "High Place," with its small apse, was both a martyrium, as its domical covering signified, and a ciborium above the actual altar that was located beneath the wooden dome.

The scene which was on the dome is reproduced upon two Syrian patens of the sixth century, one from Stûmâ (Fig. 33), a small town south of Aleppo, and the other from a North Syrian tomb at Rîhā (Fig. 34). On the Rîhā paten, which is in the Dumbarton Oaks Collection at Washington,[85] the ciborium over the altar is a curious, nichelike form decorated with a conch. Although there appears to have been an explicable confusion on the part of the craftsman as to whether he was depicting a ciborium over an altar or the apse back of it, the shape is that of a slightly bulbous and pointed dome.[86] In contrast, the domical shape is more clearly presented on the Stûmâ paten, where it is supported, not by columns, but by the two figures of Christ himself.[87] The inconsistencies between the scenes on the two patens can be

[83] A study of the Sion Church and its influence upon Christian art is being prepared by A. M. Friend, Princeton University, and the scholars at Dumbarton Oaks, Washington, D.C.

[84] Vincent and Abel, *Jérusalem*, II, 456 n. 5; the translation of the Armenian description by M. N. Bain reads, "To the right of the church the chamber of the mysteries, and a wooden cupola in which is imaged the sacred supper of the Saviour. In it an altar at which the liturgy is celebrated." Later this chamber is described by Daniel (Vincent and Abel, *op.cit.*, 479) as approached by a flight of steps on the south side of the church and as being covered by a vault, which Phocas (*P.G.*, 941; Vincent and Abel, *op.cit.*, 480) says was to the right of the church and up sixty-one steps, having a cupola supported on four arches.

[85] H. Peirce and R. Tyler, *L'Art byzantin*, II, 1932-34, fig. 144.

[86] The arcuated covering over Christ may have been a Syrian convention for showing a royal and divine presence, as has been suggested by D. F. Brown ("The Arcuated Lintel and Its Symbolic Interpretation in Late Antique Art," *A.J.A.*, XLVI, 1942, 398); at the same time it is apparent that the arch in both Hellenistic and Roman art frequently had a heavenly meaning (A. B. Cook, *Zeus*, II, 160); hence it is possible that the artist was consciously trying to combine the celestial symbolism of an arcuated lintel, an apse and the dome.

[87] J. Ebersolt, "Le Trésor de Stuma au Musée de Constantinople," *Revue archéologique*, series 4, XVII, 1911, 411ff., pl. VIII; Peirce and Tyler, *op.cit.*, fig. 140/a; the style, workmanship and iconography of the paten indicate that it belongs to the great period of Syrian art between the end of the fifth century and the first half of the sixth century, and not to the beginning of the seventh century where Ebersolt dated it.

explained by the fact that the craftsmen, in their effort to show the mystical implications of the event and its domical setting, were confronted with the problem of representing both an actual event which was supposed to have taken place under a symbolic ciborium and a scene which was located in the *Coenaculum* upon the dome itself. Since there was no ciborium over the altar in the "High Place," because the wooden dome was both a ciborium and the celestial covering of the martyrium as a cosmic house, the designer of the Rîhâ paten seems to have endeavored to combine the aspidal niche of the chamber with the idea of a ciborium, while the other craftsman on the Stûmâ paten was more concerned with emphasizing the heavenly canopy suspended above the communal altar. The floral patern around the canopy on the Stûmâ paten is a stylized ornament presumably intended to suggest the idea of rustic construction and thereby indicate to the initiated the underlying meanings of the domical shape as a god-given ancestral shelter, a cosmic house, tegurium, and kalubé, which in so many other scenes (Fig. 70) was also a sepulchral ciborium and the ideal abode of the martyred dead in a celestial paradise.

9. CATHEDRAL, ETSCHMIADZIN (c. 483 A.D.)

The early use of the wooden dome was not limited to any one region in the Near East. The evidence for a wooden dome of the fifth century on the cathedral of Etschmiadzin is important to the history of domical architecture because in Armenia, where the domical church became the standard type in stone construction after the seventh century, there are clear indications that many of the stone forms were sculpturally reproduced from wooden prototypes.[88] In his *History of Heraclius* Sebios does

[88] S. Der Nersessian, *Armenia and the Byzantine Empire*, 1945, 60; H. F. B. Lynch, *Armenia, Travels and Studies*, 1901, I, 264; Strzygowski, *Die Baukunst der Armenier und Europa*, 1918, 334, 340. Regarding the possible wooden origin of the domical form, Strzygowski (*op.cit.*, II, 614-625) recognized the derivation of early stone architecture from wooden prototypes whose wooden domical tradition had survived in the Ukraine and South Russia, but advanced the theory, without any convincing arguments, that the Armenian dome had first originated on the primitive wooden house of Central Asia where it was translated into sun-dried brick in North Iran before being introduced into Armenia. Grabar (*Martyrium*, I, 182-183, 328-330, 378-379) believes that the domical architecture of Armenia developed with the Cult of Relics and was derived from established martyria types, popular in the Near East, which went back to classical models. Since the early Armenian churches are so clearly sculptural reproductions in stone of forms which must have originated in wood and since the influence of these wooden prototypes are persistently evident throughout the history of Armenian architecture, there seems little reason for introducing a hypothetical brick dome as a transitional stage of development. Instead, it seems more reasonable to suppose that there was an old and persistent wooden, domical tradition in Armenia which from the seventh century on, when the Transcaucasian region began to be powerfully influenced by the domical martyrium churches of Asia Minor, Syria and Palestine and at the time when there was probably an exodus of stonecutters, as well as Christians, from Syria, the native domical tradition naturally combined with the domical tradition of the Mediterranean martyria which had already been translated into masonry vaults. As late as the twelfth century Armenian stone ribs at Hahpat (J. Baltrušaitis, *Le Problème de l'ogive et l'Arménie*, 1936, figs. 11, 12, 18) and Horomos (fig. 7) were literally and sculpturally imitated from wooden prototypes even to their irregular intersections and the use of wooden pegs. Miss Der Nersessian (*op.cit.*, 59) points out how frequently the word "domed" occurs

not say that it was a dome of wood which in 618 was replaced on the cathedral by one of stone. He merely records that they "took away the timbered roof"; but, later in the tenth century, John Kathlikos refers to the timbered dome (*Zpaïdharq kempet*) of the cathedral.[89] Since this evidence for a fifth century wooden dome has been generally accepted, it is surprising to find Creswell stating that the Armenian cathedral had a conical timbered roof like the Marneion and the Holy Sepulchre because *kempet* was a word used for domes with polygonal and conical exteriors.[90] The significant fact is not that the Etschmiadzin cupola may have been covered with a protecting conical or polygonal roof, as were so many Roman domes and perhaps the early wooden domes of the Caucasus region, but that it had a monumental carpentry roof whose domical shape was undoubtedly symbolic and traditional over the sacred dwelling of God.

10. CHURCH (MARTYRIUM?) OF S. STEPHEN, GAZA (fifth or sixth century)

The most conclusive evidence for the Syrian use of a wooden dome of pine-cone shape is furnished by Choricius of Gaza in his detailed description of the church of S. Stephen.[91] In reading his elaborate account, it must be recalled that Gaza was the city where the pagan Marneion, destroyed in 402 A.D., had a "puffed-up" wooden dome, "rising on high," and where Rufinus, an architect of Antioch, constructed on the site of the heathen temple a cruciform church that was probably domical. The translations of the passage of Choricius on this church of S. Stephen have been misleading because the church is described as a three-aisled basilica, and the translators have adhered to the usual conviction that a wooden dome was therefore impossible.[92] Since neither Hamilton nor Abel fully understood Choricius' pretentious and literary architectural phraseology, they mistook his geometrical and technical description of the dome for some kind of indefinite ornament. The translation which will be used in this study was carefully prepared by Mr. Glanville Downey, a specialist on the architectural usage of late Greek writers, and the full text of his translation will be included in the appendix.

It is necessary, in order to follow Choricius' somewhat involved method of description, to begin with him at the east end of the church where he praises the apse. Starting with its *hollowness beginning on the pavement itself*, he says it rose with *constant width*, as an apse should, up to the springing of the apsidal arch, above which *the remainder is drawn together gradually in breadth, harmoniously with the arch*. In the next paragraph, his eye having been drawn up from the elaborate marble and

---

in the early Armenian church literature and how the Armenian text of the Septuagint, instead of following the Greek which says, "to dwell in houses with coffered ceilings," has "to dwell in domed houses."

[89] *Histoire d'Héraclius par l'évêque Sebèos*, ed. Macler, 1904, chap. xxv, 77; Der Nersessian, *op.cit.*, 60.

[90] Creswell, *Early Muslim Architecture*, I, 85.

[91] Choricius of Gaza, *Opera*, ed. Foerster-Richtsteig (Teubner), 1929, "Laudatio Marciani," II, 37-46.

[92] R. W. Hamilton, "Two Churches of Gaza as Described by Choricius of Gaza," *Palestinian Exploration Fund, Quarterly Statement*, 1930, 178-191; F. M. Abel, "Gaza au VIe siècle d'apres le Rhéteur Chorikios," *Rev. bibl.*, XL, 1931, 23ff.

mosaic decorations of the apse, he undertakes to describe the crowning feature of the church. His first line, *On one hand—the highest, I mean—there rests a novel shape* (σχῆμα), Hamilton assumed referred to some ornament. In describing the "striking shape" which he saw on the topmost course of the church, Choricius attempted to show his technical knowledge of geometric shapes, for he writes, *Geometrical knowledge, I understand, calls this a half cone.* In order to make it clear that he is referring to a pine cone, and not a geometric cone, he introduces a bit of Greek mythology.

Although his method of describing the theoretical construction of this truncated pine cone becomes somewhat involved by his desire to show off his mechanical knowledge, it is evident that he is not describing ornamental "disks," as Hamilton translated κύκλοι, when he writes, *A carpenter, cutting circles* (or what we would call the ribs of the framework), *five in number, from the material which his craft furnishes him* (i.e. wood), *cutting each of them equally in two, and joining nine of the slices* (or sectors of circles) *to each other by their tips, and also joining them by their middles* (i.e. the place where they had been cut equally in two) *to the band which I just now mentioned was the highest* (course of church). Having prepared this skeleton framework, the carpenter *sets upon them pieces* (or panels) *of wood, which he hollows out* (to the required curve of the pine-cone shape), *equal in number to these* (the ribs), *which begin in a broad fashion from below and gradually become narrower as they rise up to a sharp point, so as to fit the hollowing of the surface, and drawing together all the tips into one, and bending them gently* (in a gradual curve), *he produces a most pleasing spectacle.* In spite of the geometrical affectations and literary circumlocutions of his manner of writing, it is evident that Choricius was describing in great detail the construction of a wooden dome which consisted of nine sections and whose panels were curved out like a pine cone before they came together at the top in a point.

Having had his carpenter start out with five theoretical circles, he asks what was done with the half-circle which was not used in the dome. *This part then*, he explains, *is divided equally* (into two quarter sections) *and* (one) *part of it being placed on one side of the nine* (i.e. the dome), *and the other part on the other* (side), *an apsidal vault* (ἀψίς) *of the same material* (i.e. wood) *is formed on both sides,* (each) *hollowed out in front.* In other words, having visualized his curved shape in the abstract terms of a geometrician's sections, Choricius has endeavored to say that the central dome of wood over the crossing of the church, which it will be noted from the account may have had melon-like gores, was flanked on either side by supporting half-domes of wood which theoretically did have the vertical section of a quarter circle. The church then was similar, in plan at least, to the church of the Nativity at Bethlehem (Fig. 149) after it was rebuilt with a tri-apsidal east end. That it was a martyrium is indicated not only by the dome but by Choricius' reference to "the second feast of the martyr."

11. S. SERGIUS, GAZA (THE "EUDOXIANA"?) (407 A.D. or later)

Choricius also described a church of S. Sergius at Gaza which he makes clear was domical and cruciform in plan. Unfortunately, in praising this sanctuary, he does not

39

refer either to the shape or construction of the dome and makes no mention of when it was built.[93] It has been thought that it was dedicated in 532 A.D. at the time when the orator delivered his encomium. I, however, have already endeavored to strengthen Leclercq's suggestion that S. Sergius was the famous first church of Gaza, the Eudoxiana, built by the Antiochene architect Rufinus and originally dedicated to Holy Easter on the day of the Resurrection in 407 A.D.[94] If these two structures, both cruciform, were the same church, then it is unlikely that the mosaic in the apse of the Virgin and Child flanked by "a pious group" on either side, and the New Testament scenes seen by Choricius on "the roof" were contemporary with the early fifth century dedication. They were probably not added until after the Sion Church was built and decorated.

In either event the dome was a striking feature of the church because the sixth century eulogist writes, "I fairly marvel at the roofing of the church," and then goes on to say, "On the interior of the structure, composed of four piers, is adjusted a polygonal prism forming a circle which carries very high up the spherical dome, second to none, its beauty being superior to all others." From this account of Choricius, Gabriel Millet thought that S. Sergius was a cruciform church with domes over the crossing and four arms,[95] but Abel, Hamilton and Leclercq consider it to have been a cruciform church with a dome only over the crossing.[96]

12. CHURCH, MAHOYMAC OR MAÏOUMAS, PORT OF GAZA

The port of Gaza also had a domical church, sufficiently renowned so that it was depicted as religiously characteristic of the city in a topographical mosaic at Ma'in, which is southwest of Madaba in Transjordan.[97] Little is known about this church at Ma'in, but the mosaic (Fig. 36) shows that Mahoymac had an imposing church whose dome was "puffed-up." This bulbous dome, which the artist apparently exaggerated as a significant characteristic of the structure, is partially concealed by the hemisphere of the apse, as was the dome of the *Domus aurea* on the mosaic at Yakto (Fig. 29). The mosaic, then, is graphic evidence that the bulbous dome, a shape which must have been constructed of wood, was used by the Christian builders of Syria. It is impossible to agree with Doro Levi's suggestion that the building might be the famous Marneion, flanked by two porticoes.[98] At the time when the mosaics were executed there was no reason why any Christian artist should endeavor to preserve the memory of that destroyed and hated center of paganism. The date of the mosaics is late, for an inscription in the church refers to their restoration in 641/2 A.D.

[93] Choricius, *op.cit.*, "Laudatio Marciani," I, 17ff.; Abel, *op.cit.*, 15; Hamilton, *op.cit.*, 187; Cabrol, *Dict.*, XIV, col. 1499.

[94] Cabrol, *Dict.*, XIV, cols. 1496, 1500.

[95] G. Millet, "L'Asie mineur," *Rev. archéol.*, series 4, V, 1905, 99ff.

[96] F. M. Abel, "Marc Diacre et la biographie de saint Porphyre, évêque de Gaza," *Conférences de Saint-Étienne, école pratique d'études bibliques*, 1909-10, 1910, 264 n. 1.

[97] R. de Vaux, "Une mosaïque byzantine a Ma'in," *Rev. bibl.*, XLVII, 227ff., pl. XIV/4.

[98] Doro Levi, *Antioch Mosaic Pavements*, I, 623.

13. "CHURCH," BA'ALBEK

Eutychius records that the Caliph al-Walīd in 691 A.D. carried off a golden kubba from a church at Ba'albek and reerected it over the Sakhra at Jerusalem.[99] If reliable, this reference to what must have been a gilded wooden dome at Ba'albek is of great significance to the history of domical architecture in Syria. It is not likely that Eutychius was referring merely to a domed baldachin, as has been suggested,[100] and yet it is difficult to associate this dome with any known church at Ba'albek. It would have had to be about 20 m. in diameter to fit the Qubbat-aṣ-Sakhra. The Christian church, built within the temenos of the pagan temple, was somewhat less than 16 m. wide and has no indication in its plan that it was domical. The wooden dome taken to Jerusalem was probably over the hexagonal forecourt of the Great Temple because there is evidence that this court was roofed over with wood sometime during the Christian period, and there is a reference in Michael the Syrian to one of the pagan buildings at Heliopolis having been turned into a church of the Virgin in 525 A.D.[101]

14. THE ISLAMIC WOODEN DOME

The account of Eutychius links up the Islamic use of the wooden dome with the Christian tradition in Syria. The present wooden dome of the Qubbat-aṣ-Sakhra was built to replace a former dome destroyed in 1022 A.D. Its somewhat bulbous and pointed form (Fig. 38), however, resembles the pine-cone shape referred to in the descriptions of the Marneion and the church of S. Stephen at Gaza. Since it is known that in 903 A.D. the Sakhra had a similar dome consisting of an inner shell of wood planking and an outer wooden cupola with (gilded) lead sheathing,[102] it is reasonable to assume, as Creswell has demonstrated, that the original dome, built by Syrian workmen between 685 and 705 A.D., was "exactly like the present one" (Fig. 37) and that the shape and construction of the Dome of the Rock were directly influenced by the Holy Sepulchre, which the Arabs admired and desired to rival. In view of this traditional relationship between the two great domical sanctuaries of Christianity and Islam at Jerusalem, it is significant to find in the twelfth century that the Sakhra, after having been converted from a mosque into the *Templum Domini*, was depicted on the Latin seals (Figs. 218-227) in combination with the Holy Sepulchre.

The Great Mosque at Damascus at present has a stone dome over the haikal (Figs. 39, 40). In 705 A.D., however, when al-Walīd remodeled an existing structure into a congregational mosque which would rival the finest churches of Syria, and especially the Qumama, or church of the Holy Sepulchre, this mosque, built by "Rumi and Coptic craftsmen, inhabitants of Syria and Egypt," which became one of the wonders

[99] Eutychius, ed. Pocoke, II, 372-373; Creswell, *Early Muslim Architecture*, I, 78.

[100] Clermont-Ganneau, *Recueil d'archéologie orientale*, III, 89-90.

[101] Krencker, *Die Wallfahrtskirche des Simeon Stylites . . .* , 20; Krencker, *Röm. Mitt.*, XLIX, 1934, 86; E. Diez, *Die Kunst der islamischen Völker*, 1915, 15; T. Wiegand (ed.), *Baalbek*, II, 1923, 129ff. For reference to church of the Virgin see p. 105.

[102] Creswell, *op.cit.*, I, 63.

of the Arab world, had three wooden domes over the haikal or transept.[103] According to the twelfth century account of Ibn Jubays, the main dome, the "Dome of the Eagle," was "round like a sphere, and its structure is made of planks, strengthened with stout ribs of wood." An indication of the extent to which the Arabs in building these domical mosques were carrying on a Syrian tradition is indicated by the name, Qubbat as-Nasr, or Dome of the Eagle, which was given to this dome. The idea of associating an eagle with a kubba went back to the celestial implications of the domical shape on the imperial tombs where the dome was surmounted by an eagle (Figs. 17-21), to the sacred conoid stone of Emesa whose heavenly implications were indicated by an eagle (Figs. 127, 137), and to the Syrian conception of the eagle as a sun symbol and emblem of immortality.[104]

Furthermore, in the Great Mosque at Damascus, the mosaics, which were executed by Syrian craftsmen working for al-Walīd, show various towers and buildings with bulbous and pointed domes (Figs. 41, 42) which were undoubtedly characteristic of the Syrian architectural tradition. De Lorey, in describing these mosaics, says, "This type of dome is, in fact, originally of Syria and Palestine,"[105] and M. Van Berchem points out that architectural motifs of this kind must have been part of the stock-in-trade of Syrian workmen and hence preserved an architectural tradition which was typically Syrian.[106] There is also one Christian mosaic from Khirbit Mukhayyat on the Dead Sea which shows domical towers (Fig. 44) on the façade of a church.[107]

The weakness of the wooden dome as historical evidence of its early adoption by the Arabs is the fact that it had to be frequently rebuilt. The egg-shaped wooden cupola on the Dome of the Chain presumably preserves the form and construction of the eighth century structure even though it was rebuilt in the thirteenth century. By 1035 A.D. the large Aqsa mosque at Jerusalem is known to have had a dome over what in a Christian church would have been the crossing (Fig. 43). Creswell believes that this eleventh century rebuilding respected the plan and construction of the mosque of al-Mahdi, who about 780 A.D. rebuilt an earlier mosque which either al-Walīd or 'Abdal-Malik had erected like a Christian basilica with a domical crossing.[108]

The Arabs, when they conquered Syria, brought little with them from Arabia except their language, their religion, and their ritual. Their first mosques were crude shelters of reeds and wood covered with thatch and mud. The Prophet had set them a standard of severe simplicity and condemned the Christians and Jews for using the tombs of their martyrs and prophets as places of worship. And yet, by the end of the

---

[103] *Ibid.*, 113ff.

[104] F. Cumont, "L'Aigle funéraire des Syriens et l'apothéose des empereurs," *Revue de l'histoire des religions*, 1910. The eagle, bird of the sun and charged with carrying souls, particularly royal souls, to heaven, was in Syria a funerary emblem and at Antioch the protector of the race.

[105] Eustache de Lorey, "Les Mosaïques de la Mosquée des Omayyades à Damas," *Syria*, XII, 1931, 341ff.

[106] Creswell, *op.cit.*, I, 251.

[107] P. Lemaire, "Mosaïques et inscriptions d'El-Mehayet," *Rev. bibl.*, XLIII, 1934, 385-401, pl. XXVI/1; Crowfoot, *Early Churches in Palestine*, 141-144, pl. XXIV/b.

[108] Creswell, *op.cit.*, II, 119-126.

seventh century, they had begun to make the kubba an architectural symbol of their religion. Syria, therefore, must have furnished them with both the incentive and the craftsmen to erect their domical mosques and sepulchres.

The first mosque in Syria was a simple structure of reeds and teakwood at Bosra, a flourishing Christian city where the cathedral, a martyrium church, undoubtedly had an imposing gilded dome of wood. It was the wooden dome on the cathedral of Bosra (Fig. 49), according to Herzfeld, which inspired the Arabs to rebuild their mosques with similar symbolic and imposing domes.[109] No single church, however, like the cathedral of Bosra or the Holy Sepulchre at Jerusalem, could have given rise in so short a time to a domical style of architecture unless the dome was already a common and impressive feature of religious architecture in Syria. Only a deeply-rooted belief in the symbolism of the domical shape in both the popular cultures of Syria and Arabia explains why the Arabs so quickly appropriated the domical structure for much the same purposes as those of both pagans and Christians, that is, a place of worship, a seat of authority, an audience hall where proclamations were read, and a memorial or venerated tomb for rulers and saints. As the Arab conquest spread, this religious interest in the dome was strengthened by the domical baldachins and palaces of the imperial tradition, by the domical audience halls of the Sassanian kings, and by the religious importance of the dome in India, but in the beginning of Islamic architecture it was Syria and Palestine which gave the structural dome to Islam.

The most significant factor in this rapid assimulation of domical architecture was the existence among the Arab tribesmen, prior to their conquest of Syria and Palestine, of a native domical ideology, comparable to that of other primitive cultures, which had its origin in the religious use of an ancestral tent of a round and domelike appearance. When Eisler suggested that the Arabs, in common with other Semites, had the tradition of a domical religious habitation, "The Shepherd Tent of the World" which resembled the tent sanctuaries on Assyrian reliefs (Fig. 149), the idea was considered unlikely because the ordinary Arab tent was in no way similar to this type of shelter.[110] A careful study, however, of pre-Islamic sanctuaries, based upon early Arab sources, has demonstrated that the customary shrine of the ancient Arabs, in which they housed and transported their *bait*, or baetyl, was a round qobba tent with a domelike top that was made of red leather.[111] These qobba tabernacles, whether fixed or portable, went back in origin to a remote Semitic past when an ancient type of tent was set up by the tribal chieftain either beside, or over, the tribal idol. Portable pavilions, of the kind seen in a religious scene on a relief of the first century B.C. from the Temple of Bel at Palmyra (Fig. 147), were transported on the backs of camels and were often carried into battle as a kind of palladium. The qobba, as a sacred and cosmic shelter,

[109] E. Herzfeld, *Jahrb. d. preuss. Kunst.*, XLII, 1921, 121.

[110] R. Eisler, *Weltenmantel und Himmelszelt*, II, 594, 605.

[111] H. Lammens, "Le Culte des bétyles et les processions religieuses chez les Arabes préis-lamites," *Bulletin de l'Institut français d'archéologie orientale du Caire*, XVII, 1920, 39-101; Lammens, "Les Sanctuaires préislamites dans l'Arabie occidentale," *Mélanges de l'Université Saint-Joseph*, Beirut, XI, 1926, 39ff.

was also set up over the burial place of ancestors and famous dead, and even among the pre-Islamic tribesmen there was the custom of equating *bait* with *qobba* and hence of thinking of the domical sanctuary as the manifestation of divinity. Hence the Islamic *kubba*, which came to be used for domes and domical structures, was like the English word *dome*, the Roman *tegurium*, the Syrian *kalubé*, and the Indian *vihâra* in having been originally a house concept.

III · THE MASONRY DOME
AND THE MORTUARY TRADITION
IN SYRIA AND PALESTINE

THE reason why there has grown up the almost ineradicable impression that Syria and Palestine, apart from the unexplained phenomenon of Islamic architecture, did not influence the development of domical architecture in the Near East as did Asia Minor, is that the early explorers and more recent excavators, all more or less convinced that the dome was primarily a utilitarian form of masonry vaulting only, discovered nothing to prove that domes of brick, stone, or volcanic scoria were constructed upon the churches of these countries before the time of Justinian. Hence they assumed, depending upon which side of the *Orient oder Rom* controversy they supported, that the domical tradition was an importation either from Byzantium or Iran. Unaware of the old and popular veneration of the domical shape in Syria, convinced that the wooden dome was something of a "paradox," or an impossibility because of the present absence of timber, and half believing that the dome was in some way connected with the exotic architecture of the Orient, most scholars proceeded to restore the central churches with pyramidal and conical roofs of wood or with vaults of light volcanic scoria. In spite of the fact that masonry domes were used upon Roman baths and other buildings in Syria, it is no solution to the problem of restoring the large central churches to conclude that it would have been easy to construct large domes in volcanic scoria because the available evidence does not justify this assumption.[1] When the size of many of the central churches and the thin-

[1] Volcanic scoria, because of its lightness, is commonly thought to have been used extensively, but there is very little evidence of its having been used for large pagan domes and, as yet, no evidence that it was used in the construction of Christian domes. Some of its structural advantages for vaulting were offset by the necessity of carefully protecting it from moisture. It is difficult to tell from the ruins what was considered to be the maximum size of domes constructed of this stone and what was the required thickness of supporting walls. There was apparently a massive pagan dome of unspecified masonry over the square entrance hall of the Roman baths at Gerasa; it was 15 m. in diameter and carried on walls 2 m. thick (C. H. Kraeling [ed.], *Gerasa, City of the Decapolis*, 1938, 23, pl. XXVI). The largest vault of volcanic scoria recorded by Butler was on the South Baths at Bosra (Butler, *Syria*, II, A, 260-263, ill. 230); it was a very flat dome of eight gores over an elongated octagon, 15 m. by 12.75 m., and was carried on walls varying from 2.3 m. to 3 m. in thickness. These walls, which Butler shows as having been carried up well above the impost of the dome, were probably intended to conceal the actual dome by a protecting roof in the usual Roman manner. The dome of volcanic scoria on the kalubé at Umm-iz-Zetum (Fig. 121) had a span of 5.80 m., while the one at Shakka (Fig. 122), which was undoubtedly constructed of the same material, had an average span of 7.90 m. The masonry domes on the two circular rooms in the baths at Shehba were made of rubble cement, 9 m. in diameter, and were on walls 1.20 m. thick (Butler, *Architecture and Other Arts*, 384, fig. 134). With the exception of the brick dome of 6.66 m. on the church of Ḳasr ibn Wardān (Fig. 46), dating from 561-564 A.D., the dome with a span of 5.15 m. on the church of S. John the Baptist at Jerusalem (Fig. 189) and the church of Hagia Sophia at Edessa which Justinian rebuilt with a masonry dome, there is no other specific evidence of masonry domes on churches.

45

ness of their supporting walls are taken into consideration, it is found that lofty domes of the necessary span would have been impractical in volcanic scoria.

On the other hand it is readily comprehensible why the early scholars, who studied the ruins of Syrian architecture without excavating any of the churches, thought that the central structures should once have been vaulted with domes of either brick or stone. By the fourth century, when there began to be so much Christian building in the cities and towns of this then prosperous country, there was what appeared to be convincing archaeological evidence that the Christians had a remarkable heritage of masonry construction. For centuries the native stonecutters had so fully mastered the difficulties of intricate stereotomy that in addition to constructing half-domes of the finest dry masonry they had, by the second century, perfected the spherical pendentive as a means of fitting a flat handkerchief dome onto the rectangular spaces of their tombs, baths and gateways.[2] Under Roman supervision and probably with the aid of itinerant craftsmen from Italy, the Syrian builders had learned to construct domical vaults of volcanic scoria, like concrete, upon their private and public baths. Hence, if monumental domes were to be built, the Christian craftsmen of Syria should have been fully equipped to erect them in cut stone, volcanic scoria and brick. But did they?

It was one thing for the Syrian builders to erect relatively small domes over low tombs, one-story gateways and baths where the disintegrating thrusts of the vault could be firmly embedded in adequate abutment, and it was a totally different problem in a country suffering from severe earthquakes to raise free-standing domes of great span and height on thin walls and slight columnar supports. To the extent that the domical shape had come to have a deep mystic and celestial meaning to the Christians, it would have been religiously undesirable to conceal the domes on the exterior, as the Romans did, by enclosing walls or heavy abutment. Actually, however, we have no evidence of the masonry dome having been used upon the churches of Palestine and Syria before the period of Justinian.

A. The Brick Dome

Strzygowski, in his effort to derive all the elements of Christian architecture, and especially the dome, from the brick architecture of Mesopotamia and Iran, set up the false hypothesis that Antioch, as an outpost of the East, was the disseminating center of a brick architectural tradition in Syria.[3] His far from objective thesis rested upon the assumption of a sixth century date for the palace at Mschatta and the belief that the buildings of Kasr Ibn Wardān were of Mesopotamian rather than Byzantine derivation.[4] The issue was of great importance to the history of Near Eastern architecture because the only known brick dome in Syria was on the church of Kasr Ibn Wardān, and the only two centers of brick construction were the castrum at il-Anderin of 558/9 A.D. and Kasr Ibn Wardān of 561/64 A.D. His thesis therefore collapsed, and

[2] Creswell, *Early Muslim Architecture*, I, chap. VII; Crowfoot, *Early Churches in Palestine*, 105.

[3] Strzygowski, *Kleinasien*, 121-131.

[4] Strzygowski, "Mschattâ, II," *Jahrb. d. preuss. Kunst.*, XXV, 1904, 239-240.

the Eastern origin of brick domical architecture was left in a theoretical vacuum, when it was clearly recognized that Mschatta had to be dated much later and that il-Anderin and Kasr Ibn Wardān were imperial foundations built in the Roman manner with baked bricks of Byzantine dimensions.

The dome of Kasr Ibn Wardān is instructive because of its shape and the fact that it was the result of the introduction of imperial vaulting methods in the sixth century. Nothing but debris remains of the palace dome and only a fragment of the dome over the church. The plans (Fig. 45), however, show that they were of the same dimensions and were massive vaults of narrow span, 6.66 m., carried upon brick piers of 1.6 m., which are dimensions very different from those which would have been necessary for domical roofs to have been used upon the other central churches of Syria.[5] Although the dome which Butler restored upon the church (Fig. 46) has some exterior buttressing up to the haunch, it is more likely that the actual dome continued the pendentive-like curve of the drum and was even more concealed, for such was the structurally safer method commonly used by the Roman and Early Byzantine masons.

Looking back, it is difficult to understand why Butler and others, on the limited evidence of this one site, came to associate the brick dome with the churches of the region. Although, in discussing the brick construction at Kasr Ibn Wardān and il-Anderin, Butler wrote, "I have looked in vain for ancient brick in the mediaeval and modern architecture of Syria,"[6] nevertheless he restored church No. 3 at il-Anderin (Fig. 47) with a free-standing, conoid dome of *sun-dried* brick.[7] Also he assumed that the round church at Fa'lul (Fig. 48), dated 526/7, must have had a brick dome because the debris contained "masses of masonry in brick and mortar, the bricks being of the same kind seen in the vaults and domes of Kasr Ibn Wardān and the half-dome of the Great Church at il-Anderin," which he should have added were constructed of baked bricks. Such evidence, however, is not sufficient grounds for accepting a brick domical tradition in Syria. The light, sun-baked dome which he restored on the church at il-Anderin with a diameter of only 4.15 m. might have withstood the violent earthquakes of this region for a few generations, but it is very doubtful whether a similar, free-standing dome with a span of about 7.00 m. and with its clerestory wall supported on a circular colonnade would have been practical on the church at Fa'lul.[8]

B. The Stone and "Concrete" Dome

Small domes of cut stone and light domes of volcanic scoria were common in the pagan architecture of Syria after the Roman domination of the country. They were, however, usually concealed in the Roman manner on the exterior and always con-

[5] H. C. Butler, *Syria, Publications of the Princeton University Archaeological Expeditions to Syria in 1904/5 and 1909*, II, 1919-20, B, I, 26-54; *Early Churches in Syria*, 1929, 168.

[6] Butler, *Syria*, II, B, I, 43.

[7] *Ibid.*, 56; *Early Churches*, 169.

[8] Butler, *Syria*, II, B, I, 95-96; although he

drew the plan (ill. 113), which had a diameter of 14.95 m., without an ambulatory, he wrote that it must have had "a circle of columns within the circular wall," thereby indicating, as is shown in Fig. 48, that it had a dome of about 23 feet in diameter.

structed, as in the baths of Brad and Gerasa, upon comparatively low and massive structures. Therefore, when the large and important cathedral at Bosra, 512/13 A.D., was first restored by De Vogüé and Brünnow with a free-standing hemispherical dome of stone and then by Butler with a more lofty conoid one, there arose the question of precedent and the still more serious question of whether such domes were structurally possible in a country of severe earthquakes.[9] Butler's dome, modeled upon the tomb of Bizzos and the cupola of the near-by church of S. George at Zor'ah, had an astonishing span of 24 m., rose to a height of about 60 feet and was supported on a relatively thin drum with walls only about 1 m. thick.[10]

Scholars at once began to suspect that the interior of the cathedral at Bosra must have had an inner and smaller ring of supports, and Herzfeld, when he restored it, insisted that these inner supports originally carried a wooden dome which was one of the Syrian prototypes for the later domical mosques of Islam.[11] When excavated it was found that the church had an inner quatrefoil of piers and columns (Fig. 49) with a central square something over 12 m. wide, and that there was no evidence of its having been roofed with anything except wood.[12] Since the cathedral was also a martyrium,[13] it is significant to find that its inner shape, a quatrefoil, was one of the earliest types of martyria.[14] Like the martyria at Korykos (Fig. 180), Antioch (Fig. 170), Seleucia Pieria (Fig. 182) and Resafa (Fig. 184), it was the sepulchral implications of the plan which gave more importance to the center of the church, under its symbolic dome, than to the eastern sanctuary. There is no historical justification for restoring this martyrium church with a pyramidal roof of timbers or for disregarding both the results of the excavations and the evidence for a Syrian wooden dome by presupposing that it might have had a dome of volcanic scoria, because the debris showed that masonry vaults of volcanic scoria were only used on the small apsidal niches and it is more than doubtful that a lofty dome of about 40-foot span could have been carried on such light interior supports.[15]

The fact that all excavation and study of the interiors of central churches at Gerasa, Antioch and Resafa have revealed no debris of masonry domes raises the question

[9] De Vogüé, *Syrie centrale*, I, 63-67; II, pls. 22, 23; R. E. Brünnow and A. von Domaszewski, *Die Provincia Arabia*, 1904-09, III, 30-35; E. G. Rey, *Voyages dans le Houran*, pl. IV; Creswell, *Early Muslim Architecture*, I, 72-74.

[10] Butler, *Syria*, II, A, 281-286, ill. 248, pls. XVI-XVII.

[11] Herzfeld, "Mschattâ, Ḥîra und Bâdiya," *Jahrb. d. preuss. Kunst.*, XLII, 1921, 119, Abb. 4.

[12] J. W. Crowfoot, *Churches at Bosra and Samaria-Sebaste* (British School of Archaeology in Jerusalem, Suppl. Paper, 4), 1937; *Early Churches in Palestine*, 37f., 94ff., fig. 7.

[13] E. Littmann, D. Magie and D. R. Stuart, *Syria, Publications of the Princeton University Archaeological Expeditions to Syria in 1904/5 and 1909*, III, 1921, *Greek and Latin Inscrip-*

tions, A, 4, no. 557; "Under the most God-beloved and most holy Julianus, archbishop, was built and completed the holy Church of Sergius, Bacchus and Leontius, martyrs who received the prize and triumphed gloriously."

[14] See p. 117; Grabar, *Martyrium*, I, 176-194.

[15] Crowfoot (*Churches at Bosra.*, 13, 18) reported that masses of scoria were found in the debris where the exedrae were, but that none was found in the center of the church; after having at first come to the conclusion that "it is highly improbable in fact that it had a dome of any kind," he later (*Early Churches in Palestine*, 105) accepted the presumption of a wooden dome. A recent effort to restore this church with a square tower and pyramidal roof is discussed on page 118.

whether the dome seen by De Vogüé and Butler on the martyrium church of S. George at Zor'ah (Fig. 51), built in 515 A.D. and influenced by the near-by cathedral at Bosra, can be accepted as proof that such free-standing domes of stone or "concrete" were constructed on Syrian churches during the Early Christian period. When De Vogüé first published this church, it was considered to be the only extant original church dome in Syria. He described its pointed dome (Fig. 50), with a span of 10.15 m. and supports 0.7 m. thick, as made of stone *en blocage* and said that it was "contemporary with the primitive construction."[16] His drawing has the interior octagon constructed of carefully locked stones and brought to a 32-sided drum by means of stone squinches *at the top of the clerestory.* This could not have been the same structure seen by Butler a generation later, because Butler's interior photograph has the octagon brought to a circular clerestory drum by the gradual warping of the crude stone courses *in the spandrels of the arcade,* and his exterior photographs (Fig. 52) give clear indications of much rebuilding.[17] Butler, however, described the dome as "of concrete" and "lined with plaster which was unquestionably ancient." Another generation later, in 1938, Krencker published a photograph of the interior in which there is *no warping* of the octagon and the stone squinches are now *beneath the clerestory.*[18] In fact the whole clerestory is quite different from the one drawn by De Vogüé. Also, by this time, as a result of extensive repairs made after 1926, the church had a wooden dome (Fig. 53) covered with zinc. It is, therefore, inconceivable that a dome which in modern times had to be rebuilt two or three times in less than three generations could have originally stood for about fourteen hundred years.

Once the antiquity of this masonry dome of S. George at Zor'ah is questioned, as it has been,[19] then the similarity and presumable relations beween it and the metropolitan church at Bosra lead to the conclusion that its original roof was made of wood. It is no proof, of course, that its original wooden roof was dome-shaped to note the use of wooden domes with zinc sheathing on the martyrium church of S. Elias (Fig. 56) at Zor'ah, dated 542 A.D., and on the near-by sixth century martyrium (Fig. 58) at Chagra.[20] Even if these two domes, like the present wooden dome on S. George at

---

[16] De Vogüé, *Syrie centrale*, II, 61. That this central-type, domical structure was also a martyrium is established by an inscription (Waddington, *Inscriptions de Syrie*, 2498; cited by De Vogüé on p. 62) recording how in "this magnificent monument" was "placed the precious relic of the holy conquering martyr George."

[17] Butler, *Architecture and Other Arts*, 411-413.

[18] Krencker, *Die Wallfahrtskirche des Simeon Stylites in Kal'at Sim'ân*, pl. 18/c.

[19] F. P. T. Sarre and E. Herzfeld (*Archäologische Reise im Euphrat- und Tigris-Gebiet*, 1911-20, II, 31 n. 2), Rivoira (*Lombardic Architecture*, 1910, I, 84, II, 15 and *Moslim Architecture*, 97), Crowfoot (*Early Churches in*

Palestine, 98), Wulff (*Altchristliche und byzantinische Kunst*, I, 253) and Watzinger (*Denkmäler Palästinas*, II, 134) have questioned the antiquity of the masonry dome and suggested that the original dome was built of wood. Creswell (*Early Muslim Architecture*, I, 85f.), on the other hand, pointed out that the dome seen by De Vogüé could not have been later than 1805, when Seetzen visited the building, and took the position, because of the lack of wood in the Hauran, that the church always had a masonry dome.

[20] Jean Lassus, "Deux églises cruciformes de Hauran," *Bulletin d'études orientales de l'Institut français de Damas*, I, 1931, 23ff.; "Les monuments chrétiens de la Syrie septentrionale," *Atti del III Congresso internazionale di*

Zor'ah, are modern, they refute the usual arguments advanced against the use of the wooden dome in a region as barren of wood as southern Syria and the neighborhood of Mesopotamia where domes were formerly thought to have originated, because of the lack of timber. In fact they strongly suggest that modern builders have again discovered that wood, even if it has to be imported, is the easiest and safest material for reproducing the traditional domical shape upon the central type of church.

What, then, is the evidence for the masonry dome in Syria and Palestine? Apart from the relatively low domes on Roman baths in Syria, some cut-stone cupolas on a limited group of Palestinian tombs which will be considered in the next section, and some small masonry domes on Tychia and kalubés to be taken up under the Graeco-Roman kalubé, there were few domical vaults and no archaeological evidence of a free-standing masonry dome (or, for that matter, of any large, buttressed, and partially concealed domical vault) having been constructed on any Syrian church prior to the sixth century. There is nothing to support the assertion, so frequently made, that there were masonry domes on such Constantinian churches as the Holy Sepulchre and the *Domus aurea*. In fact, after the "Great Church" at Edessa was completely rebuilt, following the flood of 524 A.D., with funds of Justinian, the wonders and symbolism of its dome were described in a Syrian hymn which says, "there is no wood at all in its roof which is constructed entirely of stone," thereby indicating that stone domes were very much of an innovation.[21]

Actually we are left with the fifth century tomb of Bizzos at Ruweha (Fig. 61) as the only extant free-standing dome of masonry. It was this dome which influenced Butler in his restoration of the churches at il-Anderin (Fig. 47) and Bosra. The tomb, which is located to the south of the east end of the church, has a pointed, slightly bulging, and definitely conoid, shape and is made of magnificently cut stone, fitted together without mortar and set upon a square chamber.[22] Its interior (Fig. 59), like that of certain pagan tombs (Figs. 78, 80) in western Palestine, is cruciform, with the burials in the four shallow arms, or niches. It was the theoretical prototype of the later Islamic *weli* and furnishes solid proof that the free-standing Syrian dome was not hemispherical, like the Roman dome, but was pointed and somewhat "puffed-up," resembling the pine-cone shape so specifically referred to in the descriptions of the wooden domes of Syria and Palestine.

C. The Domical Mortuary Tradition in Syria

The tomb of Bizzos raises the questions whether the domical shape had an established mortuary symbolism adopted by the Christians and whether any connection

---

archeologia cristiana, 1934, 480; *Sanctuaires chrétiens de Syrie*, 1947, 147-148.

[21] A. Dupont-Sommer, "Une hymne syriacque sur la cathédrale d'Édesse" (Codex Vaticanus Syriacus 95, fol. 49-50), *Cahiers archéologiques*, II, 1947, 29ff., verse x.

[22] De Vogüé, I, 113-114; II, pl. 91; M. van Berchem and E. Fatio, *Voyage en Syrie* (Mémoires de l'Institut français d'archéologie orientale du Caire, 39) 1914-15, I, 204, II, pl. XLIII; Butler, *Architecture and Other Arts*, 247-248; Creswell, *Early Muslim Architecture*, I, 310.

existed between its conoid shape and the similar conelike domes of wood which were symbols of a heavenly abode on Christian martyria. Ever since the late Stone Age there had been a widespread veneration of the round and dome-shaped tomb as the reproduction of an ancient, ancestral and god-given shelter. At an early date in different parts of the ancient world this instinctive desire to present and make permanent the revered shape of a primitive shelter as an eternal home of the dead gave rise to various domical traditions: in India it was preserved in the reliquary stupas of the Buddha; among the Scythians the tomb began as a burial in the domelike tents of the living which were then imitated in the buried wooden sepulchres and finally translated into masonry vaults;[23] it persisted in round tombs of North Africa[24] and in the round barrows of the Germanic North where the actual burial chamber beneath the tumulus (Fig. 62) was at times a careful reproduction of the circular wicker hut,[25] or was made more permanent as a domelike cabin of overlapping logs;[26] and it was common during the second millennium throughout the Mediterranean from Crete to Iberia, as is shown by its reproductions in the rock-cut (Fig. 64) and corbeled (Fig. 63) tholos tombs.[27] This sepulchral house concept, which gave so much content to the domical shape regardless of its construction, was continued by the Etruscans (Fig. 65), from whom the Romans derived many of their funerary customs and much of their mortuary use of the dome.[28]

It was because of this undying religious veneration for an ancient house form that

[23] While there is extensive bibliography to show that nearly all ancient cultures had at one time the custom, or the memory, of burials in the house before they developed the tradition of constructing special, eternal homes for the dead in imitation of the ancestral dwellings of the living, the clearest evidence for the importance of the round and domelike hut in the early mortuary traditions are the hut urns of northern Europe, the Mediterranean, Egypt and Japan (M. Ebert, *Reallexicon der Vorgeschichte*, "Wohnungsbestattung," xiv, 443-445, "Hausgrab," v, 215; M. Hoernes, *Natur- und Urgeschichte des Menschen*, 1909; F. Behn, *Hausurnen*, 1924; W. B. Bryan, *Italic Hut Urns and Hut Urn Cemeteries*, 1925; E. B. Smith, *Egyptian Architecture as Cultural Expression*, 1938, 24-27; S. Shimada and K. Hamada, *Nan-shan-li* (Archaeologia Orientales, iii), 1933; O. Mori and H. Naito, *Ying-ch'êng-tzǔ* (Arch. Orient., iv), 1934; K. Hamada, *Megalithic Tomb Ishibutai*, 1937. The influence of the prehistoric round house upon the funerary and religious traditions of the Celts has been traced by A. H. Allcroft (*The Circle and the Cross*, 1927), while the evolution of the masonry tomb from the nomadic round tent among the Scythians has been outlined by M. Rostovtzeff (*Iranians and Greeks*

in South Russia, 1922, 47, 49).

[24] L. Frobenius,"Der kleinafrikanische Grabbau," *Praehistorische Zeitschrift*, viii, 1916, 1-84; O. Bates, *The Eastern Libyans*, 1914.

[25] G. Lechler, "The Evolution of Prehistoric Architecture," *Art Quarterly*, 1943, 207, Fig. 51; A. E. van Giffen, *Bauart der Einzelgräber*, 1930, ii, pl. 85 and "Ein neolithischer Grabhügel mit Holzkonstruction in Harendermolen," *Prae. Zeit.*, xiv, 1922, 52ff.

[26] J. H. Holwerda, "Das alteuropäische Kuppelgrab," *Prae. Zeit.*, i, 1909, 374-379, and "Neue Kuppelgräber aus der Veluwe," *Prae. Zeit.*, iv, 1912, 368ff.

[27] O. Montelius, *Civilisation primitive en Italie depuis l'introduction des metaux*, 1895-1910; V. G. Childe, *Dawn of European Civilization*, 1939, 22, 203ff.; S. Xanthoudidos, trans. by J. P. Droop, *The Vaulted Tombs of Mesara*, 1924; A. Evans, *The Palace of Minos*, 1921-35, ii, chap. 34; J. Déchellette, *Manuel d'archéologie préhistorique celtique et gallo-romaine*, i, 1928, 411.

[28] W. Altmann, *Die italischen Rundbauten*, 1906, 4-16; L. Canina, *L'Antica Etruria marittima*, 1846-51, ii, pl. ci; Å. Åkerström, *Studien über die etruskischen Gräber*, 1934, Abb. 31, 34, 37, 38, 42; A. Minto, *Populonia*, 1943, 76-117.

the rock-cut tombs in various parts of the Mediterranean preserve the somewhat bulbous and pointed shapes of wicker and thatched cabins, shapes like those described upon the Syrian churches and later continued upon the Islamic mosques. At an early date in the laborious process of transforming a transient hut into an eternal stone dwelling for the dead, the domical shape of the round tomb, whether rock cut or constructed by corbeling, undoubtedly acquired both a celestial and cosmic significance. Some such belief in the symbolic relation between an ancestral dwelling and a heavenly abode was presumably intended by the builders of the tholos tombs of Mycenae (Fig. 63), in which the carefully carved conoid shape of the corbeled interiors it is thought were studded with rosettes as stars.[29] A similar relationship was more fully developed by the third century B.C. when the beehive dome of a Bulgarian tholos tomb at Kazanlak (Fig. 66) was carved and decorated.[30] The heavenly character of the tomb is revealed by the bands of decoration, the lower one presenting the funerary banquet at which the dead wears the crown of immortality and the upper one depicting three celestial chariots, which probably indicate an apotheosis and reflect the influence of early Italian grave symbolism.[31] There was a widespread and persistent use of a dome-shaped house of the dead in many regions, from the Danube to Iberia and Ireland. The most striking example is a house grave-stele (Fig. 67) from the Saar Basin during the late La Tène period, because its conoid dome is so similar to the Syrian tomb of Bizzos (Fig. 61) and the Islamic weli.[32]

These primitive beliefs, associated with a traditional round house, were present in the Hellenistic and Roman heroä which were erected to the memory of dead heroes; they contributed to those classical ideas regarding the omphalos, which saw in its conoid shape the dwelling of a legendary king, the tomb of Dionysus and the abode of departed spirits; and they also survived in the Roman conceptions of the mundus. M. Porcius Cato wrote, "The mundus gets its name from the 'sky' above our heads;

[29] G. Perrot and C. Chipiez, *Histoire de l'art dans l'antiquité*, 1882-1911, VI, 637, pl. VII; A. J. B. Wace (*British School at Athens, Annual*, XXV, 350) admits the possibility; Cook, *Zeus*, II, 2, 1150.

[30] A. Frova, "Le Pitture di Kazanlak," *Arti figurative*, I, 1945, 105-122, pl. XLVIII; C. Verdiani, "Original Hellenistic Paintings in a Thracian Tomb," *A.J.A.*, XLIX, 1945, 402-415, figs. 1-13; a number of other tholos tombs of this type have been discovered in Thrace, the one at Mezek (B. Filov, "The Bee-hive Tombs of Mezek," *Antiquity*, XI, 1937, 300-305, fig. 2) dating from the fourth century B.C.

[31] The chariot as a vehicle for transmitting souls to an eternal sphere was of great antiquity. Very similar to the decorations of the tholos are the bands of chariots driven by Nikes, but carrying such symbolic figures of immortality as Herakles and Dionysos, which were commonly represented in combination with funereal repasts on Hellenistic tomb phialai (G. M. A. Richter, "A Greek Silver Phiali in the Metropolitan Museum," *A.J.A.*, XLV, 1941, 372). Other references to the chariot are cited by Mrs. A. Strong (*Apotheosis and After Life*, 1915, 167, 226ff.), who also quotes an oracular utterance made to the Emperor Julian which, although late, preserves the same idea of chariots and an ancestral home as is depicted in the Bulgarian tholos. It reads: "Then when thou hast put off the grievous burden of mortal limbs, the fiery car shall bear thee through the midst of the eddying whirlwinds to Olympus; and thou shall come into that ancestral home of heavenly light, whence thou didst wander to enter the body of man" (Eunapis, *Hist.*, fr. 26).

[32] E. Linckenheld, *Les Stèles funéraires en forme de maison*, 1927, 30, fig. 19; other examples pl. III/5, 7, and pl. IV/4, 5.

indeed its shape resembles the sky."[33] By Hellenistic and Roman times this inherently mystic association of round and domical shelters with departed spirits had become so general that a domical tholos (Fig. 25), or aedicula, was a customary symbol in cemeteries and funereal gardens to provide a shelter for the soul in an idyllic hereafter.[34]

To these traditionally Western concepts regarding the mortuary significance of the domical shelter was added another, Eastern, pattern of ideas which, during the late antique period, contributed to the growing interest in the domical shape. As far as Rome was concerned, the real impact of these Eastern ideas came, probably during the reign of Nero, when the cosmic tent of Alexander the Great was adopted as an imperial symbol and heavenly covering over the Roman emperors in their role of a divine being and cosmic ruler. The round and presumably domelike tent of Alexander the Great with its celestial decorations, which was the immediate prototype of the imperial baldachin (Figs. 144, 146), went back in the Orient to the "heavenly" audience tents of Achaemenid and Indian rulers. This conception of the universe as a tent form in which the Son of Heaven appeared, an idea that was not new to the classical world when Alexander took it over, gave a new impetus to domical symbolism at Rome and throughout the Empire. After the construction of the Golden House of Nero, where the kosmokrator dined and gave audiences beneath a revolving and astronomically decorated cupola of wood, the dome became an essential element in imperial palace architecture. Also, the *velum*, or tent motif, which is sometimes called a "carpet" and "fan" pattern, became a celestial symbol upon imperial domes and other types of vaults and continued to remain a traditional decoration upon Roman, Christian, and Renaissance domes.[35]

The celestial baldachin, or tent shelter, was also taken over into mortuary imagery as a symbol of a heavenly dome. In the sepulchre, for example, of M. Clodius Hermes (Fig. 68), which was part of the catacombs of S. Sebastiano, the tent is painted on the ceiling.[36] In this scene of apotheosis the heroic figure of the dead, in the midst of a crowd of onlookers, is depicted rising heavenward through the opening in the top of a domelike tent with its four fringed lobes. This pagan tomb painting will later help to explain why the Christians used the word *skene* to designate the martyrium of S. Babylas at Antioch as an ideal dwelling in the afterlife.[37] In fact, from the time when Christianity began to think of its martyrs as the successors of the classical heroes and to visualize its Heavenly Ruler in the formal terms of a Roman imperator, all the cosmic meanings associated with the domical baldachin began to have a profound

[33] Cook, *Zeus*, III, 431; Cato, *Notes on Cases of Civil Law*; H. Funaioli, *Grammaticae Romanae Fragmenta*, 1907, 14. That the mundus was an underground, domical and tholoid structure, a prehistoric tomb, which was prominent in the Roman beliefs regarding the afterlife is discussed by Cook, *op.cit.*, 429-442.

[34] P. Grimal, *Les Jardins romains*, 1943, 332; see Chap. II n. 52.

[35] Representations of this tent pattern on the ceilings of the *Domus aurea*, Hadrian's villa, Pompeian frescoes, etc., and its history as a celestial symbol are well illustrated in Karl Lehmann's "The Dome of Heaven," *Art Bulletin*, XXVII, 1945, 1-27.

[36] F. Wirth, *Römische Wandmalerei vom Untergang Pompejis bis ans Ende des dritten Jahrhunderts*, 1934, 190, pl. 50.

[37] See p. 109.

influence upon a Christian imagery which was endeavoring to express the invisible by means of the visible.

Because of their preoccupation with a life after death, the Christians naturally continued the antique habit of visualizing an ideal abode for the dead as a rustic tegurium which the gods had given to man in a golden age when all was peace and happiness. By the fourth century, when they were able to develop a more monumental architecture, the Christians were also deeply influenced by the great domes which the Roman emperors had adopted as the crowning feature of their mausolea and stamped upon the imperial coins as the cosmic feature of their *aeternae memoriae* (Figs. 17-21). It should become increasingly evident why the Christians, dependent as they were upon imperial forms and antique habits of thought, came to attach so much significance to the domical shape as a sepulchral symbol.

During the Proto-Christian and Early Christian periods, when so much religious enthusiasm was centered in mortuary chapels and oratories built over the relics of saintly heroes, the Christians began to adopt for these simple martyria the Roman types of tombs and memorials along with their easily assimilated domical ideology. This process can be seen, perhaps as early as the end of the third century, in the frescoes of a Sardinian tomb, near Cagliari, where the symbolic scene of Jonah cast overboard and devoured by the sea monster who represented the evils of mortal existence is depicted.[38] The religious implications of the theme culminate on the end wall where the soul of Jonah, as a babe, is carried by the Lamb of God and transported to an ideal tegurium (Fig. 70), which is both his mausoleum and his eternal home in a heavenly paradise. The domical tegurium of rustic construction is clearly a shepherd's hut, which is also the lowly abode of the Good Shepherd, and on it, instead of the celestial eagle of the imperial mausolea (Figs. 17-21), is the Dove of Peace. Even in rendering the appearance of the symbolic tegurium, the artist was aware of the imperial meanings which could be attached to its domical shape, because he introduced into the ordinary interlace of wickerwork a band of scale ornament, taken from the tiles which frequently protected the domes of imperial tombs, memorials and aediculae (Figs. 18, 22). That the mortuary shelter of Jonah was imagined as located in a garden scene of paradise, and hence similar to the tomb of Lazarus (Fig. 23) and the Sepulchre of Christ (Fig. 10), is made evident by the two trees, one an olive tree of peace and happiness, and the other a palm which, according to De Rossi, signifies Jerusalem.

In the process of formulating their new art the Christians made little effort to differentiate very clearly between the various types of ritualistic shelters which they borrowed from the pagans. The ciborium, which usually had a domical canopy like the baldachin, they frequently called a tegurium.[39] Although the ciborium became the

---

[38] De Rossi, "Cubicoli sepolcrali cristiani," *Bollettino di archaeologia cristiana*, III, 1892, 130-144, pls. VI-VIII.

[39] Du Cange says, "Tegurium quod ed ciborium vocatur." What came to be the ciborium

was frequently designated tegurium (with all its various spellings: tiburium, tugurium, tigurium, tiburinum, and cyburiam, etc.) in the *Vita Symmachi* (498-514 A.D.), the *Vita Honorii, Vita Gregorii* and *Vita Sergii*. For specific

ritualistic covering over the altar, which in the East was also thought of as the tomb and throne of Christ, it was first used as a sepulchral shelter over the relics and remains of the dead, with the result that throughout the Middle Ages it retained both its sepulchral and heavenly symbolism.[40] Because the content went with the form and purpose of a religious shelter, and not with its method of construction, the stone reliquary built beneath the altar and in the center of the cruciform tomb crypt of S. Demetrios at Saloniki (Fig. 69) was made domical like a sepulchral tegurium.[41] For this reason it is necessary to restore the original martyrium of S. John at Ephesus (Fig. 83) as a monumental ciborium, a symbolic replica of the tomb and heavenly dwelling of Christ, with a dome, which would then explain why it was later rebuilt as the domical crossing of a cruciform church.[42]

During the first centuries of Christianity not all the reliquary chapels, oratories and early martyria were domical and central structures with circular, polygonal, square, quatrefoil and trefoil tomb plans. Between the fourth and sixth centuries, however, largely because of the growing popularity of the Cult of Martyrs, the domical tomb-types, which the Christians had taken over from Roman sepulchral architecture, were enlarged into monumental martyria and churches, as was the martyrium of S. John at Ephesus. The assimilation of pagan ideas in this process of creating a new architecture accounts for the fact that a starry dome (Figs. 14, 71, 73) over a tomb was visible

---

references see J. Braun, *Der christliche Altar*, II, 1924, 189-191, and Cabrol, *Dict.*, III, "ciborium," cols. 1588ff.

[40] Because of the early use of the ciborium as a ritualistic and symbolic covering over the body or relics of martyrs, and its figurative identity with tegurium, the domical tomb of Lazarus on the gold-glass (Fig. 23) and on the fourth century silver casket of Brivio in the Louvre (P. Lauer, "La 'Capsella' de Brivio," *Mon. Piot.*, XIII, 1926, 229ff., pl. XIX; H. H. Arnason, "Early Christian Silver of North Italy and Gaul," *Art Bulletin*, XX, 1938, 215f., figs. 21-23) was both a tegurium and ciborium. In the sixth century Gregory of Tours described the covering over the altar in the rotunda of S. Andrew at Rome as a *ciborium sepulchri* (*M.G. SS. rer. Merov.*, I, 504, cited by Braun, *op.cit.*, II, 190) and in Byzantine art the funeral of a saint usually shows the body beneath a domical ciborium. As late as the fifteenth century Symeon of Thessalonica (*De sacro Templo*, 133ᵛ: Migne, *P.G.*, CLV, col. 341) says κιβώριον symbolizes the tomb of Christ. In 1023 A.D. when the encyclopedia of Rabanus Maurus was illustrated, "de sepulchris" was pictured as a domical ciborium (A. Amelli, *Miniature sacre e profane dell' anno 1023, illustranti enciclopedia medioevale di Rabana Mauro*, 1896, pl. XCVIII) in much the same way

that "de sepulchris" in the *Agrimensorum Romanorum* was illustrated presumably by the Holy Sepulchre (Fig. 13). The variety of symbolic meanings associated with this ritualistic covering, but only specifically used for the ciborium from the twelfth century on, is indicated by the names given to it: *conopaeum, caelatura, coelum, tentorium, supratentorium, divum, umbella quam coelum dicunt*, and *mappula* (Braun, *op.cit.*, II, 270).

[41] G. A. Soteriou, 'Αρχ. 'Εφ., 1929, 239-241, figs. 72-74.

[42] The first structure at Ephesus was a square, monumental and ciborium-like chapel over the relics of S. John, which in the fifth century was enlarged by four arms into a cruciform martyrium and rebuilt in the sixth century by Justinian with domes over the crossing and arms (Grabar, *Martyrium*, I, 77, 154, 357; J. Keil, "XVI. Vorläufiger Bericht über die Aufgrabungen in Ephesos," *Jahresh. d. öster. arch. Inst.*, XXVII, 1931, Beiblatt, fig. 47). If the basic thesis of this study is sound, it should show that the masonry dome which Justinian had erected over the crossing and original tomb chapel was not the result of the introduction of domical roofing from Byzantium, but evidence that the fifth century martyrium and original chapel had a domical covering, presumably made of wood.

proof that all who were purified and faithful unto death were assured of an ideal and heavenly home more everlasting than anything enjoyed by a Roman emperor in his cosmic *Domus Dei*.

Something of the mystic nature and appeal of this domical ideology is seen in the way the concept of the dome was carried over from the tomb to the baptistery. At first the baptistery was an ordinary rectangular room, or chapel, usually with a small apse;[43] and it was this type of baptistery which, with a few exceptions, remained standard in Syria throughout the Early Christian period.[44] During the fourth century in Italy, however, the Christians began to construct their baptisteries like domical mausolea and martyria.[45] This radical change, which probably began with either the Lateran baptistery or the baptistery of the Holy Sepulchre and then spread in the course of the fifth century, illustrates the growing appeal of domical symbolism. Because the Christians had been in the habit of using their burial places as baptisteries and their baptisteries as martyria,[46] they transferred the imagery of the tomb, or martyrium, as a heavenly tegurium to the font house, which they then visualized as a symbolic, cosmic shelter in a sylvan paradise where animals drank at the Fountain of Life. In the Lateran baptistery, which was perhaps the first to be constructed like a martyrium with a celestial dome, golden harts stood around the edge of the font for the same reason that animals were pictured in the manuscripts about the tempietto over the sacred waters and that harts and trees were combined with a woodsman's hut to denote paradise in the martyrium at Seleucia Pieria (Fig. 94). At the same time this artistic symbolism was given deeper content by the Church Fathers who had established a mystic equation which made baptism a reexperience of the death and resurrection of Christ.[47] Hence, by means of this relation between the baptistery and the tomb of Christ, and because of the growing interest in domical symbolism, not only was the house of purification, like the house of the dead, transformed into a domical and heavenly dwelling, but in

[43] R. Krautheimer, "Introduction to an 'Iconography of Mediaeval Architecture,'" *Journal of the Warburg and Courtauld Institutes*, v, 1942, 22.

[44] See p. 104.

[45] Krautheimer, *op.cit.*, 26-31; P. Styger, "Nymphäaen, Mausoleen, Baptisterien," *Architectura*, I, 1933, 50ff.; Grabar, *Martyrium*, I, 202, 203, 385 n. 2, 446.

[46] The evidence for this relation of tomb and baptistery is very conclusive (Krautheimer, *op.cit.*, 28); not only have tombs been found in many baptisteries, as in the baptistery of the Arians at Ravenna (G. Gerola, "Il Restauro del battistero ariano di Ravenna," *Studien zur Kunst des Ostens*, 1923, 114), but the prevalence of the practice is shown by its prohibition in 578 by the Council of Auxerre (F. W. Unger, "Uber die christlichen Rund- und Octagon-Bauten," *Bonner Jahrb.*, XLI, 1866, 38);

the use of the martyrium as a baptistery is established at Nisibis (Grabar, *Martyrium*, I, 79), in Africa (*ibid.*, 446), by the baptism of Severus of Antioch in the martyrium of S. Leontius (Lassus, *Sanctuaires chrétiens de Syrie*, 228), and by Prudentius (*Peristephanon*, VIII, v. 1ff.; Migne, *P.L.*, LX, cols. 430ff.); and the relationship is shown by the fact that the baptistery at Jerusalem was connected with the Anastasis rather than the basilica. An indication of when this relationship was recognized in Syria is the fact that a baptistery was added onto the cruciform martyrium of S. Babylas at Antioch-Kaoussie early in the fifth century.

[47] Krautheimer, *op.cit.*, 27-33, with references to the writings of S. Paul, S. Basil, S. Augustine, Hilarius of Poitiers, the Pseudo-Augustine, Leo Magnus, and Anselm of Canterbury.

Byzantine architecture, where the martyrium church supplanted the basilica, "the baptistery was absorbed by the cupola church."[48]

The domical mortuary tradition, however, like the domical baptistery, was not native to Syria, for neither in Syria nor farther east in Mesopotamia and ancient Persia were there any round tombs whose domical shape preserved the memory of an ancient house.[49] Instead, in Mesopotamia, the earliest brick tombs were tunnel-vaulted imitations of the ancestral rectangular reed shelters with hoop roofs.[50] From earliest times the natives of Syria and Palestine buried their dead in natural grottoes, like the caves and pit dwellings of their ancestors, and even after there had evolved an elaborate ritual of offerings, libations and sacrifices, which strengthened the conception of the tomb as a house of the dead, they continued to carve out underground burials.[51] In the first century B.C., as a result of outside influences largely from the Hellenistic-Roman culture, there began to appear a great variety of sepulchral stone monuments—towers, classical tempiettos and rectangular structures with pyramidal tops—erected above the tomb chambers.[52] It is possible that before the introduction of these monumental tombs there had been transient ritualistic shelters, like rustic cabins and tents, which served as places of worship for the underground burials. Certainly before the first century B.C. there is no evidence of domical tombs in Syria.

The first extant, free-standing, tomb monument of a domical shape is the monolithic cylinder at 'Amrith (Fig. 74), which is a curious grave stele standing above the underground chamber.[53] Formerly it was thought to have been erected by the Phoenicians, but it is now attributed to a period perhaps as late as that of Herod the Great, along with the Nabatean tomb towers, the "tomb of Absalom" with its concave, conical roof, and the "tomb of Zacharias" with the more common pyramidal top.[54] Regardless

[48] Grabar, *Martyrium*, I, 392.

[49] In tracing the evolution of domical architecture it is impossible to overlook this fact, that the round and dome-shaped tomb, which was so common in both India and the Mediterranean, was completely absent from the sepulchral traditions of Mesopotamia and Iran until the Islamic conquest. The one, or more, crudely shaped rubble domes, which C. L. Woolley (*Ur Excavations*, II, 1934, 229-237) uncovered on square tombs at Ur, left no tradition and were probably constructed to protect their flat, timbered roofs.

[50] W. Andrae, *Das Gotteshaus und die Urformen des Bauens im alten Orient*, 1930, 60-72.

[51] I. Benzinger, *Hebräische Archäologie*, 1927, 133, 205-210; P. S. P. Handcock, *The Archaeology of the Holy Land*, 1916, 302-326; A. Lods, *La Croyance à la vie future et le culte des morts*, 1906, 184ff.; R. A. S. Macalister, *A Century of Excavation in Palestine* (1925), 256ff.; C. Watzinger, *Denk. Paläs.*, I, 77f.

[52] Watzinger, *op.cit.*, II, 71-74.

[53] Perrot and Chipiez, *Histoire*, III, 151-152, fig. 95; E. Renan, *Mission de Phénicie*, 1864, pl. 13.

[54] The pyramid was a common form of memorial and grave monument in Syria and Palestine from the Hellenistic period down to Roman times. While it retained something of the sun symbolism which characterized it as the *ben-ben* of ancient Egypt, it had acquired a variety of uses and meanings; R. Vallois (*L'Architecture héllenique et hellénistique à Délos*, I, 1944, 394f.) who gives an excellent bibliography, says that the pyramidal towers of Syria were either tombs or heroä, and shows that in many instances they were religious monuments, like classical tholoi, consecrated to the cult of emperors, legendary heroes and even divinities; and M. J. Lagrange (*Études sur les religions sémitiques*, 1903, 206) says they were frequently used as grave stele and called *naphchâ*, meaning "soul" or "person." Although it is easy to see why scholars should have thought that the pyramid form, which was as common to the Syrian memorials as the

of its date, it is not comprehensible enough to contribute much to domical history, unless it was a stone version of a qobba tent which the ancient Arabs frequently erected over the tombs of their ancestors. Apart from this sculptured stele, all the other domical tombs between the first century B.C. and the fourth century A.D., when the Christians began to build martyria, occur in Palestine and indicate a Roman influence coming in from Egypt. At Tall Hinnom, near Jerusalem, there are a number of rock-cut tombs, such as the "Ferdus er-Rûm" (Fig. 75), which have flat domical roofs decorated with lotus rosettes over the reception hall, or main room, of the tombs.[55] A similar square tomb chamber (Fig. 76) covered with a shallow dome which is without either a squinch or pendentive at the corners, but constructed of finely cut masonry, occurs at 'Amman.[56] The dome of this undated pagan tomb, which is eighteen feet in diameter, was supported on walls about five feet thick and completely concealed on the exterior.

The other domical tombs of Palestine, whose fine masonry resembles the Roman construction of the Antonine period at Ba'albek, have cruciform plans within a square tower, and their domes, which are almost wholly concealed on the exterior, are fitted to the interior square by carefully executed spherical pendentives. Of these the tomb at Qusayr an-Nuwayis (Fig. 78), near 'Amman, which is assigned to the late second or early third century, has perhaps the earliest known cut-stone dome with pendentives.[57] Another similar tomb with pendentives, dated 193-211 A.D., was discovered at Sebastya (Fig. 79), which is evidence that the masons of this region were well acquainted with domical construction.[58] Other square tombs with cruciform interiors, which are believed to have had interior domes, have been located in western Palestine at Kades (Fig. 80), Beisan, Teiâsîr, Khûrbet Zanûtu and Es-Semû'a.[59] Inasmuch as

dome was to the Roman ones, should have been used upon Christian martyria, there is no evidence that the Christians took over its symbolism and established a pyramidal roof tradition.

[55] R. A. S. Macalister, "The Rock-cut Tombs in Wâdy er-Rababi, Jerusalem," *Palestine Exploration Fund, Quarterly Statement*, 1900, 225ff., and 1901, 147, 215; Watzinger, *op.cit.*, 63; K. O. Dalman, "Uber ein Felsen grab im Hinnomtale bei Jerusalem," *Zeitschrift des deutschen Palästina-Vereins*, LXII, 1939, 190-208. These shallow rock-cut cupolas, fitted to a square chamber without squinches or pendentives, are the same as the cupola in the Gabbari tomb of the Roman period at Alexandria (*Bull. Soc. Arch. Alex.*, N. 3, T. 4. 6; R. Delbrueck, *Hellenistische Bautem in Latium*, 1907-12, II, 79, 102).

[56] Creswell, *Early Muslim Architecture*, I, 308, fig. 364; C. R. Conder, *The Survey of Eastern Palestine*, 1889, 43-45, pl. opp. p. 44; Watzinger, *op.cit.*, II, 99.

[57] Creswell, *op.cit.*, 313-314, fig. 382; Conder,

op.cit., 172-174; Watzinger, *op.cit.*, 101, Abb. 9 (plan); a recent photograph (N. Glueck, *Explorations in Eastern Palestine*, III [Annual of the American Schools of Oriental Research, XVIII-XIX], 1939, 175, fig. 57) shows that its dome projected a little above the flat roof and had a flamelike finial.

[58] Creswell, *op.cit.*, 315, fig. 386; R. H. Hamilton, "The Domed Tomb at Sebastya," *Quarterly of the Department of Antiquities in Palestine*, VIII, 1938, 64ff.; G. A. Reisner, C. S. Fisher and D. G. Lyon, *Harvard Excavations at Samaria*, 1908-10, I, 1924, 220-223, figs. 148-152.

[59] At Kades (Conder and Kitchener, *Survey of Western Palestine, Memoirs*, 1881-83, I, 228; C. W. Wilson, "Remains of Tombs in Palestine," *Pal. Expl. Fund, Quart. St.*, 1869-70, 69; Watzinger, *op.cit.*, 100, Abb. 8 [plan], Taf. 34 [view]) the four arms are covered with tunnel vaults and the central square, something over 3 m. in span, had a cut-stone dome on pendentives. Beth-Sean (*Survey of Western Palestine, Memoirs*, II, 110; Watzinger, *op.cit.*, 99 n. 3);

the tower tomb at Hass in Syria, which De Vogüé (Fig. 81) and Butler published as having had a free-standing dome, was in partial ruins, it seems more likely that it had only a concealed dome over the central square of its cruciform interior.[60] At Hierapolis (Fig. 82) are the remains of a large octagonal structure which was undoubtedly covered with a heavy masonry dome.[61] Although it was probably a martyrium of the fifth century, and not a tomb, it is so similar in plan and construction to what is known of the mausoleum of Constantine at Constantinople that it shows how even on the northeastern border of Syria the imperial type of mausoleum was adapted to Christian use as a martyrium.

The sepulchral evidence, therefore, indicates very strongly that before the Peace of the Church the domical tomb in Palestine and Syria was of Hellenistic and Roman derivation, probably first introduced into Palestine by way of Egypt. This conclusion, when taken in conjunction with the similarity of the Holy Sepulchre and the martyrium at Hierapolis to the imperial mausolea, sustains Grabar's assertions that all the early martyria in the Near East were adaptations of the sepulchral architecture of Rome.[62] Were there no other evidence of domical traditions in these regions it would be difficult to understand how in the Christian period Syria and Palestine, after having borrowed the mortuary dome from the West, could have assumed an important role in transforming the domical tomb into a martyrium, and why Syrian churchmen, as Grabar says,[63] should have been influential in bringing about the change which led to the Byzantine adoption of the domical martyrium church in place of the gable-roofed basilica.

Moreover, it is still necessary to explain the free-standing, conoid dome upon the late fifth century tomb of Bizzos (Fig. 61) and to account for its similarity to the Islamic weli. This one extant Christian tomb could not have been the prototype of the hundreds of subsequent Arab weli and domical oratories, like the tombs of Sarah, Joseph and Rachel (Fig. 84), which became so common in Syria and which both Christians and Arabs looked upon with such reverence. The appearance in Egypt during the fourth and fifth centuries at Bawit, Bagawat (Fig. 86) and Kharga (Fig. 87) of so many square mortuary chapels and oratories covered with brick domes undoubtedly contributed to the growing popularity of the domical tomb in the Christian and Islamic East.[64] While the appearance of the Egyptian chapels is all part of the development of domical interests, there is still the question in Egypt, as in Syria, of why this type of religious monument became so popular, for again there is no evidence that the dome was of any significance in the sepulchral architecture of Pharaonic Egypt.

---

at Teiâsîr (*Survey*, II, 245; Watzinger, 100) there is some doubt as to whether the crossing of its cruciform plan had a groin vault or cupola; at Khurbet Zânûta (*Survey*, III, 410; Watzinger, 99 n. 3) there is no extant evidence of dome, but it is supposed to have had one; at Es-Semû'a (*Survey*, III, 413; Watzinger, 99 n. 3) the square interior had a vault which has fallen.

[60] De Vogüé, *Syrie Centrale*, II, pl. 72; Butler, *Architecture and Other Arts*, 246-247, fig. 99.

[61] See p. 102.

[62] Grabar, *Martyrium*, I, 197ff.

[63] *Ibid.*, 313, 322, 377.

[64] *Ibid.*, 82-85, 357-358.

What accounts for the tomb of Bizzos and made Syria so receptive to the mortuary symbolism of the dome was her own native domical traditions. Not only did the Christians of Syria and Palestine inherit an old religious belief in the symbolic implications of the domical shape, which will be taken up in the next chapter, but also Syria had a primitive type of domical shelter, which was there to serve as a model at the time when the Christians were taking over the late antique beliefs in a domical tomb as a divine and ancestral type of tegurium. The first step, then, in reconstructing the domical ideology of Syria is to start with the history of the qubâb hut and see why it came to serve as the model for the tomb of Bizzos, influenced the mystic thinking of Syrian churchmen and served as a model for the Islamic weli.

A second important factor, less easy to demonstrate, in accounting for both the Christian and Islamic adoption of the mortuary dome was the pre-Islamic Arab tradition of a domical religious shelter. Prior to the Islamic Conquest, when many Arabs were already established in parts of Syria and Palestine, the tribesmen had a primitive type of domelike tent, known as a qobba, which they used as a portable sanctuary and erected over the graves of ancestors and famous dead.[65] Hence, they, like Syrians, were already conditioned to the religious significance of the domical shape. The fact that their ancient form of tabernacle and tomb shelter was called a qobba, which was the same as qubâb, does not mean that both types of primitive shelter had the same origin. The Syrian qubâb was primarily a rustic hut of reeds, branches and thatch, whose shape had been translated into pisé, brick and stone, while the Arab qobba was originally a leather tent which was not imitated symbolically in masonry until after the Arabs had adopted the architectural traditions of Syria and Egypt. Both were presumably called by the same name because of their curved and cuplike shape. Both also serve to show how complex were the origins of domical beliefs which in so many cultures went back to an ancestral form of dwelling.

[65] H. Lammens, "Le Culte des bétyles et les processions religieuses chez les Arabes préislamites," *Bulletin de l'Institut français d'archéologie orientale du Caire*, XVII, 1920, 92.

IV · DOMICAL FORMS
AND THEIR IDEOLOGY

I
T HAS already become evident that there were many different religious beliefs, associated with the domical shape and the primitive round shelter, which were deeply imbedded in the conservative and superstitious imagination of various communities. By Christian times in the eclectic civilization of Syria all of the domical beliefs were readily assimilated and attached as mystic overtones of meaning to the imagery already present in the culture. In her own heritage Syria had an indigenous type of primitive shelter which was considered to be an ancestral, god-given dwelling such as the Romans saw in their tegurium, the Indians in the vihâra, the Libyans in the maphalia,[1] the Arabs in the qobba and the Hebrews in the tent, or tabernacle, of Moses. Many pagan communities of Syria and Palestine had for centuries worshipped heavenly divinities as conoid baetyls whose form was probably derived from a house concept. Hence the local veneration for the conoid shape as an ancestral hut, a divine stone, an inner tabernacle and a cosmic house readily combined with Hellenistic ideas regarding the tholos and omphalos, with the Roman conceptions of the dome as a mortuary symbol, a celestial covering and royal baldachin, and with the other symbolic beliefs, such as those of the celestial helmet, cosmic egg and pine cone. Because of the location of Syria at the head of the trade routes to the East, it is also probable that the older domical beliefs of India, which so closely paralleled those in the West and went back in origin to similar house concepts, were contributing factors even before Christian thought and monastic life took on so many characteristics of Hindu mysticism.[2]

A. The Ancestral Shelter: Qubâb Hut and Kalubé

The Syrian shelter of round and domical shape is known as a qubâb.[3] It is still peculiar to certain parts of Syria and can be traced back certainly to the eighth century

[1] The maphalia, which was a nomadic dwelling and shepherd's hut among the Libyans, had mortuary associations as early as Herodotus (IV, 190), who in describing the burial rites says the maphalia was made of reeds, intertwined with asphodels; by the Roman period it was frequently depicted upon sarcophagi. Full bibliography: E. Müller-Graupa, "Mapalia," *Philologus*, LXXIII, 1914-16, 302-317.

[2] H. Lester Cooke, Jr. is preparing a study of domical beliefs in India.

[3] The early and underlying shelter concept of *qubba* is indicated by the various meanings of the word which are given by E. W. Lane (*Arabic-English Lexicon*, 1863-93) as: "a round tent or pavilion, any round structure, a small round tent of a particular kind, what is raised for the purpose of entering thereinto, a dome-like or tentlike covering (of a woman's camel-vehicle); a dome or cupola of stone or bricks, a building covered with a dome or cupola." According to G. E. Miles, who has helped me in preparing this note, the unscientific Arabic lexicographers intimate that it came from the Arabic root *qbb* with the meaning of "collect, or gather together, the extremities of a thing." Professor Wolf Leslau, however, says, "The meaning of Arabic *qubba* is best represented in Syriac and Aramaic *qubbeta*, 'tentorium; palatium cupola ornatum; fornix coeli, altaris, etc.' Inasmuch as many technical expressions for construction, building, etc. are taken from Aramaic, the Arabic *qubba* is considered as an Aramaic loan word (S. Fraenkel, *Die aramä-*

61

B.C. and, perhaps, even to the fourth millennium. The well-known Assyrian relief from the palace of Sennacherib at Koyunjiq (Fig. 91) presumably preserves the appearance of these Syrian qubâb dwellings in the eighth century B.C. For a long time it was thought that this one relief from Nineveh furnished graphic proof of the existence of domical structures in Mesopotamian architecture. It has also been suggested that the domical buildings on this relief are Indian shrines which the Mesopotamian world undoubtedly knew.[4] Without denying the close similarity of the buildings on the relief to Indian religious structures, any direct relationship seems most unlikely, first, because of the distances involved and, second, because the relief was primarily devoted to depicting a scene of Assyrian prowess in transporting overland a carved stone statue. At all events the scene with its mountains covered with olive trees and evergreens could not have been native to the flat plain of the Mesopotamian valley. Instead, it represents a foreign village, probably in the foothills of the Lebanese mountains, where the Assyrians obtained much of their stone and their finest timber. Furthermore, it should be noted that the direct trade route from Nineveh to the Lebanon passed directly through the districts of Homs and Hama where settlements of similar houses are numerous today (Fig. 88). In Assyrian times the only reason why Mesopotamian craftsmen should have included a small village in a scene of royal power was that such domical villages were recognized as characteristic of the distant mountainous and wooded land of Syria.

The modern Syrian domed huts are of two types (Figs. 92): the more primitive form having a "beehive," or conoid, shape set directly upon the ground, and the later form having a dome raised upon a rectangular chamber just as it is upon the Assyrian relief, the tomb of Bizzos, and the Arab weli. All the qubâb villages are at present concentrated into two widely separate regions, one along the eastern highlands of North Syria and the other at the headwaters of the Euphrates Valley in the northwestern highland zone of Assyria.[5] Both groups, located on the outer and culturally retarded borders of regions that were formerly wooded, are survivals in their use of the domical shape of a primitive round reed and wattle hut such as is depicted on the fourth millennium sherd (Fig. 90) from Arpachiyah in northwestern Assyria.[6] The huts on this piece of painted pottery are combined with trees in a scene whose religious implications will be considered later.[7] To see the origin of the Syrian type of shelter, it is only necessary to compare the profile of a group of modern qubâbs with the Arpachiyah sherd and then with the modern survivals of the prehistoric Egyptian round house from Nubia (Fig. 93), where the traditional huts of the Shilluks are

ischen fremden wörter in Arabischen, Leiden, 1886, p. 288)." These Aramaic meanings, especially "the vault of heaven" and the implication of a covering over the altar, again illustrate the early symbolic significance of the domical shape.

[4] E. Diez, Die Kunst Indiens, 1925, 43; E. B. Havell, The Ancient and Mediaeval Architecture of India, 1915, 95.

[5] E. Banse, "Die Gubâb-Hütten Nordsyriens und Nordwest Mesopotamiens," Orientalisches Archiv, II, 1911-12, 173ff.; L. Speleers, "Les Tépés hittites en Syrie du Nord," Syria, VIII, 1927, 42ff.

[6] M. E. L. Mallowan and J. C. Rose, Prehistoric Assyria, 1935, 32, fig. 20.

[7] See pp. 65, 73.

grouped as a religious shrine. Because of desiccation the primitive dwellings of pliable materials in Syria and northern Mesopotamia were translated at an early date into more permanent pisé, brick and small stone construction.

It has already been pointed out by Banse that the qubâb house could not have originated in the brick architecture of Mesopotamia because these domical villages are never found in the alluvial plain of the Tigris and Euphrates, where rectangular flat-roofed houses of brick were common from the fourth millennium.[8] Further confirmation of their origin in materials other than brick has been furnished by the excavations of prehistoric Arpachiyah where a few round and domical pisé houses, or shrines, occur as either survivals or intrusions among the rectangular brick buildings of this very ancient Assyrian town.[9] That they once existed over wide areas of mountainous and wooded regions in Asia Minor, and at a very early date had acquired sufficient religious significance to have been carved laboriously in solid rock, is shown by the so-called "cones of rock" (Fig. 89), cut and hollowed out in imitation of round hut villages, which have been found in southern Cappadocia and Syria.[10] Another

[8] There is slight evidence that the earliest dwellings in Mesopotamia were circular reed huts, but before the fourth millennium B.C., when the houses and temples of Mesopotamia were becoming rectangular, brick structures with flat, timbered roofs, the ordinary dwellings made of pliable materials were rectangular and had hoop roofs (Andrae, *Das Gotteshaus und die Urformen des Bauens im alten Orient*, 1930, 60-72, Abb. 61; E. Heinrich, *Schilf und Lehm*, 1934). In fact, there is no evidence to sustain the belief that the dome originated in the brick architecture of this region. Apart from one crude rubble dome found by Woolley upon a burial tomb at Ur, there are no indications of domes having been used upon houses, tombs and temples. As an adaptation presumably of the earliest round house, some partially buried granaries were covered with brick domes. (Andrae, *op.cit.*; Henrich, *Fara*, 1931, Taf. 3.) At Ur the excavators thought they had uncovered indications of mud domes in the fragments of bituminous lining which adhered to the corners of four square compartments of a cistern (Woolley, *Ur Excavations*, II, 237); but it was admitted that these domes, if they existed, had neither structural nor expressive value because they must have been fake domes of mud, moulded on baskets, which were concealed under flat, timbered roofs (Woolley, *Antiquaries Journal*, XIII, 1933, 371). A circular well and rectangular shaft at Tell Asmar, dating about 2150 B.C., were both covered with intersecting half-domes of laminated bricks (H. Frankfort, S. Lloyd and T. Jacobsen, *The Gimilsin Temple and the Palace of the Rulers at Tell Asmar*, 1940, 80). In spite of this evidence, which indicates only that the brick dome was used for a few utilitarian purposes, Woolley suggested that the central chamber of the Nin-gal temple and the Dublalmah sanctuary at Ur, both dating from the Kassite period about 1400 B.C., might have had domes, although he admitted that "material proof is lacking" (*Antiq. Jour.*, V, 1925, 371ff.; VII, 1927, 408). Apparently the myth regarding the Mesopotamian origin of the masonry dome started in 1867 when Victor Place mistook the Assyrian representations of tents for structural half-domes and restored the palace at Khorsabad with fine Islamic domes rising for no reason out of its flat roof.

[9] The circular structures uncovered at Arpachiyah had diameters up to 7 m., but it is not clear whether the larger ones were covered with pisé or thatch, because only one had enough of its walls standing to show the curve of its clay dome, which curiously would have had a clearance of only 1.5 m. at the center. In describing these structures Mallowan notes the occasional traces of carbonized wood in the pisé, indicating "that some timber was used"; but he does not specify whether the carbon was found in the tholos or in the rectangular vestibule (Mallowan and Rose, *Prehistoric Assyria*, 25-31).

[10] Perrot and Chipiez, *Histoire de l'art*, IV, 787, fig. 389. These stone replicas of the qubâb huts of Syria and northern Assyria are sometimes called Hittite, presumably because they have been found in Cappadocia and Syria, in the district between Kodja-dagh and Kurddagh.

proof that they were an upland and primitive type of shelter is the fact that the sur-vivals of this round-house tradition translated into brick construction, which have been uncovered in ancient Mesopotamia, have been found only in the northernmost part of the valley.[11] On the analogy, then, of similar round huts in Sardinia, ancient Gaul, India, Ireland, North America and other parts of the world, which are known to have originated in thatch, bamboo and other pliable materials and then at a much later date to have been translated into stone construction, the qubâb huts of Syria are stone, brick and pisé replicas of the ancient round and domelike shelters of straw, reeds and wattle which at one time were common throughout the wooded regions of North Syria.

The persistence of the domical tradition has also been shown by the villages of the second and third centuries A.D. which Schlumberger discovered northwest of Palmyra, where the houses consisted of square chambers of stone covered, like the qubâb huts, with domes of sun-dried brick.[12] The sanctuaries in these villages were domical like the houses. The outline of one of these cult houses, preserved on a graffito, is, from the description, very similar to the rectangular domical house on the Assyrian relief from Nineveh, the tomb of Bizzos and the weli or mortuary kubba of the Arabs. Archaeological evidence has thus established the existence of a domical house and shrine tradition in Syria. At the same time it must be assumed that the prototype of these brick, pisé and stone qubâb huts, which was a kind of kalubé made of pliable materials, continued to be used by the woodsmen and shepherds of North Syria. The persistence of this type of rustic shelter helps to explain some of the domical shrines of pagan Syria and the importance of the conoid shape on Christian monuments. Moreover, it suggests an explanation for one of the Christian reliefs discovered in the Martyrium at Seleucia Pieria.[13]

The relief preserves the appearance of this Syrian type of rustic shelter (Fig. 94), for the cabin is made of flexible materials, bound together and bent over to form its

[11] Apart from granaries, the only other strict-ly round building so far discovered is at Nuzi which was not far from Arpachiyah on the northern border of Mesopotamia. This struc-ture, dating from the fourth millennium, was first made of pisé and later rebuilt in brick. Be-cause its walls were vertical and thin, the ex-cavator, overlooking the probability of its hav-ing had at this time a curved roof of thatch, says it was "too slight to have resisted the thrust of a dome" and hence must have been open or flat-roofed (R. S. Starr, *Nuzi*, 1937-39, I, 9). The discovery of a curvilinear structure from the early Tell-el-'Obeid period and a larger "round house" from Stratum XVII at Tepe Gawra, which was in the neighborhood of Arpachiyah, suggests very strongly the sur-vival of a venerated round-house tradition of the north which had already begun to be modi-fied by the multiple-room and flat-roofed brick architecture of the south (E. A. Speiser, "On Some Recent Finds from Tepe Gawra," *Bul-letin of the American Schools of Oriental Re-search*, LXII, 1936, 12; A. J. Tobler, "Progress of the Joint Expedition to Mesopotamia," *ibid.*, LXXI, 1938, 22).

[12] D. Schlumberger, "Neue Ausgrabungen in der syrischen Wüste nordwestliche von Pal-myra," *Archäologischer Anzeiger*, 1935, 595-633.

[13] One of the sculptured fragments found in the debris around the central platform or "Place of Commemoration" of the martyrium: dowel holes on the exterior face of the semi-circular exedra indicate that these reliefs were revetments on the vertical side of the raised platform and belong to the second period of construction, which was in the sixth century (R. Stillwell [ed.], *Antioch-on-the-Orontes*, III, 1941, no. 480, pl. 27).

pointed and domelike roof. The fact that it is combined with the sacred tree and hart shows that it was intended to represent a symbolic kalubé. This idea of an ancient rustic dwelling of a divinity in combination with a sacred tree, or grove, was common to the religious traditions of many parts of the ancient world, and probably older in Syria and Asia Minor than it was in Greece and Rome; but by the sixth century when this relief was carved for a Christian martyrium it is only the shape and construction of the rustic shelter which is Syrian. The tradition of a primitive habitation as an ideal abode in combination with a sacred tree and wild animals had become so popular in Roman art and literature that the Christians, largely through the influence of Virgil and Ovid, had come to think of such a scene as symbolizing the heavenly home of the martyred dead in a sylvan paradise.

The appeal of this theme, which went back to the early beginnings of religious art in various countries, was largely inspired for the Christians by the Eclogues of Virgil where the ancestral tegurium (Fig. 96) was a symbol of the peaceful and ideal life "in our rude fields and lowly cots" where the woods ring with happiness, "the wolf plans no ambush for the flocks," and "kindly Daphnis loves peace."[14] This Roman idealization of a golden past and veneration of an ancestral shelter, as in Ovid's praise of the good old days "when Rome was new, when a small hut sufficed to lodge Quirinus," and when "Jupiter had hardly room to stand erect in his cramped shrine,"[15] became for the Christians an expression of their own longing for a celestial abode and a symbolic representation of their own lost paradise. Hence the subject of the shepherd's hut was taken over by Christian sarcophagus carvers in Rome, by tomb painters in Sardinia (Fig. 70) and by ivory carvers (Fig. 100) in the Syro-Palestinian area.

The memory of a god's hut in his sacred grove was too old and common in the ancient world to be attributed to any one source. The scene on the fourth millennium pictograph from Arpachiyah (Fig. 90) presumably depicts divine huts in formal combination with sacred trees. On the early Buddhistic reliefs (Fig. 98) similar round and domelike huts were the sanctified abode of the Gotama and his disciples when they lived a holy and ascetic life in the Deer Forest of Benares.[16] Also both the sanctuary of Buddha and the Indian fire temple (Figs. 138, 142) were represented as primitive, thatched dwellings in combination with sacred trees, while the golden dome of the Buddha Gaya, itself a celestial symbol, was identified with the spreading banyan, or amalaka, tree where the gods dwelt. The process by which the ancient shelter with its domical shape acquired its symbolic importance on the religious architecture of

[14] Vergilii Romanus, *codicis Vaticanus* 3867, fols. 6, 16, 44, 45; *Eclogues* (Loeb), II, 28f.; V, 6of. The extent to which the late antique and Early Christian periods drew upon the *Eclogues* and saw in the "lowly hut" a symbol of the past is illustrated by the coins of Constantius II and Constans, designed to commemorate the eleventh centenary of Rome in 348 A.D., on which a soldier holds by the hand a little shepherd, or woodsman, emerging from a rustic tegurium with a tree behind it (H. Mattingly, "Fel. Temp. Reparatio," *Numismatic Chronicle*, series 5, XIII, 1933, 182-202, pl. XVII/15-25).

[15] Ovid, *Fasti* (Loeb), I, 198-202; II, 293ff.; III, 183ff.

[16] Relief at Mardan (A. Foucher, *L'Art gréco-bouddhique du Gandhâra*, I, 1905, fig. 189, p. 374; other examples, figs. 190, 191).

India was essentially the same as what is suggested to account for the evolution of domical ideas in Syria: the vihâra, or woodsman's hut, which the gods had first made and in which the Buddha had lived, was translated into wood carpentry and later, after stone construction had been developed or introduced from Hellenized Bactria, was reproduced in stone as a religious dwelling, a traditional type of sanctuary and a reliquary.[17]

In Palestine and the Near East the ancient idea of a sacred tree in combination with a religious habitation was taken over by the Christians in order to show the sacredness of holy places.[18] Following the precedent of Hellenistic funereal gardens (Fig. 25), the divine and ideal character of their martyria was indicated by the trees which went with a martyr's abode, as can be seen in the representation of the martyrium of S. John the Baptist at Alexandria (Fig. 31) and that of S. Athenogenes on an ampulla from Alexandria (Fig. 153). For the same reasons both the Holy Sepulchre (Figs. 8, 9, 10, 14) and the tomb of Lazarus (Fig. 23), it has been seen, were frequently presented as a tegurium, domical tholos, or memoria in a *paradisus* or funereal garden.[19]

This veneration for a rustic cabin of domical shape is again illustrated by an ampulla from Egypt on which the thatched cabin of conoid shape (Fig. 99) is the abode of the holy martyr Athenogenes.[20] According to the legend, a hind entered the sacred hut and offered itself as a disciple of the holy man. That this lowly hut was visualized as an ideal dwelling of God in the afterlife is indicated by another ampulla (Fig. 153) which shows the same saint standing beside his domical martyrium.[21] His hut, then, like the kalubé on the relief from the martyrium at Seleucia Pieria, was a symbolic martyrium. At the same time it was similar in shape to the sculptured stone naos (Fig. 101), or inner sanctuary, of a Ptolemaic temple which, in turn, reproduced a very ancient Egyptian type of hut shrine.[22]

That there existed in the religious traditions of Syria a similar idea of an ancient habitation, round and domelike, which God had given to man in a remote and happier past, is shown by the scene of the Sacrifice of Isaac (Fig. 95) on the walls of the Jewish Synagogue of 245-256 A.D. at Doura-Europos.[23] Unlike the customary representations of Abraham's Sacrifice, a dwelling is included in the scene; according to Du Buisson, the domical structure in the background is not a tent, but a Syrian qubâb hut such as the artist might have seen frequently along the eastern borders of Syria and hence believed to have been an ancestral shelter in the land of Abraham.[24] It symbolizes the

[17] Foucher, *op.cit.*, 99-145.

[18] Grabar, *Martyrium*, I, 71-74.

[19] See p. 27.

[20] Dresden ampulla (R. Pagenstecher, "Zu den Germanenhütten der Markussäule," *Germania*, III, 1919, 57, Abb. 3; *Die griechische-ägyptische Sammlung von Sieglin*, III, 1913, Abb. 106/2); an ampulla from Thebes in the Berlin Museum shows thatched construction similar to that on the relief from Seleucia Pieria (O. Wulff, *Altchristliche und mittel-alterliche . . . Bildwerke*, I, 1909, no. 1402, Taf.

LXIX; C. M. Kaufmann, *Ikonographie der Menas-ampullen*, 1910, 143-144).

[21] Wulff, *op.cit.*, no. 1403, pl. LXIX; Kaufmann, *op.cit.*, 143; Strzygowski, *Hellenistische und koptische Kunst*, 1902, 39, fig. 24.

[22] E. Baldwin Smith, *Egyptian Architecture*, 121, pl. XXXII, 4.

[23] R. du Mesnil du Buisson, *Les Peintures de la synagogue de Doura-Europos*, 1939, 22-27, fig. 20, pl. XIII/2.

[24] *Ibid.*, 24.

temple of Yahweh, for the Jews also had the tradition of a primitive habitation which had been given to man by God. In an early text, found at Sâlihîyeh, near Doura-Europos, and in the later Arab *Chronicle of Tabari*, it is related that Abraham was instructed to build a sacred dwelling for Yahweh which he was unable to keep from collapsing until he had undertaken to sacrifice his son.[25] Hence the dome-shaped dwelling was meant to denote a symbolic ancestral shelter, the one which God first brought from heaven in order to honor Adam and then took away until after the earth had been purified by the Deluge.

It is unfortunately impossible to accept Du Buisson's interpretation of the Doura scene without some qualifications because, in the scene of the Sacrifice of Isaac on an incised glass medallion (Fig. 97) of inferior workmanship from Trier, there is also a domical structure behind the altar.[26] Whatever the exact derivation of these shelters may have been, it is curious to find them only upon these two representations of the Sacrifice in the two regions where there was an old and established domical tradition, and to have them presumably symbolizing the house of God in a scene of personal sacrifice. Regarding the specific origin of the dwelling of Yahweh on the Doura fresco, it is not necessary to decide whether it depicts a Roman tegurium, an ancient Syrian kalubé like a modern qubâb, a Semitic qobba, or a Jewish ohel such as Eisler endeavored to show was the cosmic and ritualistic "Shepherd's Tent of the World" (Fig. 149) and which he believed the ancient Hebrews derived from Mesopotamia.[27] All these beliefs in a cosmic house as an ancestral shelter were much too common in the late antique period to be traced back to any one local type of dwelling, although they were all interrelated in the general heritage of ideas which contributed so much to the mystic symbolism of Syria and Palestine. Nevertheless, it should be realized to what extent all classes who had inherited any belief in the sacredness of an ancestral shelter, and had seen the symbolic house of Yahweh on the Jewish frescoes or the kalubé on the Christian relief at Seleucia, were accustomed to associate the conoid shape of the qubâb huts with the celestial House of God.

B. The Sacred Kalubé

The idea of a kalubé as a simple, ancient and sacred shelter was expressed by Philostratus when he wrote, *For once on a time this god Apollo dwelt in quite a humble*

---

[25] *Ibid.*, 25 n. 3; *Revue des études juives*, XCIX, 1935, 119-120; Chronicle of Tabari, composed at Bagdad in first part of tenth century (ed. H. Zotenberg, I, 1867, XXVII-XXVIII, 84-86).

[26] J. Wilmowsky, *Archäologishe Funde in Trier*, 1873, 32, 40, Taf. II; C. M. Kaufmann, *Handbuch der christlichen Archäologie*, 1922, fig. 123; E. Krüger, "Einige spätromische Glasgefässe aus dem Treverergebiet," *Provinzialmuseum Trier, Jahresbericht*, 1928, 206ff., Taf. xv/1, 2; W. Neuss, "Die Anfänge des Christen-

tums im Rheinlande," *Rheinische Neujahrblätter*, 1933, 43, Abb. 19; Cabrol, *Dict.*, I, fig. 54.

[27] See p. 84. As a result of the studies of Lammens on the pre-Islamic cult tent (*Bulletin de l'Institut français d'archéologie orientale*, XVII, 1920, 39-101) and Morgenstern on the primitive Hebrew religious tent (*The Ark, the Ephod and the "Tent of Meeting,"* 1945), it must be assumed that the dwelling of Yahweh in the scene of the sacrifice of Isaac is a qobba.

habitation; and a little hut [καλυβή] *was constructed for him to which the bees are said to have contributed their honeycomb and wax, and the birds their feathers.*[28] In the pagan communities of Syria there were various types of humble habitation, such as arboreal huts, tribal tents and portable canopies, which had survived since primitive times, or had been introduced from adjacent regions, as the traditional dwelling, inner tabernacle, or ritualistic ciborium of a local divinity. These revered shelters, as the coins show, continued to be used for the actual dwelling and festivals of the gods even after the temples had been rebuilt with the magnificent porticoes and gabled façades of the classic style. Some of these honored tabernacles were conical in shape, others were pyramidal, and a few had a hoop roof, but most of them were either domical or had a cupola beneath a protecting conical roof. By usage the shape and purpose of these traditional cult shelters acquired such powerful meaning in the religious thought of every community that the Christians, when they came to enshrine their own altars, tombs, relics and thrones, naturally appropriated the pagan forms for their ciboria, baldachins and festival shrines. Both the shape and symbolism were taken over into the architecture and art in much the same way that the Christians, who had been accustomed to seeing the official representative of the State beneath a ciborium (Figs. 103, 144, 146), adopted the royal baldachin and presented their Heavenly Imperator (Fig. 115) and his Queenly Mother (Fig. 114) enthroned, like Roman and Byzantine rulers, beneath a celestial canopy.

The peoples of Syria and the Near East, it must be realized, were fully conditioned to a religious reverence for the domical shape as a manifestation of a divine presence. This is most clearly shown by the pagan coins on which the actual tabernacle, rather than its enclosing temple, is so frequently depicted. The celestial god on a coin of Laodicea ad mare (Fig. 102) is presented as an eagle in his domical shrine,[29] while over a pair of altars in Pisidia (Fig. 104), on which the stars and moon denote their heavenly character, the sacred ciborium is a domical tent.[30] A similar tent appears as a tabernacle of Canopus (Fig. 105) on coins of Alexandria[31] and also occurs as a heavenly baldachin (Fig. 143) above a Sassanian deity on a coin executed under strong classical influence.[32] Another type of inner shrine on a coin of Pisidia (Fig. 107) has fringes and a reticulated fabric pattern, showing that its domical form was a divine

[28] *Life of Apollonius* (ed. Loeb), VI, x. In his discussion of *Kalubai* Oelmann (*Bonner Jahrb.*, 127, 1922, 227-235) disregards the roof shape and identifies it with the liwan house.

[29] Laodicea ad mare, Philip sen. (*British Museum Catalogue of Coins, Galatia, Cappadocia and Syria*, 262, no. 111, pl. XXXI/7).

[30] Sagalassos (F. Imhoof-Blumer, *Kleinasiatische Münzen*, II, 1920, pl. XIV/11; *Brit. Mus. Cat. Coins, Lycia etc.*, p. 244, nos. 23, 24). The arch which here appears above the altars of the Dioskouroi and occurs so frequently over gods and goddesses was a sky symbol (Cook, *Zeus*, II, 362f., 365f.), but at the same time it

was a numismatic convention for representing the curved canopy of the ciborium which was the inner sanctuary and heavenly abode of the divinities. The celestial character of the domical canopy is sometimes emphasized by giving the arched form a border of stars, cusps, or jewel-like disks.

[31] *Numi Augg. Alexandrini* (*Coll. G. Dattari*), 1901, pl. XXXIX/1132.

[32] Herzfeld, *Iran in the Ancient East*, 1941, fig. 406, p. 319. Here the disks of the domical canopy, or cosmic tent, which Herzfeld says was a Hellenistic convention, are over the god Hormizd.

tentorium.[33] Of all these tent shelters in Syria and Asia Minor the most important was the gigantic baldachin over the Altar of Zeus (Fig. 106) at Pergamum.[34] The coins show it as a puffed-up and bulbous shape resembling the dome on the church of Mahoymac (Fig. 36) and the Parthian sanctuary on the arch of Septimius Severus (Fig. 228) at Rome. To the thousands who saw this baldachin at Pergamum above the renowned altar of the supreme sky god, or who handled the Roman coins, its domical shape undoubtedly had a celestial meaning. Furthermore, this Hellenistic altar and the Parthian structure suggest that the other open-air altars and fire temples of Syria and Persia must have had similar ritualistic coverings such as is indicated by my tentative restoration of the fire temple of Ba'al Shamīn (Figs. 123, 124) at Sî'.

In Syria the shrines of Tyche (Fig. 108) at Tyre[35] and of a veiled goddess (Fig. 110) at Arca[36] were portable tabernacles with dome-shaped tents, while at Antioch the covering of the famous Tyche of the city (Fig. 109) was again presumably a portable ciborium with a domical covering.[37] In each city these Tychia appear to have followed a local tradition, for the domical kalubé of the Tyche of Damascus (Fig. 111) has an out-curving flange which could only have resulted from its curved roof having been constructed on a framework of pliable materials.[38] This type of rustic shrine with a flanged dome, which also occurs over a celestial eagle on a tabernacle (Fig. 113) at Laodicea ad mare in North Syria,[39] was taken over by the Christian ivory carvers of the "Syro-Palestinian," or "Palestinian-Coptic," school and used as a ritualistic shelter. It occurs as a baldachin above the Enthroned Christ as the Heavenly Ruler on the Murano book cover (Fig. 115) and over the Enthroned Virgin and Child (Fig. 114) on another ivory panel where its celestial symbolism is clearly indicated by the incised stars; it is also used as a symbolic and divine martyrium for the tomb of Christ (Fig. 117) and as a heavenly shelter over Daniel in the Lions' Den (Fig. 116). Closely related to this ritualistic kalubé with its flanged dome of double curvature is the baldachin above the Enthroned Mother of God (Fig. 118) upon the crudely carved lintel of 554/5 A.D. from Ruweha[40] and the rustic shelter pictured as the tomb of Christ on the Rabula Gospels (Fig. 10). All these presumably native forms of domical covering are quite different from the schematic and semicircular shelter (Fig. 119) on a basalt

[33] Antioch in Pisidia, Gordianus (Imhoof-Blumer, *Kleinasiatische Münzen*, II, 362, no. 25, pl. XII/20).

[34] Pergamum, Septimius Severus (*Brit. Mus. Cat. Coins, Mysia*, 152, no. 315, pl. XXX/7; Cook, *Zeus*, I, 119 n. 2 for bibliography).

[35] Tyre, Trebonianus Gallus (*Brit. Mus. Cat. Coins, Phoenicia*, 283, no. 437, pl. XXXIV/3; C. H. Hill, "Some Graeco-Phoenician Shrines," *Journal of Hellenic Studies*, XXXI, 1911, 62, pl. IV/23).

[36] Caesarea ad Libanum, Elagabalus (*Brit. Mus. Cat. Coins, Phoenicia*, 109, no. 6, pl. XIII/7; Hill, *op.cit.*, 63, pl. IV/31); the decoration beneath the ciborium may represent a balustrade, as has been suggested.

[37] Antioch, Trebonianus Gallus and Volusian (*Brit. Mus. Cat. Coins, Galatia, etc.*, 229, no. 656, pl. XXVI/5).

[38] Damascus, J. Domna (*Brit. Mus. Cat. Coins, Galatia, etc.*, 284, no. 11, pl. XXXIV/9); another version of the Tyche shrine at Damascus (Fig. 112) has the same type of roof (*ibid.*, 287, no. 26, pl. XXXV/3).

[39] Laodicea ad mare, Caracalla and Plautilla (*Brit. Mus. Cat. Coins, Galatia, etc.*, 260, no. 95, pl. XXX/14).

[40] J. Lassus, *Inventaire archéologique* (Documents d'études orientales de l'Institut français de Damas), 1935-36, 121-122, pl. XXIII/2; *Atti del III Congresso internazionale di archeologia cristiana*, 1934, 479, fig. 1.

lintel from Querâté,[41] which as a ciborium in combination with the tree and cross was intended to denote a symbolic sepulchre, a martyrium and an ideal dwelling in paradise, as did the tegurium in the scene of Jonah (Fig. 70) and the tholos (Fig. 23) in the Raising of Lazarus.[42]

C. The Monumental Kalubé of Masonry

In the evolution of the ancient styles of architecture, stone temples at first took form as the result of a desire to translate a traditional cult house of impermanent construction into a more imposing and everlasting monument of masonry. While most of the religious and mortuary stone architecture of Syria was under strong classical influence during the period of Roman domination, some of the native kalubés were monumentalized and their domical roofs reproduced in either cut-stone or volcanic scoriae. The evidence for this transformation of the domical shape from a rustic hut, or sacred tentorium, into stone is naturally limited by the ruined and roofless remains of Syrian architecture. It has been suggested that the round temple at Ba'albek, where the domical shape is concealed in the Roman fashion under a protecting roof, and the sanctuary at Rahle were dedicated to some local Tyche, or the Cult of the Caesars, and for that reason reproduced the domical shape in sculptured stone masonry.[43] Although there is only one domical building which is referred to in the inscription as a kalubé, there must have been many similar cult houses dedicated to some local divinity, or to the daemon of an emperor.

The kalubé of 282 A.D. at Umm-iz-Zetum has a square liwan-like central hall (Fig. 121) covered with a dome and flanked on the façade by projecting walls (Fig. 120). The dome, which was 5.80 m. in diameter, was adjusted to the square plan by means of overlapping stone squinches at the corners. This relatively small dome of volcanic scoriae had collapsed at the time when De Vogüé saw the building, so that he restored it with a Roman hemispherical vault, as he did the dome at the tomb of Bizzos.[44] Later Howard Butler reported that the remains of the original dome were standing in one corner to the height of a meter and clearly showed that its curve "was not a semi-

[41] Lassus (*Inventaire*, 17-19, fig. 18) suggests that the building is a kiosk, or a ciborium symbolizing the temple of Jerusalem.

[42] See p. 27.

[43] The Tychaion, known as the Temple of Venus, dates from the second or third century and had a shallow, three-quarter dome of cut stone with a span of 8.92 m., which was heavily buttressed at the haunches and concealed under a conical extension of the gable roof (T. Wiegand, *Baalbek*, II, 1923, 90-109, Abb. 165-166, Taf. 63-64). Very similar to the Baalbek temple was the sanctuary at Rahle, near Damascus, which had a horseshoe apse of cut stone, nearly three-quarters of a circle and with a span of 4.90 m. (D. Krencker and W. Zschietzschmann, *Römische Tempel in Syrien*,

1938, 226ff., pls. 94-96). While admitting that it may have been a nymphaeum, Krencker suggests that it was an audience hall, or kalubé, devoted to the Cult of the Caesars (p. 280). The circular aedicula of six columns over the sacred well in the forecourt of the great temple at Baalbek has an interesting dome (Wiegand, *op.cit.*, 1921, I, 95-96, Abb. 69-71); the exterior roof of this monopteral well house, which resembles the tempietto over the Fountain of Life in Christian art, is a concave cone, decorated with a tentlike pattern and surmounted by a pine cone; but the interior of the stone roof, very much like the choragic monument of Lysicrates, is cut to a domical shape.

[44] De Vogüé, *Syrie centrale*, 43, pl. 6/4, 5.

circle."[45] Therefore it probably had a conoid shape. The sacred character of the building is established by the inscriptions on the front wall which read: *Good Fortune! The community of the village and of the god built the sacred kalubē . . .*, and *Good Fortune! For the preservation and victory of our lord Marcus Aurelius Probus Augustus, in the seventh year was built the sacred kalubē of the community of the village, successfully.*[46]

A similar cult house at Shakka (Fig. 122) was restored by both De Vogüé and Butler as a domical *kalubē*.[47] De Vogüé described the central hall as a cubical chamber, 8.15 m. wide, with stone squinches like the corner supports at Umm-iz-Zetum; but neither De Vogüé nor Butler mention the material of the fallen dome which they saw in the debris. It is significant to the development of domical architecture in Syria that about 360 A.D. this pagan sacred structure was turned into a mortuary chapel, dedicated, according to the inscription, to S. George and his martyred companions.[48] Another building of the same type was discovered by Butler at il-Haiyât (Fig. 125), which he described as a *kalubē* in "excellent preservation" and restored with a conoid dome.[49] At Chabba in the same region the building, which has been described as a kalubé of trefoil plan with a cupola, is much more doubtful.[50] Since the inscription at Umm-iz-Zetum indicated that some of the domical shrines in Syria were at least in part devoted to the worship of a divine emperor and that the domical baldachin was a form of royal setting, De Vogüé, when he published the third century palace at Shakka, recognized the probability of the religious or ceremonial use of the domical hall, 8.93 m. by 10.20 m., which he said was covered with a *coupole barlongue* constructed of a *mélange de blocage et de claveaux appareillés.*[51]

D. The Conoid Baetyls and the Ancestral House Concept as a Manifestation of Divinity

Like turns unto like, and even a new religion had to make its appeal to those habits of thought which were already a part of the cultural environment. For centuries the peoples of Syria and Palestine had attached divine and celestial meanings to the domical shape of their tabernacles. At the same time they were accustomed to see in the royal baldachin, with its curved canopy enriched with gold and precious stones,

[45] H. C. Butler, *Syria*, II, A, 361.

[46] Littmann, Magie and Stuart, *Greek and Latin Inscriptions in Syria*, III, A, 357f., no. 765/12, 13.

[47] De Vogüé, *op.cit.*, 41ff., pl. 6/1, 2, 3; Butler, *Architecture and Other Arts*, 396.

[48] De Vogüé (*op.cit.*, 43) tells of finding indications of a Christian altar under the cupola and of an inscription (Waddington, *Inscr. Syr.*, no. 2158) on the lintel of door which says that in the 263rd year of the era of Shakka (about 368 A.D.) Bishop Tiberinus dedicated the building as a martyrium to S. George and

his companions.

[49] Butler, *Architecture and Other Arts*, 397f., figs. 142, 143.

[50] J. Mascle (*Le Djebel Druze*, 1936, 63ff.) describes a kalubé, but Rey calls it an unfinished temple and Dussand, Dunand and De Vogüé do not mention it. It is probably the same structure which has been called a nymphaeum and which Butler (*Architecture and Other Arts*, 383, fig. 133) restored as an apsidal pavilion, suggesting that it might have been a kalubé.

[51] De Vogüé, *op.cit.*, 49.

a symbolic seat of authority and a heavenly covering above a god-like and universal ruler. By the fourth century, when so many were already converted to Christianity, they were also beginning to adopt for their martyria the Roman conception of a sepulchral dome as an ideal and spiritual abode. Another and even more important factor in the formation of a Christian domical mysticism was the long-established veneration of the Syrian masses for a conoid shape, which for centuries their ancestors had worshipped as the form of sacred stones and hence as the embodiment of the supernatural.

The maṣṣebâh of ancient Syria and Palestine was both the living presence of a divinity and the spiritual abode of the dead.[52] At the same time that those stones which were believed to be an animate and active god were frequently called by the Greek word *baítylos*,[53] among the Hebrews they were known as *bēthēl*, which meant "House of God" and implied, perhaps, that their shape had once been associated with a primitive house concept. By the second and third centuries the most sacred baetyls of Syria had a conoid shape, presumably derived from the ancient domical hut, or kalubé.

The most famous center of the cult was at Emesa, or modern Homs, which was east of Antioch in the region of the conoid qubâb settlements and near Ruweha where the Christian tomb of Bizzos had a similar conoid shape. In his temple at Emesa the sky god El-Gabel, or Jupiter Sol, was worshipped in the form of a conoid baetyl.[54] On the coins this stone is depicted as if it were the divinity within his columnar temple (Fig. 128). Combining the evidence from the various representations, the conoid stone was set upon a rectangular base (Fig. 126) and surrounded by a chancel rail (Fig. 127). The celestial nature of the divinity was made manifest by the eagle of the sky god,[55] sometimes by a heavenly star above the sacred stone,[56] and on many of the coins by the parasols (Figs. 126, 128) which shaded the stone as if it were an actual personage.[57] In origin the parasol was a portable shelter of domical shape which in the East had long been the symbolic covering of a divine and royal being. That the form of El-Gabel was considered to be like a pine cone is shown by the description of Herodianus, who wrote, *Sed lapis est maximus, ab imo rotundus et sensim fastigiatus, velut conus, color ei niger, feruntque delapsum coelo.*[58]

[52] A. Lods, *La Croyance à la vie future et le culte des morts dans l'antiquité israélite*, 1906, 201; A. Lods (trans. S. H. Hooke) *Israel*, 1932, 259-263; M. J. Lagrange, *Études sur les religions sémitiques*, 1903, 201.

[53] *Baítylos* (Cook, *Zeus*, III, 887ff.; G. F. Moore, "Baetylia," *A.J.A.*, VII, 1903, 198-208); Bēthēl (Cook, *op.cit.*, 891; O. Eissfeldt, "Der Gott Bēthēl," *Archiv für Religionswissenschaft*, XXVIII, 1930, 1-30; J. Benzinger, Pauly-Wissowa, *Real-Encyclopädie*, III, 363.

[54] A. B. Cook, *Zeus*, III, 900-907; F. Cumont, Pauly-Wissowa, *R.-E.*, V, 2219-2222; Daremberg and Saglio, *Dictionnaire des Antiquités*, II, 529-531; F. Lenormant, "Sol Elagabalus," *Revue de l'histoire des religions*, III, 1881, 310-322.

[55] Emesa, Caracalla, Fig. 127 (*Brit. Mus. Cat. Coins, Galatia, etc.*, 239, no. 15, pl. XXVII/12; Cook, *Zeus*, III, fig. 739).

[56] S. A. Cook, *The Religion of Ancient Palestine in the Light of Archaeology*, 1930, 159; A. B. Cook, *op.cit.*, III, 901.

[57] Emesa, Caracalla, Fig. 126 (*Brit. Mus. Cat. Coins, Galatia, etc.*, 239, no. 16, pl. XXVII/13); Uranius Antoninus, Fig. 128 (*Brit. Mus. Cat. Coins, Galatia, etc.*, 241, no. 24, pl. XXVIII/2; A. B. Cook, *op.cit.*, III, fig. 748; W. Fröhner, "Les Monnaies d'Uranius Antoninus," *Annuaire de la société française de numismatique et d'archéologie*, X, 1886, 193, no. 11, pl. 7/10).

[58] The quotation is from I. Eckhel, *Doctrina numorum veterum*, VII, 1828, 250; Donaldson, *Architectura numismatica*, no. 19, 72-75.

This animistic worship of a conoid shape was not limited to the region around Emesa, for on a sacred mountain near Antioch there was a somewhat similar stone of tholoid, conoid, or omphalos-like shape (Fig. 129) which, as Zeus Kasius, was enshrined in an aedicula.[59] Further south at Tyre there was a pair of conoid baetyls (Fig. 130) whose combination with a sacred tree recalls the domical shelters on the fourth millennium sherd from Arpachiyah (Fig. 90) and, therefore, suggests that the conception of divinities in this shape went back to a remote past when amorphous deities could only be visualized in the form of their sacred dwellings.[60] The antiquity of the theme and its possible relation to the domical symbolism of India is shown by a coin of Eucratides II (175 B.C.) which is almost identical with the coin of Tyre.[61] In the Hauran the ancient god of the Nabateans was Dushara, who was called the "Lord of the House."[62] He was depicted on the coins of Adraa (Fig. 131) and Bosra as a domical stone raised upon a chamber, platform or altar.[63] That the rungs in front of this raised baetyl suggest a ladder giving access to a heavenly zone would seem to strengthen the assumption that the shape of these stones went back to a house concept. While there was at Petra another "omphalos-like" stone enshrined in a niche,[64] most of the Nabatean sacred stones were rectangular,[65] a fact which again might be explained by the early adoption in this region of the rectangular flat-roofed house as the abode of the local divinities.

Contrary as it is to the opinion of those modern scholars and Roman writers who explain all baetyls as stones which had fallen from heaven, there is no question but that many of these conoid and rectangular stones, such as the stone at Emesa, were regarded as celestial divinities, sky gods manifesting themselves in house forms. It was common to worship meteorites, but not all sacred stones could have been aerolites, and quite apart from how they had come from heaven, there is still the question of how they acquired their specific conoid or rectangular shape. Following the early worship of crude fetishes there is convincing evidence from both primitive and re-tarded cultures to show the important part played by the primitive dwelling in helping men to formulate comprehensive images of both the supernatural and the universal. The habit of visualizing a spiritual power in the form of his earthly dwelling continued to be customary in Palestine and Syria at both the popular and symbolic levels. The pre-Islamic Arabs apparently equated the meaning of *bait* (baetyl) and *qobba* (its domical tent sanctuary), and when they carried their qobba into battle, like a palla-

[59] S. A. Cook, *The Religion of Ancient Palestine in the Light of Archaeology*, 157, pl. xxxiii/1; there are variants from the reign of Hadrian to the second century (*Brit. Mus. Cat. Coins, Galatia, etc.*, pls. xxxii/9 and xxxiii/3, 4, 7), like those of Elagabalus (pl. xxxiii/7) having the stone, not in the aedicula, but in the intercolumniation of the temple with the heavenly star and crescent in the gable.

[60] Tyre, Gordianus III (*Brit. Mus. Cat. Coins, Phoenicia*, 281, nos. 426, 430, pl. xxxiii/14, 15.

[61] *Cambridge History of India*, I, 1922, pl. viii/44.

[62] A. B. Cook, *Zeus*, iii, 907ff.; S. A. Cook, *Religion of Ancient Palestine*, 18.

[63] Adraa, Gallienus (*Brit. Mus. Cat. Coins, Arabia*, 15, no. 2, pl. 3/5; Cook, *Zeus*, iii, 907ff., figs. 755, 756; S. A. Cook, *op.cit.*, 160, pl. xxxiii/3.

[64] S. A. Cook, *op.cit.*, 160.

[65] *Ibid.*, 160; A. B. Cook, *op.cit.*, iii, 909; G. F. Hill, *Brit. Mus. Cat. Coins, Arabia*, xcii, xcvi, pl. xiii/7, 8.

dium, they saw in it, as the Hebrews did in their ark, the active and supporting presence of a god.[66]

Regardless of how elevated may have been the figurative means by which the priests presented the house concept of a revealed god, the Hebrew masses undoubtedly continued to identify Yahweh with his abode, for had not their fathers been instructed to erect a tent in order that "I might dwell among them"? As late as the Second Revolt they saw their ark presented on the coins (Fig. 151), like the image of Greek and Roman gods standing in their temples. Certainly the mystic Christian writers made it clear to what extent the Syrian mind was also fully accustomed to associate an invisible god with his earthly dwelling. This form of architectural revelation is revealed by the Syrian hymn in praise of the domical church at Edessa and by S. Maximus the Confessor who wrote, *Ecclesia est sacrarium Dei, templum sanctum, domus orationis, conventus plebis, corpus Christi* and *terrenum caelum inqua supercaelestis Deus inhabitat et inambulat.*[67]

E. Other Sacred and Celestial Aspects of the Domical Shape

There were other ideas regarding the value and meanings of the domical shape which were Christian adaptations of prevailing habits of thought. In order to reconstruct what the ordinary and credulous antique man in Syria thought about the domical shape at the time when Christianity was evolving a mystic language of architecture, it must be recalled that he still believed in the animate being and supernatural powers of inanimate objects, such as the parts of buildings. Hence, as long as the domical shape had a real content for him, it did not matter in the least whether it was the curved veil of a ciborium, the bejeweled canopy of a baldachin, a sacred stone or omphalos, a cosmic egg, pine cone,[68] divine helmet, parasol, or a massive vault

[66] See p. 83.

[67] "Hystorica mistica ecclesie catholice Maxime," fol. 25-26 (S. Pétridès, *Revue de l'orient chrétien*, X, 1905, 309).

[68] The habit of associating a pointed and somewhat swollen type of domical form, which had originally taken shape on primitive huts of pliable materials, with a pine cone was of great antiquity. That it had become customary to visualize the domical tholos as a pine cone, rather than like a "beehive" or "pain de sucre," is indicated by the fact that Theophrastus (*Historia plantarum*, III, 9, 6; F. Robert, *Thymélè*, 60-61) could think of no more accurate way of defining a pine cone than to call it Θολοειδής. In the fourth century Gregory described the pointed and puffed-up dome which he proposed to build upon his martyrium at Nyssa as κωνοειδής (see p. 31), and in the sixth century Choricius compared in some detail the wooden dome on the church of S. Stephen at Gaza to a pine cone (see p. 39). By the thirteenth century at Constantinople the Arabic and Persian word *machrût, machrúṭa*, for pine cone was so commonly associated with all domical shapes that Mesarites uses ὁ Μουχρουτᾶς to describe a domical chamber in the imperial palace which he calls a "Persian" work (N. Mesarites, *Die Palastrevolution des Johannes Komnenos*, ed. Heisenberg, 1907, 44, and commentary, 72).

While it is difficult to prove to what extent the Christians attached a special symbolism to the conoid dome, it is evident that the pine cone, as the fruit of the ancient Mesopotamian tree-of-life, had acquired during the antique period a mortuary symbolism involving the idea of life after death. The pine cone, which was used by the Assyrians as the finial on the posts that carried their ritualistic and dome-like baldachins (Perrot and Chipiez, *Histoire de l'art*, II, 201, 202, 205, figs. 67, 68, 70), also

above a tomb, altar, or audience hall. Ideologically it was natural for him to combine these different, though related, beliefs and to transfer meanings from one similar shape to another.

1. THE OMPHALOS

The significance, therefore, of the conoid, or tholoid, domical shape had been strengthened and enriched in Syria, with its Greek and Roman heritage, by the similarity in appearance and concept between the native baetyls and the classical omphalos.[69] This acceptance of the Greek and Roman ideas regarding the omphalos gave new overtones of meaning to the domical shape even after it had been appropriated by the Christians. In fact the complexity of beliefs already associated with the omphaloid shape helps to explain how the Christians could see such a variety of meanings in a mere similarity of shape.

Those aspects of the omphalos concept which most directly influenced the growth and popularity of domical ideology among the Christians were: (a) its sepulchral symbolism and the tradition that the omphalos at Delphi, as a round hut with a cupola,

---

occurs above the sacrificial horns at the top of the posts which support the domical baldachin over an altar in a Roman fresco (Fig. 145). Its mortuary implications in antiquity, which were combined with those of the similar phallus, are shown by its use as a finial on grave tumuli in Asia Minor (Perrot and Chipiez, v, 48ff.) and its significance as an emblem of resurrection and fertility by its frequent occurrence on Etruscan grave stele and Roman tomb monuments (B. Schröder, "Studien zu den Grabdenkmälern der römischen Kaiserzeit," *Bonner Jahrb.*, 108-109, 1902, 70ff.) and, perhaps, by the house steles (Fig. 67) of La Horgne in the Sarre Basin (E. Linckenheld, *Les Stèles funéraires en forme de maison*, 1927, pl. III/5, 7, pl. IV/4, 5) which may have derived their conoid shape from the sepulchral monuments of Italy. During the Early Christian period this funerary use of the pine cone, with its idea of new life and possible resurrection, suggests that the large finial on the mortuary tegurium of the Trivulzio ivory (Fig. 9), symbolizing the tomb of Christ, was intended to be a pine cone.

Elusive as such evidence is, it is sufficient to indicate that the Christians carried on a pagan symbolism. C. Huelsen ("Porticus Divorum und Serapeum," *Röm. Mitt.*, XVIII, 1903, 17-57) has pointed out the relation between the Roman use of the pine cone and the fact that a large bronze pine cone beneath a baldachin served as a fountain in the *paradisus* of S. Peter's. At Baalbek, in the forecourt of the great temple, there was a circular tempietto

over the sacred well which had an interior dome and a pine cone finial (T. Wiegand, *Baalbek*, I, 95-96, Abb. 69-71). As a development of this symbolism, Strzygowski ("Der Pinienzapfen als Wasserspeier," *Röm. Mitt.*, XVIII, 1903, 185-206) showed that the pine cone, which in the Byzantine period was used as a fountain in the atrium, symbolized Christ as the life-giving waters. If, therefore, the conoid form had mortuary implications, was used by the Christians as a Fountain of Life in a symbolic house of God and if there was a symbolic relation between the domical baptistery (see p. 104) and the tomb of Christ, which was also considered to be an ideal and cosmic dwelling of God, then the conoid dome of Syria and Palestine must have come to have much the same life-giving significance as the pine-cone shape had for the pagans.

[69] A. B. Cook, *Zeus*, II, 166-193, 841, 983, 1057, 1189, 1193; F. Courby, "L'Omphalos delphique," *Comptesrendus. Ac. d. inscr.*, 1914, 257ff.; G. Elderkin, *Kantharos*, 1924, 112; J. E. Harrison, "Delphika," *Journal of Hellenic Studies*, XIX, 1899, 205-251; T. Homolle, "Ressemblance de l'omphalos delphique avec quelques représentations égyptiennes," *Revue des études grecques*, XXXII, 1919, 338-358; G. Karo, Daremberg and Saglio, *Dict.*, IV, 197-200; Pauly-Wissowa, *R.-E.*, Suppl. V, 123; Roscher, *Abh. sächs. Ges.*, XXIX, 1913, 9ff.; XXXI, 1915, 1ff.; K. Schwendemann, "Omphalos, Python-grab und Drachenkampf," *Arch. f. Religionswiss.*, XX, 1920-21, 481ff.; J. N. Svoronos, *Jour. intern. d'arch. num.*, XIII, 1911, 301-316.

was the tomb of a legendary god or king; (b) the idea of the gradual transformation of the omphalos from a prehistoric shelter into a tomb and then into a shrine with rites for the departed dead, which closely paralleled the transformation of the tegurium into a Christian tomb and then into a martyrium: (c) its relation to a belief in resurrection; (d) its acceptance as the speaking manifestation of a divinity; and (e) its significance as the central point of an earthly and spiritual domain. It has already been suggested that the Holy Sepulchre, like Diocletian's domical mausoleum at Spalato, was thought of as a kind of omphalos situated at the center of an earthly and heavenly kingdom.[70] While it is impossible to agree with Heisenberg and believe that the Christians at Jerusalem preserved and used a pagan omphalos of the cult of Adonis with its beliefs in resurrection,[71] it is easy to understand how they came to associate the ideas of an omphalos with the domical tomb of Christ, the ciborium over the altar and the Mount of Calvary.

It had been customary at least since the time of Ezekiel to think of Jerusalem as the center of the world, "the omphalos of the earth."[72] After the construction of sanctuaries over the most holy places of Christianity at Jerusalem, there does not appear to have been any one monument which was considered to be *the* omphalos. In fact, there is no evidence to indicate that there was either a stone or ciborium to mark the center of the *paradisus*, where after the seventh century the omphalos was presumably located after it had become a liturgical station. Instead, several parts of the sacred complex, including Golgotha, the ciborium over the altar and perhaps the Holy Sepulchre itself, were each figuratively considered to be an omphalos in much the same way that the pagans had thought of their tholoid (tomb) symbols.[73] If there was a domical shrine on Mount Calvary prior to the seventh century, as all the evidence suggests,[74] then it is readily understood how its omphaloid shape (Fig. 167), resembling as it did both a tholos tomb and conoid baetyl (Fig. 127), gave more meaning to the prevailing beliefs that it was also the ancestral tomb of Adam, a manifestation of Christ and the holy center of the earth.[75]

Certainly a reflection of this kind of imagery and an echo of a pagan past are clearly apparent in the words of S. Maximinus who, in defining the mystical meaning of "ciborium," wrote, "Ciborium est pro Calvariae monte, ubi crucifixus est Christus: prope enim erat locus et proclivis sive sub divo, ubi sepultus est: sed quoniam in brevitate designatur crucifixo et sepultura et resurrectio Christi, in ecclesiam co-

[70] Grabar, *Martyrium*, I, 218-219.

[71] Heisenberg, *Grabeskirche und Apostelkirche*, I, 215ff.

[72] Ezek. 5, 5; 38, 12.

[73] Vincent and Abel, *Jérusalem*, II, 224ff.; A. Piganiol ("L'Hémisphairion et l'omphalos des Lieux Saints," *Cahiers archéologiques*, I, 1945, 7-14) develops the somewhat complicated theory that the troublesome word *hemisphairion*, used by Eusebius in describing the basilica, was actually an omphalos, or ciborium, marking the place of Christ's death in the apse, while the Holy Sepulchre marked the place of his resurrection; this seems to be only another way of saying what S. Maximin does when he defines the mystical meaning of "ciborium."

[74] See p. 106.

[75] From the middle of the fourth century it was customary for the Christian writers to refer to Golgotha as "the center of the earth," the *umbilicum terrae*, or omphalos (Vincent and Abel, II, 188 n. 4).

aptatur."[76] Also the same processes of thought, which in the Byzantine East led men to think of a domical church as a tomb and celestial manifestation of God, made it possible for the later Greek theologians to refer to the central point under the dome of a church as an omphalos.[77]

2. THE COSMIC EGG

Since a conoid shape is also ovoid, it follows that the East Christian's mystical interest in a gilded conoid dome as a celestial form must have been directly influenced by the pagan ideas of a cosmic egg, which not only figured so prominently in the early religions of India, Egypt, Persia and Greece, but by Roman times were essential to the heavenly symbolism of the two cults that had the greatest influence upon Christian imagery. Although the actual origins of the beliefs regarding a primordial egg and a god in the egg have little bearing upon the formation of domical ideology, it is to be noted that an egg-shaped baetyl in its rustic shrine upon an engraved gem (Fig. 132) from Minoan Crete suggests the very early importance of such concepts in the West and recalls the sacred stones of Syria.[78] The appeal to the Christians of the ovoid shape and of the earlier beliefs in a golden egg came long after these beliefs had been combined with the mortuary cult of the Dioskouri, as dispensers of immortality, and had been taken over into the cosmogony of the popular Orphic cult which was preoccupied with the afterlife.[79]

In the Orphic theogony the conception of the universe as the upper and lower halves of a vast egg, which were heaven and earth, recalls the Vedic beliefs of India which visualized the Divine One as residing in a primordial egg split into two parts, the lower, silver half being the earth and the upper, golden half resembling the gilded domes of Buddhistic and Christian sanctuaries, being the heavens.[80] At the same time that this conception of a golden half egg was so prevalent in the late antique period, the egg itself was an emblem of resurrection[81] and the belief in the universe as two halves of an egg had been taken over into the Cult of the Dioskouri, where the ovoid shape, as symbolizing heaven and earth, was identified with their helmet-like piloi.[82] How directly this symbolism of the celestial helmet, and hence of the cosmic egg, was accepted by the Christians will become apparent in the next section.

3. THE CELESTIAL HELMET

The one symbolic domical concept of great antiquity in the Near East which can be most definitely connected with Palestine and Christian writings is the idea of a

[76] *Revue de l'orient chrétien*, X, 1905, 310; J. Braun, *Die christliche Altar*, II, 274.

[77] Du Cange, *Glossar. Med. Graec.*, II, 1044.

[78] A. Evans, *Palace of Minos*, 1921-35, I, fig. 494.

[79] A. B. Cook, *Zeus*, II, 1023, 1033; R. Eisler, *Weltenmantel und Himmelszelt*, II, 410, 411, 413.

[80] Cook, *Zeus*, II, 1035; F. Max Müller, *The Upanishads, Sacred Books of the East*, I, 1879,

55; J. Eggeling, *The Satapatha-Brahmana, Sacred Books of the East*, LXIV, 1900, 12. References to egg in Persia: F. Cumont, *Textes et monuments figurés relatifs aux mystères de Mithra*, I, 1899, 163; Eisler, *op.cit.*, 410 n. 3.

[81] F. Chapouthier, *Les Dioscures au service d'une déesse*, 1935, 319; M. P. Nilsson, "Das Ei im Totenkult der Alten," *Arch. f. Religionswiss.*, XI, 1908, 530ff.

[82] Chapouthier, *op.cit.*, 308.

celestial helmet. Although it was also derived from the Cult of the Dioskouri and related to the belief in a cosmic egg, it apparently had its origin in several different cultural traditions. From Hittite times the helmet had been a celestial symbol, and at Sinjerli, where Hittite culture was finally absorbed into the civilization of Syria and the Near East, the "divine helmet" occurs on the relief of King Kalamis as a sign of royal and, perhaps, cosmic power.[83] By the classical period the sky was frequently visualized and described as a hat or domical helmet,[84] and it was Cratinas who is said to have compared the cupola of the Odeon at Athens to the helmet which Pericles always wore in public.[85]

The lasting appeal of this particular domical shape and its direct link with Christianity came when its sky symbolism was combined with that of the piloi and the cosmic egg in the Cult of the Dioskouri, which had spread throughout the Empire and was strongly established in Palestine.[86] The popularity of these ancient heroes, themselves born in an egg, came from their having become the intermediaries between men and gods, and the dispensers of immortality.[87] Therefore, when their conoid bonnets, or helmets, surmounted by stars, became the common symbol of the cult and were identified with the cosmic egg and the similar conception of the world as a globe consisting of two halves, the upper hemisphere being the radiant heavens to which men aspired and the lower half being the earth plunged in darkness from which men desired to escape, the celestial pileus gave a deeper and more spiritual meaning to the conoid shape.[88] The twin helmets of the Dioskouri appear on Roman coins (Fig. 134) as early as Augustus,[89] while in Palestine the heavenly helmet surmounted by a star (Fig. 135) occurs on the coins of Palestine during the reign of Herod.[90] The conoid piloi, bound with the wreath of immortality and surmounted by a star, has been discovered on reliefs from Samaria (Fig. 136), where the cult is known to have flourished.[91] Also closely related to these Palestinian beliefs in a celestial helmet was the Hebrew symbolism which associated the domelike miter of their high priest with the heavens.[92]

Over and above the lasting effect of all such beliefs upon the popular imagination,

[83] F. v. Luschan, *Ausgrabungen in Sendschirli*, IV, 1911, 377, pl. LXVII, fig. 273.

[84] Cook, *Zeus*, II, 385f.; Eisler, *op.cit.*, I, 64, 67; II, 582, 677.

[85] Plutarch, *Pericles* (Loeb ed.), XIII, 43. There is divergence of opinion regarding the domical shape of the Odeon, which Plutarch says was made in imitation of tent of Xerxes (O. Broneer, "The Tent of Xerxes and the Greek Theatre," *University of California Publications in Classical Archaeology*, I [1929-44], 305ff.; F. Robert, *Thymélè*, 35; and C. Picard, *Rev. archéol.*, series 6, IX, 1937, 258, who takes the position that it had a cupola).

[86] Chapouthier, *Les Dioscures au service d'une déesse*, 1935.

[87] *Ibid.*, 328.

[88] *Ibid.*, 306f.

[89] *Numi Augg. Alexandrini* (Coll. Dattari), pl. XXVIII/54. The piloi occur on the coins of other cities, but at Alexandria the Cult of the Dioskouri, which was combined with that of Isis, was especially popular.

[90] S. A. Cook, *The Religion of Ancient Palestine in the Light of Archaeology*, 193, pl. XXXIV/38; G. F. Hill, *Brit. Mus. Cat. of Coins, Palestine*, 97, 220, pls. XXIII/14, 15, 16, XXIV/1, XLII/6.

[91] Vincent, "Le Culte d'Hélène a Samarie," *Rev. bibl.*, XLV, 1936, 221-226; J. W. Crowfoot, *Pal. Expl. Fund, Quart. St.*, 1923, 23.

[92] Josephus, *Jewish Antiquities* (Loeb), III, 176 ("hemispheric lid"), 187 (symbolizing heavens).

everything connected with the Dioskouri was of interest to the Christians. As gods of the tomb and intermediaries between heaven and earth the two pagan heroes were precursors of the martyrs.[93] Therefore, the symbolism of their heavenly pileus with its cosmological meaning and its mystical explanation of an immortal life after death may explain the Christian references to the helmet in the descriptions of domical churches. The author of the Syrian hymn in praise of Hagia Sophia at Edessa wrote, "Et sa coupole élevée, voici qu'elle est comparable au cieux des cieux, *semblable à sa casque*, se partie supérieure repose solidement sur sa partie inferieure."[94] More significant, perhaps, is the poem in praise of Hagia Sophia at Constantinople where Paul the Silentiary not only uses the phrase "beautiful helmet," but also calls the dome, "rising into the immeasurable air, the great helmet, which bending over, like the radiant heavens, embraces the church."[95] This emphasis upon the celestial helmet in two poems written in praise of two Hagia Sophias, which were both rebuilt by Justinian, makes one suspect that the Byzantine Emperor had derived much of his passionate interest in domical churches from the same Syrian and Palestinian sources as had presumably given the Silentiary his mystical interest in a dome as a "beautiful helmet."

F. The Cosmic House

Underlying the development of the Christian interest in domical tombs, martyria, baptisteries, ciboria and baldachins has appeared an instinctive and popular belief in an ancestral shelter as a cosmic house. From the time when men began to visualize the unknown in terms of the known and attached so much value to mimesis, many cultures had come to think of the house, tomb and sanctuary as a replica, or symbol, of the universe.[96] Because of the religious nature of this cosmological thinking, most antique civilizations were accustomed to associate the heavens with the ceilings of their most revered shelters. Hence blue ceilings with stars had become traditional in Egyptian tombs and Babylonian palaces, and coffers decorated with stars continued to be used in Greek and Roman temples. Not all the different types of cosmic dwellings, like the hoop-roofed hut of ancient Mesopotamia and the rectangular festival tent of Ion at Delphi, were round and dome-shaped. Nevertheless, it was the prevalence and persistence of the various beliefs in the celestial symbolism of domical coverings on ancestral types of cosmic houses which were most responsible for the growing popularity of the domical shape. By Christian times this cosmic imagery had come to transcend the mortuary, divine and royal symbolism already associated with the dome.

[93] Chapouthier, *op.cit.*, 342-346; J. R. Harris, *The Dioscuri in the Christian Legends*, 1903; E. Lucius, *Les Origines du culte des saints*, 1908, 32.

[94] A. Dupont-Sommer, "Une Hymne syriaque sur la cathédrale d'Édesse," *Cahiers archéologiques*, II, 29ff., verse 6.

[95] W. R. Lethaby and H. Swainson, *The Church of Santa Sophia, Constantinople*, 1894,

42, 43.

[96] Eisler, *Weltenmantel und Himmelszelt*, II; Cook, *Zeus*, I, 751; II, 187; A. C. Soper ("The 'Dome of Heaven' in Asia," *Art Bulletin*, XXIX, 1947, 225-248) in reviewing the evidence for a ceiling of heaven in the East perhaps over-emphasizes what he considers to be Western influences.

1. INDIAN TRADITION

Among the cultures whose prehistoric ideas regarding the sanctity of a primitive round hut most directly influenced the development of domical architecture, India had a cosmic house tradition which in origin and ideology closely paralleled, if it did not influence, the growth of domical concepts in the West. By means of that instinctive process of imagery which inspired men to attach different beliefs to similar shapes, the Indians saw in the curved roof of their primitive huts a manifestation of all the other celestial ideas which they had come to associate with a domelike shape. Hence, in the same way that both the pagans and Christians of Syria were able to combine in their conception of the dome ideas of a pine cone, omphalos, baetyl, helmet, lotus, skene, kalubé and tegurium, they saw in the curved outlines of their cosmic house a golden and star-covered egg, a divine parasol, a cuplike and life-giving lotus flower, an upturned bowl and the essential profile of the sacred banyan and amalaka trees which were also the heavenly dwelling of the gods.

Although the scattered references to the cosmic house and the beginnings of religious architecture in the Brahmanas, Puranas and Sutras have not as yet been systematically studied, there appears to have been in Vedic cosmogeny two distinct traditions of a world shelter as the dwelling of the gods. The one which conceived of heaven, or the Varenna, as "four-cornered" was presumably brought into India by the conquering Aryans, while the other, which was circular, was derived from the primitive huts of the native Dravidian culture. The mystical nature of the early Indian beliefs regarding the primitive domical shelter as a cosmic and symbolic form has been explained by A. K. Coomaraswamy; and the significance of the different types of houses in Indian traditions is preserved in the *Mānasāra*, an early treatise on Indian architecture, which describes the three types of houses and modes of architecture as the Nagada, distinguished by its rectangular shape, the Vesara, by the octagonal and hexagonal shapes, the Drāvida, by the circular shape.[97] It was the round shape with its domelike roof of thatch, which was similar to the Italian tegurium and the Syrian kalubé, that was taken over as the venerated form of the early Buddhistic shrine, as is illustrated (Fig. 138) on the balustrade post of the stupa at Amarāvatī.[98]

Once the shape of the dwelling of the Divine One was translated into wood carpentry and the cosmic significance of its roof was architecturally emphasized, the golden dome became the most dominant feature, as can be seen, for example, on a relief from Bhārhūt (Fig. 139), dating from the first century B.C., which depicts the turban relic of the Buddha enshrined in the heaven of Indra, beside the palace of the gods.[99] The literalness with which the shape of the venerated hut form was preserved is apparent in a section of the Sudāma cave (Fig. 141), dating from the twelfth year

[97] A. K. Coomaraswamy, "Symbolism of the Dome," *Indian Historical Quarterly*, XVI, 1938, 1-56; W. Simpson, "Origin and Mutation in Indian and Eastern Architecture," *R.I.B.A. Transactions*, VII, 242; P. K. Acharya, *Indian Architecture According to the Mānasāra-Sil- pasāstra*, 130; idem, *The Architecture of the Mānasāra* (English trans.), XVIII, 92-104.
[98] Foucher, *L'Art gréco-bouddhique du Gandhâra*, I, 456, fig. 228.
[99] Coomaraswamy, *History of Indian and Indonesian Art*, fig. 43.

(260 B.C.) of Asoka's reign.[100] The stonecutters, in carving out of solid rock the circular and domical inner sanctuary of this cave near Buddha Gaya, were careful to reproduce the actual overhang and curves of a thatched roof.

2. THE ASIATIC TRADITION AND THE IMPERIAL BALDACHIN

The great difficulty in reconstructing the development of the early cultural beliefs in a cosmic house comes from the inevitable dissemination and mingling of such beliefs. In Greece it was probably a cultural importation of cosmological ideas which accounts for the starlike rosettes that presumably decorated the vaults of the Mycenaean tholos tombs (Fig. 63), and at a later date explains the cosmic tent of Ion at Delphi with its heavenly embroideries. By the classical period several different traditions of a cosmic and sacred tent were already established around the eastern shores of the Mediterranean. All, at one time or another, came from the East. In fact it was the "Tent-Dwellers" of Central Asia with their traditions of a round and domelike cosmic tent who account for the widespread popularity of the domical shape. These nomads of Asia had always lived, as so many of them do today, in domical, *kabitka* tents, like those described by Marco Polo, Clavijo, and other mediaeval travelers.[101] Two of these Asiatic traditions, one, the audience tent of the Achaemenid kings, and the other, the Semitic qobba, which the pre-Islamic Arabs had inherited, were most influential in the development of domical ideas in the Near East. These traditions also show the complicated nature and origin of domical ideologies.

The Achaemenid kings of Persia, who were to give the classical world its conception of a divine and universal ruler, held their audiences and festivals in a cosmic tent, although they lived for the most part in palaces built of brick and stone. According to Hesychius, their "royal tents and courts of round awnings were called Heavens."[102] The general shape and appearance of these royal tents of Persia were presumably similar to the great domical tents of the Mongol Khans, which so impressed the Western travelers in the Middle Ages, and hence were not essentially different from the vast audience tent (Fig. 148) used by the Chinese Emperor Kienling in 1793.[103] It was this early Asiatic tradition of a heavenly tent, as the place of appearance of a divine King of Kings, that was taken over by Alexander the Great after his conquest

[100] W. Simpson, "Origin and Mutation in Indian and Eastern Architecture," *R.I.B.A. Transactions*, VII, 252, fig. 118; Coomaraswamy, *op.cit.*, 18.

[101] In describing the habitations of the Mongols, both Friar John and Friar William (M. Komroff, *Contemporaries of Marco Polo*, 1928, 5, 59) tell how they were domical structures made "upon a round frame of wickers interlaced compactly" and covered "with white felt." *Marco Polo* (ed. H. Yule, 1874, I, 390) tells how the "Great Tent" of the Khan, where he spent so much of his time, "was large enough to cover a thousand people"; and Cla-

vijo (ed. G. Le Strange, 1928) describes the great pavilion of Timur as "four square in shape," three lances high and its ceiling "made circular to form a dome" which was supported on twelve posts (p. 238), and of another tent he writes, "high up, in the ceiling of the cupola of the tent . . . is seen the figure of an eagle in silver gilt, it is of great size and its wings are open" (241-242), which would suggest that it was a cosmic tent which went back to the audience "Heavens" of the Achaemenid kings.

[102] Hesychius, *s.v. οὐρανός*.

[103] *Marco Polo* (ed. Yule), I, 394 n.7.

of Persia. In the words of Plutarch (*Alexander*, III), "The Son of Heaven had a magnificent tent made with fifty gilded posts which carried a *sky* of rich workmanship."

While there may have been other traditions of a sky canopy above an enthroned ruler, it was presumably from the world tent of Alexander that the Roman and Byzantine emperors derived the jeweled and golden baldachin (Figs. 144, 146) in which they made their state appearances as a supreme being. Therefore, it was the Persian conception of a deified and universal monarch, enthroned beneath a domical cosmic tent, which inspired Nero to present himself to the empire as the incarnation of the sun god and to build his *Domus aurea* in the form of a "sun palace." His "Golden House," which introduced the dome with its celestial symbolism into imperial palace architecture, was essentially the same as the much later domical throne room of Khosro II, for in it the Kosmokrator sat beneath an astronomically decorated dome of wood which "went around perpetually day and night like the world."[104]

Furthermore, it was presumably because of the various celestial implications of the cosmic tent that the Romans adopted the "awning pattern" as a customary domical decoration[105] and that it was used in the tomb of M. Clodius Hermes (Fig. 68). Even as early as the first century A.D. the domical baldachin had become such a common attribute of royalty in the Near East that Philostratus claimed to have seen in the Parthian Empire a Judgment Hall, or audience tent, "the ceiling of which was constructed in the form of a dome like the heavens, covered with sapphire stone, this stone being intensely blue and of the color of the sky . . . and in its heights are the images of the gods in whom they believed, and they appear golden."[106] The fact that there were in Parthia such domical and cosmic throne rooms, in which the universal monarch was enthroned as a divinity, is further indicated by the building (Fig. 228) among the sculptures on the arch of Septimius Severus that record his conquest of the Parthians.

The motif of the canopy illustrates the way in which so many domical ideas spread and mingled at different historical levels. In spite of its Asiatic origin and continued use in the East, by Sassanian times the royal and divine baldachin was fully established in the West, with the result that, according to Herzfeld, it only occurs on Persian

---

[104] The cosmic significance of the *Domus aurea* and its heavenly dome have been discussed by A. Alföldi ("Insignien und Tracht der römischen Kaiser," *Röm. Mitt.*, L, 1935, 128), H. P. L'Orange ("*Domus aurea* . . . der Sonnenpalast," *Serta Eitremiana*, Oslo, 1942, 68-100) and K. Lehmann ("The Dome of Heaven," *Art Bulletin*, XXVIII, 1945, 21-22). Its relation to the throne room of Khosro II, which was built by craftsmen of the Roman Empire and also had a celestial dome that revolved above the head of the universal ruler, and the influences of this Sassanian conception of a monumental baldachin, or world house, upon Byzantine and mediaeval ideas have been

discussed by E. Herzfeld ("Der Thron des Khosro," *Jahrb. d. preuss. Kunst.*, XIV, 1920, 2-24, 103ff.) and L'Orange (*ibid.*).

[105] Lehmann, *op.cit.*, Pompeian ceiling, fig. 25; *Domus aurea*, figs. 27, 28; Hadrian's Villa, fig. 29.

[106] Philostratus, *Life of Apollonius of Tyana*, I, 25; Eisler, *Weltenmantel und Himmelszelt*, II, 614; Cook, *Zeus*, I, 262f.; Lehmann, *op.cit.*, 22. The bulbous and tentlike domical form of such a Parthian structure can be seen in the sculptures of the arch of Septimius Severus (H. P. L'Orange, *Serta Eitremiana*, 1942, 75, Abb. 1).

coins (Fig. 143) which were designed under strong Hellenistic influences.[107] On the other hand, until we know more about the beginnings of domical ideas in India, it would be unwise to assume that the scene of Buddha enthroned beneath a heavenly baldachin (Fig. 140) on a relief of Gandhara came from either Hellenistic or Iranian contacts. While the Gandhara canopy may well reflect a mingling of domical traditions, in which the peacocks appear to be substituted for the Western eagles, the Indian baldachin carefully preserves both the native ideas of thatch upon a cosmic hut and of leaves spreading from the branches of a heavenly tree.

3. PRE-ISLAMIC AND HEBREW TRADITION

Something of the similarity and intermingling of cultural beliefs regarding an ancestral and cosmic shelter which have been apparent in the Western conception of the Hellenistic baldachin and in the Eastern origins of the Buddhistic canopy again appear in the domical traditions of Palestine, where ideas of a cosmic house of God were of great antiquity. While the evolution of the Hebrew ark and tabernacle as a domelike tent and representation of the universe is confused, controversial and complicated by contradictory evidence, recent studies have clarified many essential steps. At the same time they have contributed certain facts concerning the primitive significance of the tent among the Semites which help us to understand why the dome acquired so much symbolic importance for both Christians and Mohammedans.

First of all, it has been proved that the pre-Islamic Arabs, and perhaps all Semites, had the ancient tradition of a sacred domelike tent of leather, called the qobba. It was the portable dwelling of the divine baetyls, served as a kind of palladium, or ark, accompanying them into battle and leading them on their migrations, became an emblem of clan authority, and was frequently erected over the graves of ancestors and great men.[108] The only well-preserved representation of this tent sanctuary, which was always transported upon the back of a camel and then set up alongside the chieftain's tent, occurs on a second or third century relief from the temple of Bel at Palmyra (Fig. 147),[109] which was on the outskirts of Syria where there had always been nomadic Arab tribes. Whereas in primitive times the qobba always housed the two baetyls of a clan or tribe, it has survived down to modern times among the Bedouins as the 'otfe of each clan. Although no longer containing any idols, its "tentlike shape, with a domed top has continued to be the palladium of the clan and an emblem of authority."[110] The primitive qobba was also the prototype of the "kubbe" of Islam,

[107] Herzfeld, *Iran in the Ancient East*, 319, fig. 406. The best Sassanian coins were done by Greek craftsmen.

[108] H. Lammens, "Le Culte des bétyles et les processions religieuses chez les Arabes préislamites," *Bulletin de l'Institut français d'archéologie orientale*, XVII, 1920, 39-101; *L'Arabie occidentale avant l'Hégire*, 1928, 101-179; "Les Sanctuaires préislamites dans l'Arabie occidentale," *Mélanges de l'Université Saint-Joseph*,

XI, 1926, 39ff.

[109] Seyrig, "Antiquités syriennes," *Syria*, XV, 1934, 159ff., pl. XIX.

[110] J. Morgenstern, *The Ark, the Ephod and the "Tent of Meeting,"* 1945, 24-27, 176-179. This book, which was first published in the *Hebrew Union College Annual*, XVII, 1942-43, XVIII, 1944, is an excellent study of the sacred tent in Palestine, with a full bibliography.

which Mohammed and his immediate successors continued to carry with them, both in battle and on the march, "as a sign of authority" and a revered symbol of Islam.[111]

Before the Exile the Hebrew clans had tent sanctuaries, *ephods*, which were closely related in form and religious use to the pre-Islamic qobba; and it was probably the ephod of Ephraim at Shiloh that became the ark of the federated tribes of Israel.[112] After their return from captivity, where they lost the first tradition of the ark, they were influenced, perhaps, by a Babylonian conception of a cosmic tent and by the Persian ideas of a universal ruler enthroned in his audience tent.[113] It has been suggested by Eisler that it was in the days of the Exile that the Jews derived their idea of the tabernacle as a cosmic replica of the universe from the Babylonian "Shepherd Tent of the World," which he believes may be seen in the round, ritualistic tent (Fig. 149) on Assyrian reliefs.[114] According to his translation of the Sohar, "In the middle of the house of the primordial creation is a great tree with large branches bent under the weight of fruit," which was the supporting tree-of-life, uniting heaven and earth.

Following the destruction of the temple by the Babylonians in 586 B.C. and the resultant disappearance of the ark, the original conception of the portable tent emblem was transformed into a boxlike container in which the two tablets of the law were deposited in place of the primitive pair of baetyls. After the Hebrews had returned to Judea the nature of the ark was again reinterpreted and, although an effort was made to reinstate it as a sacred object, it continued to be regarded as a container with doors for the "Tablets of Testimony." From this point on the evidence becomes confusing, and Morgenstern's theory, that the authors of the Priestly Code (and, it might be added, those who came after them) had only a vague and unreliable tradition of what the ark should be, seems to be substantiated by the different representations of the ark in the scenes in the Synagogue at Doura-Europos.[115] In the scene of Aaron and the Tabernacle it appears to combine the early tradition of domelike qobba with the paneled doors of a box-container; while in the scene of the Removal of the Ark from the Temple of the Philistines, it is a portable tent on wheels with a conical top and the paneled doors of a cabinet. In the third scene, however, where it is captured by the Philistines, the ark (Fig. 150), which is carried on poles, has a round and domelike shape, more nearly resembling a primitive qobba or ephod.[116] Here its symbolic nature as a divine manifestation and heavenly form appeared to be indicated by the wreaths about it and the spots of decoration, which may have been intended to represent stars.

[111] Morgenstern, *op.cit.*, 64-65 (216-217).

[112] Morgenstern, *op.cit.*, 114-131 (or *Hebrew Union College Annual*, XVIII, 1944, 1-17). Other articles on the ephod and ark are: F. M. Cross, Jr., "The Tabernacle," *Biblical Archaeologist*, X, 1947, 45-68; H. G. May, "The Ark—a Miniature Temple," *American Journal of Semitic Languages and Literatures*, LII, 1936, 215ff.; H. G. May, "Ephod and Ariel," *ibid.*, LVI, 1939, 44ff.; E. Sellin, "Efod und Terafim," *Journal of the Palestine Oriental Society*, XIV, 1934, 185-193.

[113] Morgenstern, *op.cit.*, 4 (156).

[114] Eisler, *Weltenmantel und Himmelszelt*, II, 605; references to Assyrian tent sanctuary, p. 595, and to the Sohar, p. 604.

[115] Morgenstern, *op.cit.*, 78-80 (230-231).

[116] R. du Mesnil du Buisson, *Les Peintures de la Synagogue de Doura-Europos*, 1939, "Aaron and the Tabernacle," pls. XXV, XXVI/1; "Removal from Temple of Philistines," pl. XXXIV; "Capture by Philistines," pls. XXVI/3, XXXIII.

In the period following the Exile and at a time when the Hebrews were thinking in terms of a universal god, it was another tent sanctuary, perhaps a tribal ephod and ancient qobba which assumed new importance. The primitive tabernacle in the wilderness, which had presumably come to have cosmic significance because it emanated from God himself and was the "dwelling place" of a universal Yahweh in the midst of his people, became the "Tent of Meeting," which was called the *miškan* and *'ohel mo'ed*.[117] In it Yahweh was thought to be enthroned like a world ruler, seated upon his throne, the ark. Beyond the theory of Morgenstern that this miškan, or holy of holies, was essentially a kind of qobba, there is little evidence and scholarly agreement as to its shape. Also, because of what appears to have been marked eclecticism in later Hebrew traditions, there is no agreement as to whether the holy of holies depicted upon the Jewish coins (Fig. 151) of the Second Revolt (66-70 A.D.) is merely a Torah shrine or the holy ark presented as a domical tent sanctuary and hence resembling in a general way an ancient qobba, a pagan tabernacle and a Christian ciborium.

Regardless of how the shape of the ark may be interpreted from the coins, there is no doubt that by the first century A.D. the Jews were accustomed to think of their tabernacle as a cosmic house. Philo in *The Special Laws* writes, "The highest, and in the truest sense, the holy temple of God is, as we must believe, the whole universe,"[118] and then in his *Life of Moses* he tells how the parts of the tabernacle symbolize the structure of the universe.[119] A little later in the first century, Josephus describes the tabernacle of Moses as "an imitation of universal nature" and its holy of holies, with its four posts, as "like the heavens devoted to God"; and he also discusses its symbolism and tells how even the dress of the high priest represents the essential parts of the universe.[120]

Unfortunately none of the accounts of this tabernacle of Moses, which was a tent hung and covered with veils, give any indication as to whether its holy of holies had a domical covering, like a qobba or heavenly hemisphere. Josephus, on the other hand, says the ark was made of "stout timber" and had a golden cover "united to it by golden pivots." His statement regarding the shape of this cover, "so even was the surface at every point, with no protuberances anywhere to mar the perfect adjustment," reminds one of the ark at Doura (Fig. 150).[121] What emerges, however, from the Hebrew evidence is the fact that the peoples of Palestine had from ancient times the traditions of a domelike sanctuary, a cosmic tent and of the domical shape as a manifestation of God.

4. EARLY CHRISTIAN AND BYZANTINE TRADITION

At the same time that the Hebrew writers were continuing to think of both the universe and the sanctuary of God in terms of a cosmic and ancient dwelling, the other peoples of Syria and Asia Minor were worshipping their gods in ancestral shelters

[117] Morgenstern, *op.cit.*, 131-161 (17-47).
[118] Philo (Loeb, VII), I, 66.
[119] Philo (Loeb, VI), II, 88.
[120] Josephus (Loeb, IV), *Jewish Antiquities*, III, 123-187.

[121] *Ibid.*, III, 134-136; at the same time that the description of a continuous surface without protuberances implies a domical shape, the dimensions indicate a rectangular shape.

which had similar cosmic implications. The degree to which it was customary for the ordinary man in Syria, around the second century after Christ, to see a heavenly meaning in the domical shape has already been illustrated by the coins. On some coins this meaning was revealed by the eagle enshrined within a tabernacle (Fig. 102), standing on a conoid form (Fig. 137), or combined with a divine baetyl (Fig. 27); and on others it was made evident by stars on a helmet (Fig. 136) and inside a tentlike ciborium (Fig. 104). Even if the tent baldachin over the altar of Zeus (Fig. 106) was not exactly a cosmic house, it was thought of as the dwelling of the ruler of Olympus. Hence, it is readily realized how this religious imagery, combined with the cosmic significance of the imperial baldachin, the Semitic tradition of the qobba and a "Shepherd Tent of the World," formed a domical heritage that Christianity had to recognize and develop, because it could not be forgotten.

Already it has become evident how traditional beliefs in an ancestral shelter— a tegurium, kalubé, and skene—as a replica of God's dwelling, underlay the Christian symbolism of a domical hut as a representation of paradise (Fig. 94), as the home of the Good Shepherd (Fig. 70), as the tomb of Lazarus (Fig. 23) and as a martyr's sanctuary (Fig. 99). Also, between the fourth and seventh centuries, when the churchmen were formulating a mystical conception of the architectural House of God as a symbol and manifestation of divine presence, and were, thereby, cultivating the imagery which was to bring about the adoption of the domical church in the Near East, Christian thought was profoundly influenced by the beliefs in a cosmic house which were still present in the Hebrew tradition and preserved in the Old Testament. Most theologians felt the necessity of reaffirming the validity of these beliefs as a means of making the future seem more real and of combatting the cosmogeny of the Ptolemaic system which undermined the authority of the Scriptures and lessened the importance of heaven. Many of them accepted with great literalness the ideas running through the book of Isaiah, where God is presented as the builder of the world. For the most part they based their imaginative structure of the universe upon the statement, "He that established heaven as a vaulted chamber ($\kappa\alpha\mu\acute{\alpha}\rho\alpha\nu$) and stretched it out as a tent to dwell in" (Isaiah, XL, 22). Furthermore, to such late antique men, accustomed to visualize an earthly kosmokrator as enthroned beneath his celestial baldachin, there was the specific implication of a vaulted covering in the words of the Prophet, "The heaven is my throne and the earth is my footstool: where is the house ye build unto me" (Isaiah, LXVI, 1).

The theologians, however, were confronted with a serious difficulty when they endeavored to present to their congregations a comprehensible cosmogeny and establish in men's minds a divine prototype for the earthly church on the authority of Isaiah and the Hebrew belief that the tabernacle, or tent of Moses, was an actual microcosmos. Because of the vagueness, contradictions and inconsistencies in the scriptural accounts, they had no authority for the exact shape of either the cosmic house or tent. Even the Jews, who had an ancient cultural tradition of a sacred and ancestral tent of domelike shape, were apparently not consistent, after their return from captivity, in regard to the shape and appearance of the ark and inner tabernacle. Nevertheless, many Early Christian writers accepted the Hebrew belief, which paralleled the classical ideas of a celestial skene, and referred to the world as a tent, without being specific as to its shape.[122] Some of them, influenced by other cosmic traditions and the reference of Isaiah to a "vaulted chamber," pictured the universe as a two- or three-storied house whose lofty roof, the "sky of skies" and the "vault of heaven," was either semicylindrical or domical in shape.[123]

The idea of a hoop roof, and hence the first idea of a tunnel vault, went back in origin to the beginnings of Mesopotamian architecture when the keel-shaped roof was taken over into brick construction from the prehistoric reed huts and used for ideological reasons on early tombs and temples.[124] Presumably this Babylonian tradition of a rectangular house with a hoop roof continued to have in the East much the same cosmic and heavenly significance as did the round and domical shelter in other cultures. In fact, the persistence of these ideas accounts for the one tunnel-vaulted chamber in Sargon's palace at Khorsabad, where the vault with its heavenly blue tiles and its yellow, starlike rosettes on the frontal arch was over the royal throne room, and not the bedchamber in the harem as Place thought.[125] Later, the same beliefs may explain why the Jews, after their return from captivity, sometimes thought of their own cosmic tent with a hoop roof, even though this idea conflicted with their own tradition of the sanctuary as a domical, qobba tent.

By the sixth century, when the author of the *Cosmas Indicopleustes* wrote what is now the fullest account of the Christian belief in the world as a cosmic house, it is evident from the contradictions in his text that he was confused by what he had been told, what he had read in the Bible and what was part of the general pattern of ideas in his day.[126] Although writing at Alexandria,[127] according to his own statement he prepared his treatise upon the tabernacle as "a type and copy of the whole world" "from the divine scripture and from the living voice" of Patricius, the Nestorian

[122] Letronne, "Des opinions cosmographiques des pères de l'Église, *Revue des deux mondes*, series 3, 1, 1834, 601-633; Marinelli, "La Geografia e i Padri della Chiesa," II, *Boll. d. soc. geo. gr. ital.*, series 2, vol. VII, 1882, 534; K. Kretschmer, *Die physische Erdkunde im christlichen Mittelalter*, 1889; P. G. Bofitto, "Cosmografia primitive, classica e patristica," *Memorie della Pontificia Accademia dei Nuovi Lincei*, XX, 1903, 113ff.; C. R. Beazley, *The Dawn of Modern Geography*, 1897, I, 287, 330; Leclercq in Cabrol, *Dict.*, VIII, 820ff.

[123] Beazley, *op.cit.*, 275ff., 330; Letronne, *op. cit.* That many theologians took Isaiah's reference to heaven as a vaulted chamber (καμάραν) to mean it was hemispherical is proved by John of Damascus, who in his chapter on "Concerning Heaven" in his *Exposition on the Orthodox Faith (Nicene and Post-Nicene Fathers*, IX, 1899, 21-22) discusses heaven as a

dome and says the idea of a hemisphere is also suggested by the words of David, " 'Who stretchest out the heavens like a curtain,' by which word he clearly means a tent."

[124] Andrae, *Das Gotteshaus und die Urformen des Bauens im Alten Orient*, 1930, 60-72.

[125] Victor Place, *Ninive et l'Assyrie*, 1867, pl. 25.

[126] E. O. Winstedt, *The Christian Topography of Cosmas Indicopleustes*, 1909; J. W. McCrindle, *Christian Topography*, 1897.

[127] M. V. Anastos, "The Alexandrian Origin of the Christian Topography of Cosmas Indicopleustes," *Dumbarton Oaks Papers*, III, 1946, 75ff. The text speaks of working with Stephen of Antioch and indicates Cosmas' indebtedness to Theodorus of Mopsuestia who was born and trained at Antioch.

known by the Syrians as Mar Abas, who had lived in Chaldaea and was "elevated to the lofty episcopal throne of all Persia."[128] Cosmas' conception of both the world and the tabernacle as a rectangular house with a tunnel vault came, therefore, from Nestorian sources, for even Theodorus of Mopsuestia, the fourth century theologian of Antioch whose teachings were so largely responsible for the Nestorian heresy, held much the same views.[129] That this whole theory originally came from Mesopotamia is indicated by the hoop roof and Cosmas' references to the cosmic mountain inside the rectangular world house.[130] Several of his phrases and figures of speech, however, when taken in combination with the inconsistencies in his account of the tabernacle, indicate that he was also accustomed to think of the heavens and the cosmic house as domical. Not only does he in one place describe the sky as a cupola (ὡς θόλος λουτροῦ μεγάλη), but, having referred to the first heaven as a vaulted chamber, he goes on to compare it to the spacious roof over a bath and "with the arena-like (πέλμα) space below."[131]

The importance which was being attached to domical concepts in the Near East is, of course, no more proved by this confusion in Cosmas' imagery than it is disproved by his own belief which came from Nestorian sources. Since there was no scriptural authority for the shape of the cosmic house, it was a question of how the majority of theologians, faced with the necessity of presenting a clear image of the celestial home, could best describe the cosmic tent and heavenly vault in their sermons. In view of all the celestial implications of the domical shape, which it has been seen were part of the popular heritage in Syria, it is evident that many of them and their congregations must have been thinking of the dome when they were talking about the vault of heaven. Even from what little is preserved in their writings, we know that a number of prominent Syrian churchmen pictured the universe as a domical house.[132] Of these the most important was Diodorus of Tarsus, who was one of the most influential religious teachers living at Antioch shortly before the martyrium of S. Babylas was built.[133] He wrote, "Two heavens there are, one visible, the other invisible; one below, the other above: the later serves as the roof of the universe, the former as the covering of our earth—not round or spherical (like the former), but in the form of a tent or arch."

Verbally this architectural conception of the universe, formulated in terms of a domical heaven of heaven rising above the nearer, tentlike covering of the earth, gives the impression of being only a vague and unconvincing combination of images derived from Isaiah. Once it is visualized, however, in relation to a domical church in which

[128] McCrindle, op.cit., book II, 24.
[129] Migne, P.G., LVI, 433; Eisler, Weltenmantel und Himmeltzelt, II, 625; Winstedt, op.cit., 6; John Philoponus, On Creation, III, 9.
[130] Eisler, op.cit., II, 626-632, Fig. 76.
[131] Winstedt, op.cit., IV, line 8, p. 130; Eisler, op.cit., 623; Grabar, Cahiers archéologiques, II, 1947, 58; Migne, P.G., LXXXVIII, 181, 380.

[132] Beazley (pp. 275ff.) and Winstedt (Introduction) list the churchmen who refer to the world as a domical house.
[133] Fragment, "Against Fate," in Photius, Bibliotheca, cod. 223 (Migne, P.G., CIII, 829, 878), and On Genesis (Migne, P.G., XXXIII, 1562-1580); also Beazley, op.cit., p. 352; Eisler, op.cit., II, 625.

the congregation stood when they were listening to sermons on God's creation, it becomes perceptually real and comprehensible. If the reader, with his mind temporarily conditioned by this mystic imagery which presented the church as a replica of the universe, will look up into a dome, such as that on Hagia Sophia (Fig. 154), he will see in the pendentives, made by the circular impost of the dome and the four arches, which this age considered to be the four sides of the earth (see p. 90) a curved shape that resembles a four-sided tent pegged down at the corners; and then through the opening in the top of this apparent covering he will see beyond a heavenly dome, which appears suspended from above because of the halo of light that shines in from the clerestory windows.

While it is impossible to argue from this view into a sixth century dome that Syrian churchmen, like Diodorus, formulated their architectural cosmogeny at Antioch with similar domical churches in mind, their writings, nevertheless, indicate that they did present their cosmogeny to the people by means of domical architecture. At the beginning of the fifth century, another Syrian churchman, Severianus of Gabala, who was undoubtedly influenced by Diodorus, said, "God made the higher heaven . . . higher than this visible heaven, and, as in a house of two stories."[134] Curiously enough this particular quotation comes from the book of Cosmas, who quotes him at great length "as a witness to confirm . . . my work" without realizing that they are not in agreement on the shape of the world house. In a subsequent passage, again quoted by Cosmas, Severianus, who is illustrating the earth's movement in relation to the sun, says, "Suppose a dome to be placed over the church." From the way in which Severianus carefully orients this dome in his sermon, as if he were pointing to the four sides, it is evident that both he and his audience were familiar with domical churches and accustomed to associate them with the universe.

Since both Severianus and Diodorus were trained at Antioch there arises the presumption that much of this cosmic imagery took shape at Antioch in specific relation to the lofty wooden domes, decorated with stars, which rose over the *Domus aurea* and the martyria, such as S. Babylas. This presumption would then help to explain why both S. John Chrysostom and Theoderet should have referred to the body of Bishop Meletius and the relics of S. Babylas, buried together in the domical crossing of the martyrium, as "tent mates."[135] Furthermore, if this mystical interest in the domical shape was formulated in Syria, and presumably at Antioch, we can more clearly account for the domical cosmogeny of the Syrian hymn which was written in praise of Hagia Sophia at Edessa.[136]

The original church at Edessa, begun in 313 A.D., was enlarged in 327/8 and at

---

[134] Winstedt, *op.cit.*, book x, C-16, p. 424; McCrindle, *op.cit.*, 335, 340; Severianus of Gabala, *Orations on Creation*, no. 3 (Migne, P.G., LVI, 447-456).

[135] See Chap. v. Sect. 23. pp. 109-110.

[136] A. Dupont-Sommer, "Une Hymne syri-aque sur la cathédrale d'Édesse," *Cahiers archéologiques*, II, 1947, 29-31; Grabar, "Le Témoignage d'une hymne syriaque sur l'architecture de la cathédrale d'Édesse au vie siècle et sur la symbolique de l'édifice chrétien," *ibid.*, II, 41-67.

some time before 345/6 became known as Hagia Sophia.[137] After it had been seriously damaged by the great flood of 524 A.D. it was rebuilt by Bishop Amidonius with imperial funds furnished by Justinian. It was this church which is praised in the *Sougitha*, a Syrian hymn which was probably written in the seventh century. The importance in it of a mystical architectural symbolism and the dogmatic assurance of its imagery make very evident that its ideas of a domical cosmic house of God must have been long established and generally accepted in Syria. It starts out by comparing the construction of the church by Amidonius and his two builders, Asaph and Addäi, to the erection of the Hebrew tabernacle of Moses. While the author was, therefore, undoubtedly influenced by the Jewish tradition of a cosmic tent and also by the *Mystagogia* of S. Maximus and the *Areopagitica* of the Pseudo-Dionysus, as Grabar has pointed out, his ideas of the relation of the world and the church all go back to the writings and beliefs of those fourth century Syrian theologians who were connected with the Church of Antioch. There is also the strong suggestion that his conception of the earthly house of God was indirectly, and unconsciously, influenced by the traditional Syro-Palestinian habit of associating a conoid house form with the manifestation of a living and ever-present god.

How fully the Christians had accepted the beliefs in a cosmic house is shown by the way in which the *Sougitha* presents the domical church at Edessa both as the image of God and as a replica of the universe, for the "Essence," it says, resides in the Holy Temple and *in effect, it is something truly admirable that its smallness should be similar to the vast World.* The dome, which it considers to be the most remarkable and exalted part of the church is described as "comparable to the Heaven of Heaven," and ornamented *with mosaics of gold, like the firmament, with brilliant stars*, while its four supporting arches are "the four sides of the World." This sense of a celestial presence in all the parts of the building, "The Essence which resides in the Holy Temple," is made evident by the references to "its marble similar to the Image not made by the hand of man," to the columns as representing the tribes of Israel, the three façades recalling the Trinity and to the light coming from the three windows of the choir as revealing to us "the Mystery of the Trinity of the Father, Son and Holy Ghost." It is also apparent in the description of the five doors representing the five Virgins, the columns standing for the Apostles, and "the nine steps leading up to the Throne of Christ denoting the nine Orders of Angels."

It is also to be noted that in the reference to the construction of the dome, it says, *There is no wood at all in its roof, which is entirely constructed of stone.* On a church of the age and sanctity of Hagia Sophia at Edessa it is impossible to believe that the sixth century builders would have made such a drastic change as the addition of a dome. In fact, there is no indication in the hymn that the dome itself was considered an innovation. The only innovation to impress the writer was its being "entirely

[137] A. Baumstark, "Vorjustinianische kirchliche Bauten in Edessa," *Oriens Christianus*, IV, 1904, 164-183; Cabrol, *Dict.*, IV, 2063; H. Goussen, "Uber eine 'sugitha' auf die Kathedrale von Edessa," *Le Muséon*, XXXVIII, 1925, 117-136.

constructed of stone." Therefore, from the reference to there having been "no wood at all in its roof," we may assume that the pre-Justinian church had a wooden cosmic dome like those on the Syrian martyria.

If the church was a theophanic martyrium, as the hymn indicates and Grabar has pointed out,[138] then its square shape surmounted by a lofty cupola made it a kind of monumental ciborium and holy of holies, like the square crossing of the fourth century martyrium of S. Babylas at Antioch, the original mortuary sanctuary over the relics of S. John at Ephesus (Fig. 83) and, for that matter, similar to the tomb of Bizzos at Ruweha (Fig. 61). Once these martyria and tombs are visualized against the Syro-Palestinian beliefs in a cosmic house, it becomes more evident why the martyria at Antioch and Seleucia Pieria must have had a dome as an architectural manifestation of the convictions of the leaders in the Church at Antioch.

The description in the *Sougitha* of "the brilliant stars," like the firmament, which decorated the vault of Hagia Sophia, is further proof of how literally the Christians had adopted earlier concepts, similar to the one that had inspired Philostratus in his account of a royal Parthian baldachin and related to the beliefs that had led to the adoption of an astral dome at Rome.[139] Most Early Christian domes, especially those in the Near East, have been destroyed, but the importance of this starry symbolism is shown by the emphasis which the Syrian writers place upon the stars as the lamps carried by angels (*lampadophores*) who inhabit the heavenly dome. Their use in tombs and martyria is also indicated by the representation of the Holy Sepulchre (Fig. 14) on a Palestinian reliquary from the Sancta Sanctorum, the vault mosaics of the fifth century mausoleum of Galla Placidia (Fig. 73), and the martyrium of the same century at Casaranello (Fig. 71). Inasmuch as the two Italian examples are in the Ravennate region where there were such close contacts with Syria and Palestine, and it has been recently shown that the iconography in the mosaics of Galla Placidia was presumably taken from a Palestinian source,[140] we may reasonably suspect that the starry dome spread from Syria and Palestine.

Much more could be added to this partial outline of the early history of domical ideas. If further evidence, however, is necessary to demonstrate why the Antiochene martyria had wooden domes, gilded like the traditional heavenly zone of Mesopotamian cosmologies and adorned with stars on the interior, it must be found, not in the results of excavations which have revealed so little in regard to the Syrian use of the wooden dome, but in the Christian mind and the inner content which it saw in the architectural parts of the House of God. Architectural mysticism, going back for its authority to the earliest beliefs regarding an ancestral shelter, was not peculiar

[138] Grabar, *Martyrium*, I, 327.

[139] The use of stars on Roman domes, such as on the vault on the Stabian baths and on the painted dome in the house of Caecilius Jucundus at Pompeii (K. Lehmann, "The Dome of Heaven," *Art Bulletin*, XXVII, 1945, 21, figs. 58, 59); the *stellata domus Jovis* (Eis-

ler, *Weltenmantel und Himmelszelt*, II, 619 n. 6); the gilded rosettes as stars on Pantheon dome (Cook, *Zeus*, III, 44ff.).

[140] W. Seston, "Le Jugement dernier au mausolée de Galla Placidia à Ravenne," *Cahiers archéologiques*, I, 1945, 37-50.

to the Syrian author of the *Sougitha*. It was part of the Christian heritage and is apparent as early as the fourth century in the *Ecclesiastical History* of Eusebius.

His "Panegyric on the building of churches, addressed to Paulinus, the bishop of the Tyrians,"[141] and delivered at the dedication of the church at Tyre, was written with the basic conviction, necessary to such architectural symbolism, that "this magnificent temple of God most high" answers "in its nature to the pattern of that which is better, even as the visible answereth to the invisible." Therefore, when he came "to the royal house," "the dazzling appearance of the workmanship," "the loftiness that reacheth heaven, and the costly cedars of Lebanon that are placed above," he drew his parallel between the actual building, the cosmic house of God and the Holy Church which was itself "the edifice the Son of God created in his own image," for, as he says, "more wonderful than wonders are the archetypes, the rational prototypes of these things and their divine models."

Because of the beliefs of the day, his statement that, "He hath builded the great and royal house composed of all, bright and full of light, both within and without," was understood by everyone to apply both to the divine prototype and the temple itself. The same was also true of his words, "Such is the great temple which the Word, the great Creator of the universe, hath builded throughout the whole world beneath the sun, forming again this spiritual image upon earth of those vaults beyond the vaults of Heaven (οὐρανίων ἀψίδων)." Although commentators and translators of Eusebius have all assumed that he was describing a basilica church, everything in his account and especially his emphasis upon "the loftiness that reacheth to heaven," "the vault of heaven," the construction of the roof with cedars of Lebanon and the specific location of the altar in the middle of the church[142] suggest that this fourth century church at Tyre was not a basilica, but a cruciform structure of the martyrium type with aisles in the four arms and with a cosmic dome over the crossing.

Much more study of the sources of Christian thought in this period is necessary before it is certain how many of the ideas in regard to the domical symbolism of the dome at first spread from Antioch and inspired the Near East during the Byzantine period to make the cosmic dome the crowning feature of the church. The domical evidence, however, conforms with Grabar's conclusions that the martyrium-type church finally triumphed in the Byzantine East largely because of the prestige of the martyria of Syria and Palestine and the influence of such mystic, Syrian theologians as the Pseudo-Dionysus and S. Maximus. If this were so, then much of the mortuary, salvational, divine and cosmic ideology, which had made the dome the transcending feature of the martyrium, must have originally emanated from Syria. What is already clear, however, is that it was ideas and not any structural and utilitarian interest in the dome, as a means of covering space, which impelled Justinian and the subsequent builders of Byzantine architecture to attach so much importance to the building of domical churches and palaces.

[141] Eusebius, *Ecclesiastical History* (Loeb, II), x, iv, 2-72.   [142] See p. 138.

All the way through the Byzantine period the theologians continued to regard the church as a replica of heaven upon earth and to see in the dome a form of great imaginative significance to man. Early in the eighth century, S. Germanos, the Patriarch of Constantinople, wrote, "The church is heaven upon earth, the place where the God of heaven dwells and moves. It represents the crucifixion, the sepulchre and the resurrection of Christ."[143] As late as the fifteenth century Symeon of Thessalonica, in his treatise *On the Holy Temple,* wrote, "The temple, as the House of God, is the image of the whole world, for God is everywhere and above all. It is to point to this that it is divided into three parts; for God is a Trinity. This was represented also by the Tabernacle, divided into three parts, and likewise by Solomon's temple, in which, as S. Paul says, there was the Holy of Holies, the Holy Place and the Atrium. Here, the sanctuary is the symbol of the higher and supra-celestial spheres, where, it is said, is the throne of the immortal God, and the place of his rest. It is likewise this that the altar represents. The heavenly hierarchies are to be found hither and thither, but they have with them priests who take their place. The pontiff represents Christ; the temple, this visible world; the vault, the visible heaven; the ground, the things which are on the earth, and the (earthly) paradise itself; the exterior, the lower regions and the earth in respect of beings which live according to reason and have no higher life...."[144]

Once the long history of pagan and Christian domical ideas begins to take shape, it becomes evident how necessary it is for the history of architecture to be freed from the purely racial, environmental and utilitarian theories regarding the origin of the dome. The Renaissance architects acquired much of their aesthetic interest in the dome, and were impelled to rank the round and domical temple above all other types of buildings, because of their admiration for Roman architecture. At the same time they were undoubtedly aware of the domical ideas, such as that of the cosmic house, which were part of their Christian heritage. Vasari, when he refers to the original Duomo at Florence which Arnolfo di Cambio planned to build with a domical crossing, speaks of it as a "universal church."[145] Although Palladio professed to admire the circular plan and domical temple because "it is, therefore, the most proper figure to shew the Unity, infinite Essence, the Uniformity and Justice of God," he explains the shape of the Pantheon, "either because, after Jupiter, it was consecrated to all the Gods; or, as others would have it, because it bears the figure of the world."[146]

Whether derived from classical or Christian sources, it was the ancient tradition of a domical cosmic house which helps to explain why Michelangelo, in designing the Medici Chapel, insisted upon having it a domical memorial, even though it blocked the whole arm of San Lorenzo. According to the most recent interpretation of this mortuary chapel, "The whole Chapel was intended to be an abbreviated image of

[143] S. Germanos, *Hist. Eccl. et mystica contemplatio* (P.G., xcviii, cols. 384-385); Père S. Salaville, *Eastern Liturgies,* 1938, 123.
[144] Translation by Salaville, *op.cit.,* 126.

[145] Vasari, Milanesi ed., I, 551.
[146] A. Palladio, *The Architecture of A. Palladio* (trans. with notes by Inigo Jones), 1742, IV, chap. XI, 7; IV, chap. XX, 28.

93

the universe, with its spheres hierarchically ranged one above the other. The lowest zone, with the tombs, is the dwelling place of the departed souls, the realm of Hades. The intermediate zone, with its rational architecture, was intended to incarnate the terrestrial sphere. The zone of the lunettes and of the cupola was intended to represent the celestial sphere."[147] It is also necessary to believe that the celestial and cosmic symbolism was in men's minds when the Church of Rome, at the very time when it was most desirous of manifesting its greatness as "the Church of the World," undertook to rebuild the old basilica of S. Peter with a magnificent free-standing cupola, which Bernini compared to the tiara of the Pope.

[147] C. de Tolnay, *The Medici Chapel* (Michelangelo, III), 1948, 63.

V · THE DOMICAL CHURCHES: *MARTYRIA*

THE shape of roofs on the central churches of Syria was in no way a matter of structural expedience. Because the Christians saw inner meanings in all the elements of architecture, their choice and use of specific forms, like domes, were not conditioned by the same kind of utilitarian and aesthetic interests as govern modern design. The previous chapters have endeavored to prove the structural importance of the wooden dome, to present in broad outline the main antique sources of domical symbolism and to show why the Christians, in their effort to create a mystic language of architectural expression, came to attach so much significance to the domical form of their martyria. By itself this background is not enough to demonstrate that the two martyria of Antioch, the one of S. Babylas at Kaoussie and the other at Seleucia Pieria, must have had soaring, gilded domes of wood.

It is still necessary to present the two martyria in relation to the gradual evolution of church architecture in the Near East and to realize that Syria and Palestine, by means of the wooden dome, had a domical tradition which was an influential factor in the development of the domical styles of both Byzantium and Islam. In order to show that the two buildings conformed to an established tradition and that the dome was an essential feature upon the martyria of these regions, they will be discussed in relation to the various types of martyria—circular, polygonal, square, cruciform (S. Babylas at Antioch-Kaoussie), quatrefoil (Seleucia Pieria), trefoil and rectangular —which are either known to have been domical or whose plans indicate a domical superstructure.[1] This involves drawing a sharp distinction between the martyrium proper and the ordinary churches which, because of the growing popularity of the Cult of Martyrs, made provisions in their side-chambers, or by means of added oratories, for relics, and so became what Lassus calls "martyrium-basilicas."[2]

Before this review is made, some reconsideration should be given to the prevailing belief that the great majority of churches were basilicas and that the domical martyrium, when it did occur, was an intrusion. This impression goes back to the publications of De Vogüé and Butler, who were limited to reporting what they saw in the unexcavated ruins of the more provincial towns and who, in reconstructing the churches, did not consider the possibilities of the wooden dome. Since their time, excavations in the larger cities have proved that the central-type martyrium was not uncommon. In fact, of the two score or more churches known to have been at Antioch and in its suburbs or its port, at least half were martyria, and of these, the three that are now best known—the *Domus aurea* and the two martyria under discussion—were central-type structures, presumably domical.[3] Of the three churches known in the

[1] Grabar, *Martyrium.*

[2] Jean Lassus, *Sanctuaires chrétiens de Syrie,* 1947, 162ff.

[3] In addition to the domical Great Church,

the martyria of S. Babylas and Seleucia Pieria and the churches of the Virgin and S. Martha, which are discussed as central-type churches, there were the "Cemetery Church," known as

sixth century to have been in the town of Zorah (Ezra), which was in the province of Arabia but under the Patriarch of Antioch, two (Figs. 53, 56) are still domical. Outside the Patriarchate of Antioch, after the fourth century, the town of Gaza and its near-by port furnishes further evidence on this ratio. Of the seven churches recorded at Gaza and Mahoymac, three are specifically described, or depicted, as domical, while the cruciform Eudoxiana should have been domical, as may have been the martyrium of S. Timothy near the Old Church outside the walls.[4] Thus we are left with the Old Church and S. Irene as probable basilicas. In view, then, of the many references in the inscriptions to martyria, of which we know nothing except their names, it is no longer possible to assume that the central and domical martyrium was not as important in Syria and Palestine as it was in Asia Minor.

The tendency to disregard the importance of the Syro-Palestinian region in the evolution of domical architecture in the Near East, and to treat the Arab use of the wooden dome as an unprecedented phenomenon, has created an inexplicable problem for the architectural historian. Even without the available evidence for the long history of domical beliefs and the use of the wooden dome in Syria and Palestine, it would be difficult to understand how the dome came to attain such preeminence throughout the Byzantine and Islamic East if it had not already existed and had mystic value upon the renowned, admired and imitated martyria of the Holy Land. Both the rapid spread of domical churches during the fifth and sixth centuries in Egypt, Asia Minor, Greece and the Balkans, and the universal acceptance of the dome after the seventh century in Armenia, northern Mesopotamia and the whole Christian and Islamic East, cannot be explained by the assumption that this whole movement was the result of the introduction of vaulting methods into all these regions from either Rome or Iran.

Regardless of where and how domical construction originated, there had to be a powerful ideological incentive to account for this widespread and radical change in religious architecture. In regions which for centuries had been accustomed to wood roofing, or which suffered from periodic earthquakes, this incentive could not have arisen from any structural interest in the difficult and dangerous technique of masonry vaulting. Instead, it must have come from the already popular beliefs regarding the mystic and cosmic significance of the domical shape, which the Christians took over and combined with the sepulchral symbolism of the Romans and the domical ideas of Iran and India. By the fourth century the Christians had two distinct types of sanctuary: one the rectangular basilica dedicated to the service of Christ; and the other the central-type martyrium built to commemorate their own heroic dead. Apart

---

the "House of Martyrs," the martyrium serving as the sepulchre of the Arians, the sanctuary of the Forty Martyrs, the martyrium of S. Stephen, and the martyria of S. Babylas, Leontius and Euphemia at Daphne. In addition there are references to other churches having been built over the tombs of martyred saints.

Cabrol, *Dict.*, I, "Antioch," 2372-2402; R. Devreesse, *Le Patriarcat d'Antioche*, 1945, 109-111; Lassus, *Sanctuaires*, 122 n. 1.

[4] Cabrol, *Dict.*, VI, 695ff. and XIV, 1477ff; Grégoire and Kugener, *Marc le Diacre, Vie de Porphyre*, LVIIIf.

from a few monumental structures like the Holy Sepulchre and the church of the Holy Apostles, which were imperial foundations, the martyria were at first small sepulchral chapels, either free standing like tombs (Fig. 152) or connected as oratories with the basilicas. After the Recognition of the Church, the rapid growth of the Cult of Relics, the traditional desire of antiquity to apotheosize the honored dead and the popular desire to partake of the sanctity and protection of the martyrs resulted in the enlargement of the early martyria. In many instances, as at Korykos (Fig. 180) and S. John at Ephesus (Fig. 83), this enlargement, instead of being a complete rebuilding, was accomplished by adding ambulatories, exedras and cruciform arms so that there would be space for the crowds to gather about the central altar in the memorial tomb chamber.

During the fifth and sixth centuries the Church, inspired by the writings of the Syrian churchmen, who attributed cosmic significance to the domical church, was desirious of cultivating the popular appeal of the celestial symbolism already connected with the domical martyrium. At the same time it was undoubtedly aware that this growing popularity of the Cult of Martyrs threatened it with a new kind of polytheism. Therefore, it began to transform the traditional types of sepulchral martyria into regular churches, devoted solely to the eucharistic service. The change was gradually brought about by adding to the central-type structure, as at Seleucia Pieria (Fig. 182), the customary eastern apse for the symbolic tomb of Christ and the side chambers for the relics and ritual, by retaining the celestial domical covering over the main body of the church, and by removing any special altars from the midst of the congregation so that nothing could compete with the regular service at the apsidal altar. This gradual fusion of two traditions, which was going on perhaps somewhat independently in different parts of the Christian East, but which was directly influenced by Syrian churchmen and the great renown of the domical martyria of Palestine, gave rise to the new type of domical church, commonly called Byzantine.

The change was augmented and strengthened during the sixth century by the centralized power of the state and the ambitious architectural interests of Justinian, which by means of imperial funds and methods of construction tended to translate this domical martyrium church into a monumental structure with masonry vaults. The religious traditions, however, with which Justinian was dealing were neither basically Constantinopolitan nor the creation of Asia Minor. The Church of Antioch was in many ways the most powerful and independent organization of Christianity, with the result that its rule and influence extended over a large area including the Euphratensis, Mesopotamia, much of the province of Arabia, and the northern regions of Isauria and Cilicia.[5] While it is no longer a question of proving that the dome had one place of origin, too much emphasis has been given to the part played by Asia Minor in this development of Byzantine architecture because of the Strzygowskian theories. As a result, not only has Syria and the influence of the churchmen trained at Antioch been disregarded, but the fact that Korykos (Fig. 180), Meriamlik (Fig. 193) and Koja

[5] R. Devreesse, *op.cit.*

97

Kalessi (Fig. 195) were under the Patriarchate of Antioch has been frequently over-looked. Therefore, in a review of the domical martyria of Syria, consideration must be given to the facts that Resafa, the sixth century metropole of the Euphratensis, Edessa, the metropole of Osrhëne, both Nisibis and Amida, the successive metropoles of Mesopotamia, as well as such Christian communities as those in Bosra, Zorah (Ezra) and Madaba, were all under the religious jurisdiction of the Church at Antioch, whose churchmen, we have seen, attached so much importance to the cosmological conception of God's universe as a domical house.

A. Circular

The form of the circular rotunda and much of its symbolic content, which the Christians had taken over from the Roman mausoleum and classical heroön, it has been seen, went back to the origins of sepulchral architecture in many separate parts of the ancient world, where a primitive and tribal dwelling had evolved into an eternal house of the dead. By the Hellenistic and Roman periods the circular structure, because of its long association in men's minds with an ancestral dwelling, with sacred repasts, funereal rites, ancestor worship and the commemoration of heroic dead had acquired varying degrees of celestial meaning as it was used for such cult houses as the skias, enagesterion, heroön, mundus, tomb and memorial.[6] The debated question of how commonly these round classical monuments were domical need not now be raised, because the *aeternae memoriae* (Figs. 17-21) of the Constantinian emperors are clear proof how important the dome was at the beginning of the fourth century in relation to the Cult of the Dead. Excellent evidence of the traditionally domical character of this type of martyrium is the Early Christian ivory in Trier Cathedral (Fig. 152), which depicts a scene of the "Translation of Relics" in a city, like Antioch or Constantinople, where the martyrium is a small, free-standing, tomb monument, with a melon-like dome, on the south side of a basilica church. That there were so few circular martyria in Syria and Palestine after the Holy Sepulchre had taken over and given such importance to the late antique tradition can be explained by the fact that the Christians made no real distinction between the circular rotunda and polygonal structures, finding it much easier to construct octagonal rather than circular memorials.[7]

1. *Jerusalem, Holy Sepulchre* (Figs. 1-3). The evidence for restoring the fourth century rotunda over the tomb of Christ with a soaring and somewhat conoid dome of wood, decorated on the interior with golden stars, has already been discussed.[8] The most reliable representation of this monument is that painted on the reliquary box from the Sancta Sanctorum (Fig. 14), for it shows an established Palestinian convention for depicting the Holy Sepulchre, which is essentially the same as the one used on two ampullae from the Holy Land. The scene of the Women at the Tomb on

[6] F. Robert, *Thymélè*, 1939.
[7] R. Krautheimer, "Introduction to an 'Iconography of Mediaeval Architecture,'" *Journal of the Warburg and Courtauld Institutes*, v, 1942, 5-9.
[8] See pp. 16-29.

phials in the Dumbarton Oaks Collection (Fig. 158) and in the Detroit Institute of Arts[9] shows a rotunda with clerestory windows, like those on the Palestinian reliquary (Fig. 14), the only difference being that the heavenly dome over the rotunda was omitted on the ampulla because of the limitations of the circular space and the presumption that its presence was too well recognized to require inclusion.

2. *Beisan* (Beth Sean, ancient Scythopolis). This fifth or sixth century circular church (Fig. 155), constructed largely of Roman materials, has a diameter of 38.80 m.[10] The fallen columns of the interior indicate that it must have had an inner circle of supports, about 10.04 m. in diameter, which Watzinger believes carried a wooden dome.[11] Abel, on the contrary, has suggested that the columns formed an interior square like the interior of two churches at Gerasa (Figs. 169, 177) and that it had a conical roof of wood.[12] Inasmuch as the span and the character of the debris make it evident that the church must have had a wooden roof, we are brought back to the original question of the symbolic importance of the domical shape. Any consideration of this question should take into account the fact that there are no Christian survivals in the Near East of conical roofs, except as coverings for domes, and no evidence that such a shape had any symbolic significance.

3. *Fa'lul.* "Built by the most glorious Diogenes" in 526/7 A.D., this circular church (Fig. 48), which has a diameter of 14.95 m., is known to have been a martyrium because in the inscriptions it is referred to as an "oratory" (εὐχτήριον), or place of prayer, of the Archangels.[13] In describing the church Butler reported that its interior was filled with debris consisting of "large masses of masonry in brick and mortar," which he considered proof of its having been "provided with a dome." It is impossible to deny the possibility of his assumption, because masonry domes were beginning to be built at this time upon Syrian churches. Since Butler suggested that there must have been an inner circle of columns to carry the dome, his plan has been modified by the introduction of an interior colonnade, which would have resulted in a domical span of about 6 m. In reviewing the evidence for probable Syrian domes it should be kept in mind that the only extant masonry dome, which is on the sixth century church at Kasr ibn-Wardān (Fig. 46), had a span of only 6.66 m. and was supported on massive piers.

4. *Antioch, Church of the Virgin.* Among the many churches erected in honor of the Mother of God after the middle of the fifth century, is one built by Justinian at Antioch[14] which was presumably domical. In 943 Ma'udi, the Arab chronicler,

[9] P. Lesley, "An Echo of Early Christianity," *Art Quarterly* (Detroit Institute of Arts), II, 1939, 215-230, fig. 1. Another variant in S. Colombano, Bobbio (G. Celi, *Cimeli Bobbiesi*, 1923, fig. 4).

[10] C. S. Fisher, "The Church at Beisan," *Pennsylvania Museum Journal*, xv, 1924, 171ff.

[11] C. Watzinger, *Denk. Paläs.*, II, 1935, 135.

[12] F. M. Abel, "Les Églises de Palestine récemment découvertes," *Atti del III Congresso internazionale di archeologia cristiana*, 1934, 504.

[13] Howard Butler, *Syria, Princeton University Archaeological Expeditions to Syria in 1904-5 and 1909*, II, B, 95ff., ills. 112, 113; Littmann, Magie and Stuart, *ibid.*, III, B, inscription 1050; Butler, *Early Churches in Syria*, 164ff.

[14] Procopius, *Buildings* (Loeb), II, x, 24.

referred to the Kanisah Maryan, which he says "is a round church, and one of the wonders of the world for the beauty of its construction and its height."[15] Not only were the Arabs most inclined to admire only the soaring, domical churches, but there are reasons leading us to believe that many, if not all, of the martyrium-type churches erected in honor of the Theotokos were domical, like her tomb at Jerusalem (Fig. 161).

In addition to these four known circular churches, the cathedral at Bosra (Fig. 49), the church of John the Baptist at Gerasa (Fig. 169), and the Tomb of the Virgin preserved on their interiors the shape of the rotunda; but since their innermost arrangements of supports had in one instance a quatrefoil plan and in the other a square, they will be taken up later.

B. Polygonal

The polygonal martyrium was originally a tomb-type taken over from the sepulchral and memorial architecture of the Romans.[16] Ideationally, however, it was considered to be essentially the same as the circular rotunda, for Gregory of Nyssa describes an octagonal plan as forming "a circle with angles" and Arculph refers to the octagonal church of the Ascension as a rotunda.[17] At the same time, many of the early Christian theologians, interested in the mystical significance of numbers, developed a special symbolism for the octagon in whose shape they saw a correspondence to the number of salvation through death and the beginning of a new life.[18] As certain early and venerated memorials which were originally mortuary types, like the rotunda, polygon, square and quatrefoil, were enlarged by additions into martyrium churches, the octagon in some cases was transformed into a cruciform church.[19] At Kal'at Sim'ân, for example, Écochard, after studying the stonework, concluded that the four great naves may have been constructed after the octagon had been built around the Stylite.[20] The presumption that these octagonal memorials of the Christian faith, which had so much inner meaning, were usually domical rests upon no specific evidence for any one building, but upon the general pattern of Christian thought, the mortuary derivations and implications of the martyrium as a celestial home, the persistent association of the symbolic dome with octagonal martyria, baptisteries and tombs, and the fact, which cannot be disregarded, that we do not know of any such early structures which were certainly not domical.

5. *Antioch, Domus aurea.* The mosaic representation (Fig. 29) and the fact that it was known to have had a gilded wooden dome in the sixth century prove that this commemorative martyrium, which was the most famous church of Antioch, was domical from the time of its erection in the fourth century.[21]

[15] G. Le Strange, *Palestine under the Moslems*, 1890, 368.

[16] Grabar, *Martyrium*, I, 141ff.

[17] Krautheimer, *op.cit.*

[18] F. J. Dölger, "Zur Symbolik des altchristlichen Taufhauses," *Antike und Christentum*, IV, 1933, 153-187; Krautheimer, *op.cit.*

[19] Grabar, *Martyrium*, I, 357-362.

[20] M. Écochard, "Le Sanctuaire de Qal'at Sem'ân," *Bulletin d'études orientales de l'Institut français de Damas*, VI, 1936, 61ff. These conclusions have been questioned by Lassus (*Sanctuaires*, 129-132).

[21] See pp. 29-31.

6. *Bethlehem, Church of the Nativity*. Although too little is known about the church which Constantine had built over the cave of the Nativity and in regard to its subsequent rebuilding, exploratory excavations (Fig. 156) have proved that it was not an ordinary five-aisled basilica, but a commemorative monument of the central type with additional space for the throngs of worshippers in its basilica-like extension to the west.[22] It is necessary to accept the conclusions of Harvey, Richmond and Vincent because the recent effort of Vionnet to resolve all the difficulties by having a series of pre-Constantinian structures completely disregards the architectural evidence.[23] According to Vincent, the original, fourth century, building had an octagonal chevet, about 18 m. in diameter, which he restored with a pointed, polygonal roof of wood. In view of the great sanctity of the site, the martyrium form of the sanctuary proper and all that the domical shape meant to Christians and Syrians, it is necessary to assume that this memorial over "the first manifestation of the Saviour's presence" was distinguished by the recognized symbol of a divine and heavenly abode. Therefore, a conoid and Syrian dome of wood has been added to Vincent's restoration (Fig. 157). It is not clear whether the available evidence makes it impossible to assume that Constantine only authorized the construction of the commemorative octagon and that before the end of the century the prestige of the site had made it necessary to enlarge the accommodations by the addition of the rectangular west end.

Regarding the subsequent history of the church, it is generally agreed that it was Justinian who had the church rebuilt with a tri-apsidal east end after it was seriously damaged by fire during the Samaritan revolt in 529 A.D.[24] Unfortunately, the only reference which associates Justinian with the work is a statement of Eutychios, the Patriarch of Alexandria, in the tenth century. The fact, however, that Sophronius, who became Patriarch of Jerusalem in 635 A.D., refers to the church as tri-apsidal, would appear to support the archaeological evidence in placing the reconstruction in the sixth century. What is still troublesome in the theoretical history of the church are the fragments of curved walls found under the pavements of the north and south transepts, which Vincent has explained, in perhaps the only way possible, as an experi-

[22] Conder and Kitchener, *Survey of Western Palestine*, 1883, III, 83-85; De Vogüé, *Les Églises de la Terre-Sainte*, 1860; E. Wiegand, *Die Geburtskirche von Bethlehem*, 1911; R. W. Schultz (ed.), *The Church of the Nativity at Bethlehem*, 1910; Leclerq-Cabrol, *Dict.*, II, 828; Vincent and Abel, *Bethléem*, 1914, Wiegand, "Die Konstantinische Geburtskirche von Bethlehem," *Zeit. d. deut. Palästina-Vereins*, XXXVIII, 1915, 89-135 and XLVI, 1923, 193-212; Vincent, *Rev. bibl.*, XVI, 1919, 297-301; Abel, *R.b.*, XVII, 1920, 602-605; R. W. Hamilton, "Excavations in the Atrium . . . ," *Quarterly Dept. of Ant. Pal.*, III, 1933, 1-8; W. Harvey and E. T. Richmond, *Structural Survey of the Church of the Nativity, Bethlehem*, 1935; Watzinger, *Denk. Paläs.*, II, 1935, 120-123; Harvey, "The Early Basilica at Bethlehem," *Pal. Expl. Fund, Quart. St.*, 1936, 28-33; *idem*, "Recent Discoveries . . . ," *Archaeologia*, LXXXVII, 1937, 7-17; Vincent, "Bethléem, le sanctuaire de la Nativité . . . ," *R.b.*, 1936, 544-574; 1937, 93, 121; Richmond, *Q.D.A.P.*, VI, 1937, 63, 66, 72; Rucker, *Oriens Christianus*, XXXV, 1938, 224-238; Crowfoot, *Early Churches in Palestine*, 1941, 22ff.; its function as a special kind of commemorative martyrium is discussed by Grabar (*Martyrium*, I, 245ff.).

[23] M. Vionnet, "Les Églises de la Nativité à Bethléem," *Byzantion*, XIII, 1938, 91ff.

[24] A. M. Schneider, "Zur Baugeschichte der Geburtskirche," *Zeit. d. deut. Palästina-Vereins*, LXIV, 1941, 74-91, who would date the tri-apsidal chevet earlier than Justinian.

mental trefoil that was started under Justinian and then abandoned. In his plan this experimental trefoil with its shallow curved walls is architecturally unconvincing. If such a plan was contemplated, it must have had rectangular corners and been the outer ambulatory of a cruciform and trefoil interior such as is seen in the plans of the martyria of Seleucia Pieria (Fig. 182), Resafa (Fig. 184) and Amida (Fig. 185). If the evidence of the limited excavations permitted, it would help to explain the popularity in Egypt and other regions of the tri-apsidal type of cruciform and domical church to assume that the first tri-apsidal rebuilding of the east end took place in the fifth century and that this renowned church was then domical like the church of S. Stephen at Gaza.

7. *Jerusalem, Church of the Ascension*. Built shortly before 378 A.D. by Poemenia, a devout Roman lady, the church was octagonal (Fig. 159), with walls 2.95 m. thick and with a diameter of 41.10 m., which had an inner ring of twelve columns with a roofing span of 20.80 m.[25] After its partial destruction by the Persians in 614 A.D. this commemorative martyrium of Imboman on the Mount of Olives was rebuilt by Modestus and according to Arculph, who made a plan of it as if it were a circular rotunda, its roof had an oculus, open to the sky. He writes: "Cuius videlicet rotundae ecclesiae interior domus sine tecto et sine camera ad caelum sub aere nudo aperta patet."[26] Also in the seventh century the Armenian account records that "on the place of the Ascension is erected, after the likeness of the Church of the Resurrection, a very beautiful cupola-shaped building, 100 ells in width."[27] Although it has usually been restored with a polygonal roof, open at the top, like the building in the mosaic of S. Pudentiana, the evidence shows that it had a cupola after the seventh century. Since it must be assumed that the ardent Modestus restored this monument, as he did the Holy Sepulchre, to its original form, there is no need to argue in a circle and insist that it originally had a wooden dome, because it had been built "after the likeness of the Church of the Resurrection." It is clear that the interior with a span of 68 feet could not have supported a masonry dome upon its light colonnade of twelve columns. Hence the assumption that it had a Syrian wooden dome open at the top.

8. *Tell Hūm*. In Capernaum there was discovered an octagonal church dating from about the middle of the fourth century.[28] It had an inner circle of columns with a diameter of 8.30 m. which Watzinger believes was covered with a wooden dome. It has been suggested by Dalman that it was a memorial chapel of the Comes Joseph of Tiberius and hence stood in the same relation to the palace as did Diocletian's tomb at Spalato and the *Domus aurea* at Antioch.

9. *Hierapolis, martyrium?* The ruined octagon (Fig. 82) with its large rectangular niches, which Koethe has shown was undoubtedly influenced by the "mausoleum of Constantine," was built sometime early in the fifth century and was probably a

[25] Vincent and Abel, *Jérusalem*, II, 360-419; Grabar, *Martyrium*, I, 282-291.
[26] Vincent and Abel, *op.cit.*, 413, IV/2; Arculphus, *Itinera* (P. Geyer, *Itinera Hierosolymitana*, C.S.E.L., XXXVIII, 1898), 246.
[27] Vincent and Abel, *op.cit.*, 413, II.
[28] Orfali, *Capharnaum*, 103, Taf. II; G. Dalman, *Palästinajahrbuch*, XVIII-XIX, 1922-23, 64f., and *Orte und Wege Jesu*, 1921, 133f.; Watzinger, *Denk. Paläs.*, II, 131f.

martyrium built in honor of the Apostle Philippus and his daughter.[29] Its restudied plan and proposed restoration by Krencker, which Koethe uses, show that its massive walls must have been covered with a masonry dome.

10. *Jerusalem, Tomb of the Virgin.* The octagonal memorial to the Virgin (Fig. 161), constructed in the imperial tradition, was built around the middle of the fifth century and had an interior colonnade with a diameter of 9 m.[30] Since it was a sepulchral monument, it must have continued the Roman tradition and been covered with a dome, as it was in the Islamic period when 'Ali of Herat described it: "The dome is supported by sixteen columns of granite and marble. . . . It was originally a church, but is now a Mashhad, or oratory, dedicated to Abraham the Friend.[31]

11. *Garizim, Church of the Theotokos.* Built by the Emperor Zeno about 484 A.D. this octagonal sanctuary had an interior span of 13 m. (Fig. 160) and an ambulatory divided into chapels.[32] It was a martyrium and place of pilgrimage not only because it possessed a relic of the rock of Calvary, but because the Virgin, after the Council of Ephesus, was honored in her quality of the Theotokos with sanctuaries of martyrium type.[33] In addition to referring to the seventeen churches which Justinian had built throughout his empire in honor of the Virgin, Procopius tells of the building of this church on the summit of Mt. Garizim by Zeno and how Justinian built fortifications around it to protect it from the Samaritans.[34] Presumably this octagonal structure, which was perhaps the first in a series of martyrium churches erected to the Mother of God, was domical like her tomb and the many later churches dedicated to her.

12. *Kal'at Sim'ân, Baptistery.* The fact that recent excavations have shown that this fifth century building, so well preserved up to the top of its drum, was a baptistery with its font in one of the apsidioles, does not mean that it may not also have been used as a martyrium.[35] Its octagon (Fig. 162), set into a rectangular exterior, has a span of about 14.78 m. These dimensions, the great height of the interior and the presence of bracket columns at the clerestory level to carry the roofing timbers all prove that it must have had a wooden roof. There would have been no necessity for these colonnettes if it had had a polygonal roof, for their location at the eight angles show that they were intended to carry the interior overhang of a dome at the corners.

[29] H. Koethe, "Das Konstantinsmausoleum und verwandte Denkmäler," *Jahrb. d. deut. arch. Inst.*, XLVIII, 1933, 198, Abb. 6, 7; Strzygowski, *Kleinasien*, XCIII, Abb. 67.

[30] Vincent and Abel, *Jérusalem*, II, 805-831; the roof was presumably always made of wood because in the twelfth century Daniel says, "Une grande église à toiture en charpente, consecrée à la assomption de la sainte Vierge ("Vie et pèlerinage de Daniel, Hégoumène Russe, 1106-1107," *Itinéraires Russe en Orient*, trans. by Mme. B. Khitro).

[31] Le Strange, *Palestine under the Moslems*, 210.

[32] Welter, *Forschungen u. Fortschritte*, 1928, p. 329; A. M. Schneider, *Deutschtum u. Ausland*, XXIII-XXIV, 1930, 83ff.; Watzinger, *Denk. Paläs.*, II, 134; Abel, "Les églises de Palestine récemment découvertes," *Atti del III Congresso internazionale di archaeologia cristiana*, 1934, 501f.; Crowfoot, *Early Churches in Palestine*, 37.

[33] Grabar, *Martyrium*, I, 325-326.

[34] Procopius (*Buildings*, Loeb, v, vii, 7, 17).

[35] De Vogüé, *Syrie centrale*, 153, pls. 149, 150; Butler, *Architecture and Other Arts*, 184-190.

The most compelling reasons for assuming that it had a celestial dome are symbolic ones, based upon the Early Christian relation between the baptistery and the tomb, or martyrium. It has already been made clear that the central-type baptistery derived its shape, and hence its mortuary, cosmic and heavenly dome, from the Roman mausolea and not from the pagan baths.[36] The ideational and structural relation between the polygonal baptistery and the polygonal martyrium, with its sepulchral origins and connotations, was much more than a matter of similarity of forms. During the Early Christian period, not only were burials frequently made in baptisteries, but baptisteries were also used as martyria.[37] As a result, Christian thought, at an early date, evolved a complicated symbolism wherein purification by water was linked with the death of the Old Adam, the martyrdom and resurrection of Christ and salvation by death.[38] Why the age came to see in the domical baptistery, as it had in the domical martyrium, the visible promise of eternal happiness and salvation in the heavenly domus of Christ, is made evident by the words of S. Basil, who said, "By imitating, through baptism, the burial of Christ" and by "being buried with Him by baptism."

The earliest baptisteries, however, were neither circular nor polygonal. Instead they were small rectangular chambers, usually with a small apse in which the font was placed. All the evidence at present indicates that the central and domical baptistery, with its mortuary implications, took shape in Italy, probably in the Lateran baptistery, and then in the fifth century began to spread to Ravenna, Syria and the East, but there is the probability that it was the Constantinian baptistery of the Holy Sepulchre which initiated the domical form. Syria, however, with two notable exceptions, continued to use the primitive type which was usually a chapel connected with the southeast corner of a church. In fact, Lassus's study of Syrian baptisteries shows how the violent controversies between the Monophysites, Nestorians and orthodox in the Patriarchate of Antioch resulted in some serious disagreements regarding the number, type and location of baptisteries and, perhaps, their use as martyria.[39] It may have been this religious conflict which explains the appearance of the polygonal baptisteries of Kal'at Sim'ân and Der Setā at a time when the symbolic dome was becoming common upon baptisteries in other parts of the Mediterranean.

13. *Der Setā, Baptistery.* This small hexagonal baptistery (Fig. 163) of uncertain date was first published by De Vogüé and can only be assumed to have been domical for the same reasons as the other exceptional baptistery at Kal'at Sim'ân.[40]

14. *Tyre, Church of the Theotokos.* A scholion in the text of Gregory of Nazianzus compares his octagonal martyrium (Fig. 28) to an octagonal sanctuary at Alexandria (Martyrium of S. John the Baptist?) and the "Theotokos naos at Tyre."[41]

[36] Krautheimer, *Journal of the Warburg and Courtauld Institutes*, v, 1942, 20-27; P. Styger, "Nymphäen, Mausoleen, Baptisterien," *Architectura*, I, 1933, 50ff.
[37] See pp. 56-57; Grabar, *Martyrium*, I, 79, 392, 445, etc.
[38] Krautheimer, *op.cit.*, 27.

[39] Lassus, *Sanctuaires*, 217-228.
[40] De Vogüé, *Syrie centrale*, 132, pl. 117; Butler, *Early Churches in Syria*, 155f., ill. 167; Lassus, *Sanctuaires*, 226.
[41] Birnbaum, *Rep. f. Kunstwiss.*, XXXVI, 1913, 192 n. 10; Watzinger, *op.cit.*, 133.

The uncertainty of the date of the annotation, which must be later than the middle of the fifth century when the Virgin was honored with the title of the Mother of God, does not allow us to attach much importance to this particular sanctuary in relation to the other domical martyria built in honor of the Virgin.

15. *Ba'albek.* The possibility that the hexagonal forecourt of the pagan temple at Heliopolis had been roofed over by the Christians and used as a sanctuary, and that its golden dome of wood had been carried off in 691 A.D. by Caliph al-Walīd to be rebuilt on the Sakra at Jerusalem has been discussed.[42] The sanctuary reconstructed out of the pagan forecourt may have been dedicated to the Virgin because there are references to such a rebuilding and dedication having taken place in 525 A.D.[43]

16. *Midjleyyā.* This octagon chapel (Fig. 164), published by De Vogüé and dated by Butler in the sixth century, was not open as De Vogüé suggested: the fragments seen by Butler show that "the interior octagon was carried up in a clerestory and was roofed in wood."[44]

17. *Zor'ah (Ezra), Martyrium of S. George, 515 A.D.* The domical history of this martyrium (Figs. 50-53), which has an interior span of 10.15 m., has already been discussed.[45]

18. *Mir'âyeh.* The interior dimensions of this small octagonal chapel (Fig. 165), or martyrium, are conjectural because the interior supports, suggested by Butler, were too deeply buried by debris to be seen.[46]

C. Square

The square, domical martyrium, which was a kind of monumental baldachin and comparable to the domical ciborium over the symbolic altar tomb of Christ, was in no sense derived from a hypothetical Iranian structure with a brick dome, such as Strzygowski endeavored to establish by comparisons with the later domical architecture of Central Asia. Instead, there is every reason to believe that it was also a late antique tomb-type, taken over by the Christians for their mortuary chapels, and in the process given the mystic meaning of a cosmic house. Between the fourth and sixth centuries it became common in Egypt at Bagawat (Fig. 86) and Kharga, while in Syria its resemblance to the native qubâb huts undoubtedly gave it an additional significance.[47] Although there are no extant examples of the square tomb with a free-standing dome in either Syria or Palestine before the tomb of Bizzos (Figs. 59-61), the type must have been common some time before the end of the Early Christian period in order to explain its widespread and persistent popularity as a heavenly abode among the Arabs. Through the Islamic period and down to the present the

[42] See p. 41.

[43] Devreesse, *Le Patriarcat d'Antioche,* 205f.; *Michael the Syrian,* IX, 16 (ed. Chabot, II, 1901, 179) and *Ps-Zacharia,* VIII, 4.

[44] De Vogüé, *Syrie centrale,* 101, pl. 63; Butler, *Early Churches,* 151; Lassus, *Sanctuaires,* 143f.

[45] See p. 49.

[46] Butler, *Syria,* II, B, 70, ill. 75; *Early Churches,* 192; Lassus, *Sanctuaires,* 142f.

[47] Grabar, *Martyrium,* I, 77-87.

domical weli, such as the tomb of Rachel (Fig. 84), has been common as a mortuary shrine and has continued to resemble the fifth century tomb of Bizzos. Even if the use of the domical tomb chapel was introduced into Syria by the Christians it was so similar to the native dwellings (Fig. 92), the celestial baetyl at Emesa (Fig. 126) and the pagan kalubé (Fig. 120) that it became and remained a popular type of mortuary shrine.

The adoption of this type of martyrium was not, however, limited to any one Christian region. It is now reasonable to suppose that in Asia Minor, for example, the fifth century square memorial over the tomb crypt of S. John at Ephesus (Fig. 83) was originally a monumental domical ciborium, whose early dome, presumably of wood, established the precedent for the two later enlargements and rebuildings as a cruciform and domical martyrium church.[48] The plan of this first, square martyrium should have the two undiscovered bases of the inner ciborium so placed that the sepulchral tegurium covered the relics. According to Grabar's theory that many Eastern churches were an enlargement by additions to an earlier martyrium, it is possible that S. Babylas at Kaoussie-Antioch (Fig. 170) was at first a square, domical tomb structure, enlarged by "exedras" into a cruciform church.[49] The highly imaginative way in which the Syrians looked upon this form of domical sanctuary as a cosmic replica of the universe and a mystic manifestation of divine presence is clearly shown by the *Sougitha*, a Syrian hymn describing the square and domical church of Hagia Sophia at Edessa.

19. *Edessa, Hagia Sophia.* The rebuilding of this square church under Justinian with a masonry dome was an effort to preserve the shape of an earlier structure, going back to 313 A.D., which presumably had a wooden dome. In describing the church the Syrian hymn refers not only to its starry vault but makes it clear that its four sides were believed to symbolize the four parts of the universe.[50] Before the significance of this Mesopotamian church can be evaluated in relation to the *Orient oder Rom* controversy, it should be recalled that Edessa was under the Patriarch of Antioch and was closely linked by religion and trade to the capital of Syria.

20. *Jerusalem, Holy Calvary.* If there was a domical sanctuary over the golden cross on Calvary in the *paradisus* between the Holy Sepulchre and the Martyrium, this one monument might well have popularized this type of memorial and its symbolical purpose. There has been much dispute about the architectural form of the chapel which stood on the mount called "Holy Calvary," "Holy Golgotha" and the "Tomb of Adam." While Vincent and Abel admitted that the cross of Theodosius may have stood under a ciborium[51] and have not refuted the arguments of Stegenšek that there was an ecclesia on the site from the time of Constantine,[52] they accepted the doubtful evidence of the mosaic of S. Pudentiana and assumed that the cross stood un-

[48] *Ibid.*, 154, 357ff.; J. Kiel, *Jahresh. d. öster. arch. Inst.*, XXVII, 1931, Beiblatt, fig. 47.

[49] Grabar, *Martyrium*, I, 359-360.

[50] See p. 90.

[51] Vincent and Abel, *Jérusalem*, II, 185ff.

[52] M. Stegenšek, "Die kirchenbauten Jerusalems im viertem Jahrhundert in bildlicher Darstellung," *Oriens christianus*, N.S., I, 1911, 280ff.

covered in the atrium with only a small chapel, or exedra, behind it. In addition to the difficulty of believing that a golden cross of such sanctity stood exposed at all times and in all kinds of weather, there is rather specific evidence to show that in the fifth and sixth centuries it was in a square and domical chapel which was essentially the same as the one built by Modestus after 614.

The reliable Anonymous in the sixth century wrote (*Codex Sangallensis*), "Et est ibi montis Calvariae ubi crucifixus Dominus fuit; et in circuitu montis sunt cancella de argento et ibi est esca ubi fuit ressucitatus per quam crux Christi declarata et ipsa crux est de auro et gemmas ornata et caelum de super aureum et deforas habet cancellum."[53] Regardless of whether *esca* was an abbreviation of *ecclesia*, or meant only an exedra, *caelum aureum* must refer to the golden and heavenly dome over the cross. Moreover, on several Palestinian ampullae (Fig. 166) the cross is depicted under what appears to be a ciborium, which was a late antique method of representing a heavenly covering.[54] The border of Apostle heads and stars shows that the cross was visualized as Christ in his celestial abode. It may be that we have a still more accurate reproduction of Holy Calvary on the sixth century mosaic (Fig. 168) in Hagia Sophia at Constantinople, which shows the jeweled cross on its mount and in a rectangular chapel surmounted by a pointed, conoid dome whose bands suggest wood construction and resemble the symbolic representation of Jerusalem (Fig. 15). Once the cruciform symbol of Christ is visualized in a tomb chapel, it is easy to see how the shape and associations of this type of memorial strengthened the old legend, which was so commonly believed in the East from as early as the fourth century, that the Holy Calvary, like a qubâb hut, was also the tomb and ancestral abode of Adam.

21. *Gerasa, S. John the Baptist.* Finished in 531 A.D., this church (Fig. 169) was a martyrium, as is indicated by its dedication, central plan and its location in relation to two flanking basilicas.[55] While it preserves, as does the cathedral at Bosra, the tradition of a circular rotunda within its square exterior, its specific memorial form is like a monumental ciborium at the center, consisting of four columns which supported the central roof. The reasons for restoring the central roof as a wooden dome (Fig. 167) are the memorial character of the building, the mortuary implications of the domical ciborium and the fact that the martyrium of S. John the Baptist at Alexandria, which was a rebuilding of the domical Serapeion, is pictured with a cupola (Fig. 30) on the mosaics at Gerasa.[56] The lightness of the supports and the absence of vaulting debris in the middle of the church make its wooden construction certain.

22. *Shakka, Martyrium of S. George.* An inscription of 323 or 368 A.D., which was discovered on the lintel of the pagan kalubé (Fig. 122), refers to the building as the

---

[53] Geyer, *Itinera Hierosolymitana*, 153ff., Vincent and Abel, II, 215.

[54] Celi, *Cimeli Bobbiesi*, fig. 9; Lesley, *Art Quarterly*, II, 1939, 226, fig. 2; the two examples of this scene on the Monza phials I believe are drawn incorrectly by Garrucci (*Storia*, VI, 1880, pl. 434/4, 8) because he mistook

the conventional serration of the arch of heaven for a wreath.

[55] Crowfoot, *Early Churches in Palestine*, 96, fig. 19.

[56] H. Grégoire and Kugener, *Marc le Diacre, Vie de Porphyre*, 137.

oecus "of the Holy Victorious Martyrs Georgios and the Saints with him."[57] In addition to this evidence that the domical kalubé had become a martyrium in the fourth century, De Vogüé found that the Christian altar had been located directly under the center of the dome.

D. Cruciform

The cruciform plan had a long history in pagan sepulchral architecture before its evident symbolism led to its adoption as a martyrium.[58] Proof that the dome was already associated with it is furnished by the Roman tomb of the Capella del Crocifisso (Fig. 171) at Cassino, which has a somewhat conoid-shaped vault of cut stone, 10.45 m. in diameter, over the intersection of the four arms.[59] The sculptural character of the stonework shows that it was not an experimental innovation. By the second or third century the cruciform tomb with a domical vault over the crossing (Figs. 78, 80) had become common in Palestine, and in the Christian period tombs with cruciform interiors were not uncommon in northern Syria, although only two of them (Figs. 59, 81) are known to have been covered with a dome.

As a martyrium the plan acquired its prestige after the construction of the church of the Holy Apostles by Constantius. In addition to the evidence which at least indicates that this fourth century martyrium, connected with the tomb of Constantine, had a wooden dome over its crossing,[60] the very fact that it and the martyrium of S. John at Ephesus were rebuilt by Justinian with masonry domes is a very strong indication that the symbolic dome was already associated not only with these two martyria, but with all cruciform martyria. This assumption is further strengthened by the fourth century martyrium at Nyssa (Fig. 27), which is known to have been domical.

By the fifth century the essential relation between cruciform plan and dome is proved by the crypt of S. Demetrios at Saloniki (Fig. 69), where a domical tegurium, as a receptacle of the relics, stands in the center of the cruciform chapel, by the domical and cruciform martyrium of the church at Ilissos,[61] and by the martyrium at Casaranello (Fig. 72), which has preserved its original dome (Fig. 71) decorated with a cross in a field of stars.[62] In the same century the tomb of Galla Placidia (Fig. 73), with its heavenly dome, is further confirmation of this symbolic relation, while Justinian's cruciform mausoleum in the sixth century is proof of its established prestige. That the Christians, as early as the fourth century, were fully aware of the inherent symbolism of the cruciform plan is evident from the references of Gregory of Nazianzus to the church of the Holy Apostles[63] and from the inscription of S. Ambrose in his cruciform church of the Holy Apostles at Milan, which read, *Forma*

---

[57] De Vogüé, *Syrie centrale*, 43; Butler, *Early Churches*, 249.

[58] Grabar, *Martyrium*, I, 152.

[59] *Ibid.*, 167 n. 2; C. Cecchelli, "Sguardo generale all' architettura bizantina in Italia," *Studi byzantini e neoellenici*, IV, 1935, 3-64.

[60] See p. 33.

[61] Sotiriou, Ἀρχ. Ἐφ., 1919, 1-31.

[62] R. Bartoccini, "Casaranello e i suoi mosaici," *Felix Ravenna*, XLIII, 1934, 157ff., fig. 6 (plan), fig. 19 (dome).

[63] Grabar, *Martyrium*, I, 152-153.

crucis templum est, templum victoria Christi sacra triumphalis signat imago locum.[64] Moreover, that the domical tomb was also a symbol of His triumph should not be overlooked in visualizing the form of these destroyed cruciform martyria.

23. *Antioch, Martyrium of S. Babylas at Kaoussie.* The report upon this church, uncovered by the Princeton excavations of 1935, was published by J. Lassus, and its identification as the martyrium of S. Babylas by G. Downey.[65] The saint was martyred in 250 A.D. and his remains, after being buried for a time in Antioch, were removed to a martyrium at Daphne and then brought back to Antioch where they were enshrined in his church at Kaoussie, "beyond the river." Inscriptions state that it was completed by 387 A.D. Since it was built by Bishop Meletius, who died in 381 and whose body was buried as a "fellow-lodger" with the remains of S. Babylas, it follows, as Downey pointed out, that the edifice "must have been well on the way towards completion before the burial could have taken place."

The central square (Fig. 170), which was the actual sanctuary and perhaps built first as Grabar has suggested, is 16.60 m. on a side with an interior span of about 13 m., and consists of four large piers, 4.50 m. to 4.78 m. on a side and varying in thickness from 1.58 m. to 1.90 m. The absence of any vaulting materials in the debris means that it must have had a wooden roof, as did the four naves which were undivided by columns and had walls only 0.70 m. thick. The church was entered at the western end and in the eastern nave were found several burials and no indication of either an altar or chancel. The fact that all four naves are at a lower level than the crossing and that inscriptions refer to them as *exedras* show that the square crossing was the sanctuary and that the arms were built, or added on, in order to provide space for those who flocked to the shrine and those who desired to be buried *ad sanctos*.

A large central platform with a semicircular west end was uncovered in the middle of the crossing. Its function as a high place upon which was located the altar will be discussed with the other Syrian examples of the central bema in the chapter on "The Place of Commemoration." Also in the crossing, but in the northwest corner, was discovered the double sarcophagus containing the remains of Bishop Meletius and the relics of S. Babylas. The reference of S. Chrysostom to this double burial shows how the age looked upon this tomb chapel as a monumental ciborium and cosmic dwelling. It was no empty figure of speech when S. Chrysostom described the two inmates of the tomb as "tent mates" (ὁμόσκηνος).[66] Most churchmen accepted both the authority of Isaiah, who said that God "established heaven as a vaulted chamber and stretched it out as a tent to dwell in," and the Hebrew tradition of the tabernacle, or tent of Moses, being a replica of the world. As a result, many theologians conceived of God's universal house, its domelike celestial roof and the salvational abode of martyrs as like a tent. *Skene*, therefore, in this cosmic and mystic sense was used for dome, or heavenly covering, in much the same way that Romans, Christians and

[64] Cabrol, *Dict.*, XI, "Milan," col. 1000.
[65] Lassus, "L'Église cruciforme de Kaoussié," and G. Downey, "The Shrines of St. Babylas at Antioch and Daphne," *Antioch-on-the-Oron-* *tes*, II, 1938, 5-48; Lassus, *Sanctuaires chrétiens en Syrie*, 123-128.
[66] Downey, *op.cit.*, 46 n. 10.

Arabs used tegurium, kalubé, maphalia and kubba to designate an ideal and heavenly dwelling in a blessed hereafter. A somewhat similar usage presumably went back to the early Greek use of skene, as a rustic shelter, which was synonymous with tholos.[67] Also a Roman variant of the same imagery has already been seen in the tomb of M. Clodius Hermes (Fig. 68) where a heavenly tent, with a crowd watching the transformation, was painted on the ceiling.[68] That the idea of referring to a double interment as "tent mates" was not peculiar to S. Chrysostom, is proved by Theodoret in his life of Theodosius, a holy man of Antioch, for he says that when Theodosius died he was buried with Aphraates in the same skene (ὁμόσκηνός τε καὶ ὁμορρόφιος) indicating again that skene was a celestial abode.[69]

By a devious and cosmic route we are brought back to the original question of restoring the shape of the roof over the center of this martyrium. In view of all that the dome had come to mean to the Christians, and its long association with the tomb, it is impossible to imagine that the square sanctuary of S. Babylas was open as has been suggested,[70] or that it was covered with a pyramidal roof of wood like so many Syrian tombs.[71] Not only is it difficult to believe that the Christians would have taken over the pyramid with its specific sun symbolism for a martyrium, but there are no monuments, Early Christian, Byzantine or Islamic which preserved any pyramidal tradition, for the pyramidal roofs in Italy, such as on the tomb of Galla Placidia (Fig. 73) and in Armenia, were to protect an interior dome. At every point where we can get behind the veil which separates us from Early Christian imagery we find evidence of the mystic habit of looking upon the domical shape as the shepherd's hut, a cosmic skene, imperial baldachin and ancestral dwelling, like the Syrian qubâb. Therefore, it is necessary to restore the martyrium of S. Babylas with a gilded wooden dome of conoid shape.

24. *Gaza, Eudoxiana*. The probability that the cruciform church, built in 407 to replace the pagan Marneion, was domical has already been discussed.[72] It is perhaps significant that it was constructed by an Antiochene architect who undoubtedly knew the martyrium of S. Babylas.

25. *Sichem*. Arculph in the seventh century left a sketch (Fig. 172) of the cruciform church over the well of Jacob.[73] It has been suggested by Grabar that the original martyrium was a square structure, similar to the crossing of S. Babylas and the first

[67] F. Robert, *Thymèlè*, 1939, 96; σκηνή was normally applied to rustic constructions of wood, but the terms Θόλος and Σκιάς were applied synonymously to rotundas, which all had a religious, memorial and at times mortuary function.

[68] P. Marconi, *La Pittura dei Romani*, 1929, 105, fig. 143; F. Wirth, *Römische Wandmalerei*, 1934, 190, pl. 50; C. Cecchelli, *Monumenti cristiano . . . eretici di Roma*, 1944, 184ff., pl. XXXII.

[69] Theodoret, *Relig. Hist.*, X, *P.G.*, LXXXII, 1393.

[70] Krautheimer, *Riv. di arch. cris.*, XVI, 1939, p. 356.

[71] Lassus, *Antioch-on-the-Orontes*, II, 34.

[72] See pp. 15, 39-40.

[73] Geyer, *Itinera Hierosol.*, 271; Arculphus, *De locis sanctis*, II, cap. 21, *De Puteo Samariae* (Migne, *P.L.*, LXXXVIII, 802); H. Graf, "Herr Professor Dehio und meine 'Neuen Beiträge . . .,'" *Rep. f. Kunstwiss.*, XVII, 1894, 128; Abel, "Le Puits de Jacob et l'église Saint-Sauveur," *Rev. bibl.*, XLII, 1933, 384-402; Grabar, *Martyrium*, I, 78, 155ff.

martyrium of S. John at Ephesus (Fig. 83), which was like a great domical and heavenly ciborium over the Fountain of Life, before it was extended into a cruciform plan to provide space in the arms for the pilgrims who gathered there. In the fourth century Aetheria mentions another sanctuary, near Charra, which was over another well of Jacob and may have been cruciform.[74]

26. *Kal'at Sim'ân, Church of S. Simeon Stylites*. The reasons advanced by Grabar for considering this famous pilgrim church, built between 460 and 490, a martyrium, and the evidence found by Krencker for restoring it with a wooden dome (Figs. 32, 36) over the central octagon have been discussed.[75]

27. *Mt. Admirable, Church of S. Simeon Stylites the Younger*. If it is necessary to believe that the great cruciform church at Kal'at Sim'ân had a wooden dome, it follows that the cruciform church of the younger Stylites (Fig. 173) built somewhat later near Antioch, had a similar dome over its crossing, for its octagonal crossing, only 8.50 m. on a side, would have been much easier to cover.[76]

28. *Jerusalem*. The Anonymous mentions a *basilica in cruce posita* which may have had a dome over the crossing of its nave and transepts as does the Aksa mosque (Fig. 43).[77] This may have been the church of the Temptation at Siloh.[78]

29. *Gaza, S. Sergius*. There is no question but that the church described by Choricius of Gaza was cruciform and surmounted by an imposing dome at the crossing. There still remains the question of whether it was a sixth century building or the fifth century Eudoxiana.[79]

E. Inscribed Cruciform

It is no longer possible to entertain the Strzygowskian theory that the domical and inscribed cruciform plan, which became so common in Byzantine architecture, had an Armenian origin. Not only was this type of plan used in the sepulchral architecture of Rome as early as the Augustan period,[80] but it had become fully established in Palestine and Syria in the Roman period. Palestinian examples of it have been seen in the pagan tombs of Amman (Fig. 78) and Kades (Fig. 80). The most developed Roman example, however, of the inscribed cruciform plan in Syria is the second century Tychaion at Mismiyeh (Fig. 174) which, like the domical kalubé at Shakka, was converted into a Christian church.[81] While there is much uncertainty regarding the form and construction of the roof over this now totally destroyed pagan sanctuary, it presumably had a kind of dome, perhaps a cloister vault, over its central crossing.

[74] *Peregrinatio* (Geyer, *op.cit.*, 68).

[75] See p. 34.

[76] P. Mécérian, *Comptes rendus de l'Ac. Inscr.*, 1936, 205; Écochard, *Bulletin d'études orientales de l'Institut français de Damas*, VI, fig. 14, p. 88; Lassus, *Sanctuaires*, 133ff., fig. 55.

[77] *Breviarias de Hierosolyma* (Geyer, *op.cit.*, 155); Grabar, *Martyrium*, I, 155.

[78] Vincent and Abel, *Jérusalem*, II, 844.

[79] See p. 39.

[80] Grabar, *Martyrium*, I, 170-175; in addition to such tombs as those of the Servilii (Rivoira, *Architettura romana*, fig. 9) and Priscilla (*ibid.*, fig. 125) he cites many examples drawn by Renaissance architects; Lassus, *Sanctuaires*, 116-120, for Syrian tombs.

[81] De Vogüé, *Syrie centrale*, pl. 7; Weigand, *Würzburger Studien zur Altertumswissenschaft*, XIII, 1938; A. S. Keck, "The Tychaion of Phaena-Mismiyeh," *A.J.A.*, XLV, 1941, 97.

The earliest known Christian use of this type of plan is the mortuary chapel of Hilarius (461-468 A.D.) which, prior to its destruction, was connected with the Lateran at Rome.[82] This oratory and the fact that the type penetrated the Balkans during the fifth century, where it was used for the church of Tsaritchin Grad in Serbia[83] and for the martyrium of Zacharius at Saloniki, suggest that it was already well known. If the little-known martyrium at Saloniki, which has a dome over the crossing, was, as Grabar has suggested,[84] "a Balkan reflection of a Palestinian cult which had spread to the West and as far as Ravenna in the fifth century," then it acquired its prestige from having been an established type of sanctuary in either Syria or Palestine. Since it occurs at Gerasa in the fifth century and became common in Syria during the sixth century, there is the possibility that the domical cruciform plan inscribed in a rectangle may have had its prototype in one of the unknown martyria of Antioch.

30. *Gerasa, Church of the Prophets, Apostles and Martyrs.* Built in 464/5 A.D. and uncovered by the Yale excavations, the church (Fig. 177) had some form of wooden roof over the crossing, which had a span of 8.80 m., because no remains of masonry were found in the ruins and, it might be added, because the columnar supports were not adequate to carry a vaulted clerestory.[85] It was rather tentatively suggested by Crowfoot that the crossing and four square corners may have been covered with wooden cupolas. There is no need to repeat the reasons why it is necessary to restore cruciform churches like this one, all more or less directly influenced by the church of the Holy Apostles at Constantinople, with a wooden dome over the center (Fig. 175). Quite apart from the mosaic of Khirbat Mukhayyat (Fig. 44), which depicts a church with domical towers,[86] there are ideological reasons for assuming that the four corners had wooden cupolas. Not only did many of the later Syrian churches have towers located at the four corners flanking the apse and western entrance, but oratories and relics were located in their chambers. In the next chapter it will be shown how the domical symbolism, originally associated with the martyrium proper, was gradually extended to the side-chambers, which had become the actual reliquary chapels after the martyria were used as regular churches and the basilicas acquired sacred relics.

31. *Resafa, "Grave Church."* There are three buildings at Resafa, which, contrary to previous reconstructions, will be presented as domical martyria. The so-called "Grave Church," lying outside the walls in the cemetery area, is the first to be considered, because it has the plan of an inscribed cross (Fig. 176). Its cruciform piers, shallow domes at the four corners of the inscribed cross, and elongated domes over the rectangular side-chambers are all important to the development of domical architecture. It has been dated in the later part of the sixth century, perhaps between

---

[82] P. Lauer, *Le Palais de Latran*, 1911, 51ff.; Grabar, *Martyrium*, I, 164.

[83] Grabar, *Martyrium*, I, fig. 57.

[84] *Ibid.*, 164, 180, 369, fig. 85; A. Xyngopoulos, 'Αρχ. Δελτ., XII, 1929, 142ff.

[85] Crowfoot, "The Christian Churches," *Gerasa* (ed. Kraeling), 256-260, plan XLI; Crowfoot, *Early Churches in Palestine*, 85ff., fig. 8.

[86] See p. 153.

569 and 582 A.D. When published by Sarre and Herzfeld and later restudied by Spanner and Guyer, it was restored without any clerestory and with a squat, pyramidal roof of wood over the central square, which has a width of 6.40 m.[87] The only reason for this restoration was the absence of any indications of a masonry dome and clerestory in the debris.

Both its date and the recent theory of Sauvaget that it was not a church but an audience hall of Alamounderos, a chieftain of the Ghassanids between 569 and 582 A.D., are based upon a crude Greek inscription which Macridy Bey saw inscribed upon the exterior of the apse.[88] It is difficult to believe that a chieftain of nomadic Christians, accustomed to living in tents, would have built a structure of this kind in a cemetery in order to hold court at the few times when the tribesmen gathered at Sergiopolis to observe the festivals of S. Sergius. While Alamounderos had his name inscribed on the sanctuary, it is most unlikely that he would have been satisfied with such a brief and curiously located inscription, if he had built the edifice for himself or contributed to its erection as a martyrium.

The finely executed stonework of Syrian character shows that the masons were working with customary forms and were not introducing flat, handkerchief domes over the corners and developing curiously elongated domes over the rectangular side-chambers either as experimental innovations or for merely utilitarian reasons. Both a structural and symbolic domical tradition lay behind their adoption here. Structurally, Syrian workmen were accustomed to fit small, cut-stone domes onto square bays.[89] Since Resafa lay on the direct trade route to the capital, and its churches were under the Patriarch of Antioch, there are strong reasons to believe that the work was done under the supervision of Antiochene builders and that there was a religious, Syrian precedent for the use of domical coverings over the corners and side-chambers, just as there was for restoring the central square with a symbolic dome of wood. In fact, it is not outside the realm of probability that the prototype for this church was one of the many martyria at Antioch.

32. *Zor'ah (Ezra), S. Elias.* The martyrium, which by an inscription is dated 542 A.D., has a cruciform plan (Fig. 54) with only the western angles brought to a rectangle.[90] The crossing, 6.65 m. E-W by 6.20 m. N-S, is today covered with a modern wooden dome sheathed in zinc (Fig. 56). The church was undoubtedly intended to be domical as it is at present; but it is impossible to agree with Lassus that it did not originally have a wooden dome because wood was too scarce. In view of all the evidence for the Syrian use of the wooden dome and the fact that "Zorava" was under

[87] Sarre and Herzfeld, *Archäologische Reise im Euphrat und Tigris-Gebiet,* II, 39-43. Abb. 152; H. Spanner and S. Guyer, *Rusafa,* 1926, 42, 66, Taf. 31.

[88] Sarre and Herzfeld, *op.cit.,* 41; Sauvaget, "Les Ghassides et Sergiopolis," *Byzantion,* XIV, 1939, 115ff.

[89] Creswell, *Early Muslim Architecture,* I,

309-319.

[90] Lassus, "Deux églises cruciformes du Hauran," *Bulletin d'études orientales de l'Institut français de Damas,* I, 1931, 13ff., figs. 1-9; "Les Monuments chrétiens de la Syrie septentrionale," *Atti del III Congresso internazionale di archeologia cristiana,* 1934, 481, fig. 4; *Sanctuaires chrétiens de Syrie,* 139f., 148, fig. 64.

the Church of Antioch, it does not follow that wood was any less transportable in the sixth century than it is today.

33. *Chagra, Martyrium*. Chagra, which is only a short distance from Zorah, has a sanctuary which its inscription calls a martyrium.[91] Although the date is missing from the inscription, its plan (Figs. 57, 58) and construction place it in the sixth century. Reconstructed after the fire which injured it during the Druze uprising of 1926, it now has a zinc-covered wooden dome. When Lassus first published the church he assumed it had an ovoid cupola of volcanic scoriae like the kalubé at Umm-iz-Zetum. It is again difficult to understand why he insisted upon a masonry dome when he admits that it would have been impossible to have placed a cupola on the octagonal dome as constructed, unless it was made of wood.

34. *Kasr ibn-Wardān, Palace Church*. The fact that the Palace church (Fig. 45), built in 561-564 A.D., was an imperial building, constructed by Byzantine craftsmen trained in the vaulting construction of Constantinople, is of great importance to Syrian architecture, because it has the only known baked-brick dome in either Syria or Palestine.[92] Its span of 6.66 m., its massive supports and the Roman manner in which the dome was concealed by buttressing on the exterior (Fig. 46) indicate that around the middle of the sixth century, and presumably under Justinian, the state was introducing the Roman hemispherical vault of masonry in place of the free-standing, conoid and wooden dome of Syria.

35. *il-Anderin, Chapel No. 3*. The small church, or chapel, restored by Butler with a pointed "concrete" dome (Fig. 47) like the one he saw on the martyrium of S. George at Zorah, has cruciform piers which divided the interior of the rectangular church into a cross with a square crossing 4.15 m. wide.[93] While it seems more probable that it had a wooden roof, as Herzfeld suggested for it and like the similar churches at it-Tûba and Resafa, it is too small to say that it could not have had a masonry dome. All that is reasonably certain is that it dated from the sixth century and had a dome over the crossing.

36. *it-Tûba, Church*. Dated by an inscription in 582/3 A.D., this church, in which Butler found one cruciform pier and two responds on the south wall, cannot be explained as a gabled-roof basilica, because a restoration of its plan (Fig. 178) shows that the western piers were so placed as to leave two square bays of about the same width as in the previous church.[94] There was no reason in this, or another similar church, to use cruciform piers spaced in square bays, if the roof was of gabled construction. In fact, it is to be noted that wherever cruciform, or T-shaped piers, occur in the churches of northern and northeastern Syria the bays are square and there are in many instances, such as at Resafa (Fig. 198) and Ruweha (Fig. 199), ideological reasons for restoring them with wooden domes. Therefore, its plan is presented as having had two wooden domes and having been comparable to several other churches

[91] Lassus, *Bulletin d'études . . .*, I, 1931, 23ff.; *Atti*, 480, fig. 3; *Sanctuaires*, 139, 147f., fig. 63.
[92] See p. 46.
[93] See p. 47.
[94] Butler, *Syria*, II, B, 19ff., ill. 17; *Early Churches in Syria*, 163f., ill. 175.

114

at il-Anderin (Figs. 200-202). It is equally possible that it had a gable roof over the western part of the nave and a single dome, as at Koja Kalessi (Fig. 194) and Bosra (Fig. 203), in front of the apse.

F. Four-lobed Cruciform

This type, which goes back in origin to the Roman use of apsidal exedrae (Fig. 179), should be taken up in conjunction with the more common trichora plan; but it is presented separately because of its cruciform character, and because it gave rise to a different form of church from the tri-lobed martyrium. Examples at Tivoli,[95] Perge[96] and, perhaps, the *tetranympheum*,[97] which Hadrian erected over the pool at Siloam, are evidence of its use in Roman architecture. Also its pre-Christian use in Syria may be indicated by the four-lobed martyrium which was constructed at Apamea out of a Roman building. The early adoption of the quatrefoil by the Christians as a form of tomb, or martyrium, in different parts of the Roman Empire is attested to by the domical mausoleum-like structure at Centelles in Spain, whose Christian scenes on the dome have been attributed to the early fifth century;[98] by the domical martyrium of S. Lorenzo at Milan, which although rebuilt in the fifth and sixth centuries, went back in origin to the fourth;[99] and by the martyrium at Athens, which was erected in the stoa of Hadrian, perhaps as early as the fourth century.[100] All other Early Christian examples, including those at Korykos, Bosra, Resafa and Amida, were in the Patriarchate of Antioch and suggest by their location, chronology and progressive changes that their Christian prototype was an early Antiochene martyrium.

The most significant example, which according to Grabar shows that the four-lobed plan was originally a tomb-type later enlarged by additions into a martyrium church,[101] is at Korykos in Cilicia.[102] Its plan (Fig. 180) and remains show that the original sanctuary was a free-standing quatrefoil over the tombs of the martyrs and that, like the original square martyrium at Ephesus (Fig. 83), it was later enclosed in a larger structure and its eastern apsidal exedra removed, or extended, in order to provide the apsidal sanctuary which would make it a church of Christ. At the time when Herzfeld and Guyer published their study of the ruins, they dated the building in the fifth or early sixth century, and insisted that the central grave structure with its four exedrae could not have been domical because the piers were not strong enough to have supported a masonry dome. Their objection to the central and original tomb-

[95] D. S. Robertson, *A Handbook of Greek and Roman Architecture*, 1929, fig. 134.

[96] K. Lanckoronski, *Städte Pamphyliens und Pisidiens*, I, 1890, 41, fig. 26.

[97] E. Wiegand, "Das Theodosioskloster," *Byz. Zeit.*, XXIII, 1914-1919, 179.

[98] F. Camprubi, "I Mosaici della cupola di Centcelles nella Spagna," *Riv. di arch. cris.*, XIX, 1942, 87-110.

[99] Grabar, *Martyrium*, I, 188; G. Chierici,

"Di alcuni resulti sui recenti lavori . . . ," *Riv. di arch. crist.*, XVI, 1939, 51ff.

[100] M. Sisson, "The Stoa of Hadrian at Athens," *Papers of the British School at Rome*, XI, 1929, 50-72; Grabar, *Martyrium*, I, 193.

[101] Grabar, *Martyrium*, I, 362ff.

[102] Herzfeld and Guyer, *Monumenta Asiae Minoris Antiqua*, II, *Meriamlik u. Korykos*, 1930, 126ff.

memorial having been what it was, a kind of cosmic dwelling with a celestial dome, of course has no validity if the symbolic cupola was constructed of wood. That the dome was always associated with this type of martyrium is further indicated in the sixth century by the "Red Church" at Perustica, which was domical, showing that this type of martyrium had the prestige to be introduced into Bulgaria.[103]

37. *Seleucia Pieria, Martyrium.* The plan (Fig. 182) and many of the mosaics of this martyrium at the port of Antioch were uncovered by the Princeton excavations at Antioch-on-the-Orontes.[104] The original construction of the church has been attributed to the fifth century. The absence of any remains of masonry vaulting and the dimensions of the central square, with a span of 12.50 m., too great to have been covered with a masonry dome on such slight supports, are ample justification for restoring it with a wooden roof. That its carpentry roof was pointed and slightly bulbous like the other conoid domes of Syria (Fig. 181) must be sustained by all that has previously been presented regarding the meaning of the dome, its mortuary association with the martyrium, and the use of wooden cupolas in the Near East. The whole building, with its golden dome, was to the Christians a mystic and monumental version of an ideal dwelling in Paradise, a kalubé or tegurium, such as was depicted on its sculptural relief (Fig. 94),[105] whose heavenly character was further indicated to the initiated by the pavement mosaics of the ambulatory wherein the pagan theme of ferocious animals in friendly combination with their natural prey, which to the Romans meant an idyllic past of love and happiness, was here a Christian symbol of the blessed hereafter.

The central quatrefoil, with its apsidal exedrae which were something over 8 m. wide, surrounded by an ambulatory of the same curvature, appears to be curiously separated from the rectangular east end. The plan has the effect architecturally of dividing the building into two ceremonially separate units, one the tomb memorial for the martyr's cult and the other the usual apsidal sanctuary where the eucharistic cult was celebrated at the altar tomb of Christ. Instead of a tomb chapel adjacent to the church of Christ, or a single domical tomb memorial, like the fourth century martyrium of S. Babylas, where the altar was on a platform in the center of the church, this fifth century martyrium suggests an effort to combine two types of sanctuary and, perhaps, two liturgical traditions. The key to this transitional type of church is the great platform filling the whole center of the martyrium proper and indicating that here, as in the early martyrium of S. Babylas, there was an altar and not just an ambon, as has been proposed. The liturgical implications of this bema and the probability that there were two altars in this church will be fully discussed in the chapter on "The Place of Commemoration." Also it will be seen in the sixth century martyria of Resafa (Fig. 184) and Amida (Fig. 185) how the experimental effort here at Seleucia Pieria to combine the domical, four-lobed martyrium with the customary

[103] A. Protitch, *L'Architecture religeuse bulgare*, 1924, fig. 4; Grabar, *Martyrium*, I, 193-194, 392.

[104] W. A. Campbell, "The Martyrion at Se-

leucia Pieria," *Antioch-on-the-Orontes*, III, 1941, 35-54, pl. x (plan).

[105] See p. 65.

church dedicated to the orthodox service led to further modifications of the plan in order to retain the symbolic features of the domical, lobed martyrium, but at the same time fully subordinated them to the liturgical preeminence of a single altar of Christ.

This gradual evolution in Syria of a domical, but orthodox, martyrium church is indicated by the changes which were made in the sixth century at Seleucia Pieria. After the fifth century martyrium had been seriously injured by an earthquake, perhaps the great one of 526 A.D., it was rebuilt with a baptistery on the north side of the eastern sanctuary and with a ceremonial chapel, probably a diaconicon, on the south side. At that time the bema in the martyrium was rebuilt and there remains the question of whether it had an altar which was used as a table of oblations in the service of commemoration. Certainly by the sixth century the relics were kept either in the baptistery or in the south side-chamber.[106]

38. *Apamea, Martyrium.* An important four-lobed martyrium with an ambulatory was uncovered in 1935 by the Belgian expedition and attributed to the sixth century.[107] Until the plan and a more complete report of the excavations have been published it is unwise to attempt to fit this building too definitely into the development of central-type churches in Syria. From what has been published it is not clear whether the whole, four-lobed structure was a Roman building taken over by the Christians, or whether only four Roman piers, which carried a groin vault of 11 m. on a side, were used. The presence of a pagan groin vault over the central square of a four-lobed martyrium would appear to contradict the basic contention of this study, that the symbolic dome was an essential feature of all such sepulchral memorials. Without any desire to force such uncertain evidence into conformity with a theory, the existence of the groin vault does not exclude an exterior, wooden dome. Since the lateral arches of the central square were the openings of the four apsidal exedrae, furnishing the abutment for the heavy masonry vault, the center of the structure would have been low and the vault would have required protection. Therefore, it is likely that a domical tower was carried up over the central vault.

39. *Bosra, Martyrium.* The cathedral of Bosra, built in 512 A.D., was a martyrium erected "under the God-beloved and most holy Julianos, archbishop," and dedicated to "Sergius, Bacchus and Leontius, martyrs who received the prize and triumphed gloriously."[108] Its plan (Fig. 49), which carefully preserved the traditional, quatrefoil type of tomb memorial, set like a sepulchral ciborium within a circular rotunda, represents a further development of the four-lobed plan in the Church's effort to transform a martyrium into a church, because here the apse and side-chambers are incorporated into the eastern side of the enclosing rectangle. The use of the side

---

[106] See p. 152.

[107] F. Mayence, "La Quatrième campagne de fouilles à Apamée," *Bulletin des musées royaux*, series 3, VII, 1935, 2ff.; *Antiquité classique*, IV, 1935, 199-204; "Les Fouilles d'Apamée," *Bulletin, académie royale de Belgique, classe de lettres*, 1939, 340; L. de Bruyne, "La Quarta campagna di scavi in Apamea . . . ," *Riv. di arch. crist.*, XIII, 1936, 332-338; Grabar, *Martyrium*, I, 346; Lassus, *Sanctuaires*, 55, 137, 153, 163, 171.

[108] See p. 48.

chambers as oratories for the relics and the original ceremonial purpose of the martyrium proper, which is still architecturally cut off by columns from the altar of Christ, will be discussed in the next chapter.[109] The main issue here is the domical character of the exterior.

Before the interior was excavated both De Vogüé and Brünnow introduced an interior colonnade and restored the church with a hemispherical masonry dome, and Howard Butler, believing he had found evidence of an interior octagon of piers, crowned his restoration with a structurally impossible masonry dome, conoid and unbuttressed, which was c. 24 m. in diameter and rose to a height of about sixty feet. Recognizing that the cathedral must have been one of the prototypes for the later Arab mosques, Herzfeld reduced the interior space and restored it with a wooden dome. After Crowfoot excavated the interior and discovered its lobed plan, he recognized the possibility that it might have had a wooden dome, but had it restored by Detweiler with a polygonal roof on an octagonal drum.[110] A recent restorer, taking the position that the cathedral was "a happy, if somewhat faulty, improvisation" by a local designer in a provincial city, has given it a western, Romanesque appearance with a square tower and pyramidal roof rising out of the center.[111]

The significance of this most recent restoration is not its accuracy, but the modern approach to the problem, which thinks of an Early Christian builder as an artistically objective and free "man who had an idea." While architects made individual contributions to every building whose erection they supervised, matters of plan, exterior form and even fenestration were of too much religious importance and too directly under both state and ecclesiastical control to be left to the discretion of an individual. The builder of the cathedral at Bosra was probably an architect of Antioch and his design was an ecclesiastical question involving symbolism, liturgy and the policy of the Church at Antioch. Therefore, the issue of whether the cathedral had a wooden dome, as it is shown here in a tentative restoration (Fig. 49), is not to be decided by modern architectural standards of functionalism and appearance. From what is known about the Christian's habit of seeing spiritual meanings in all the parts of his church, we must put ourselves back into another climate of opinion, and either restore a martyrium, like this church at Bosra, with a gilded dome or show that a pyramidal, or polygonal, roof had a comparable meaning to this age.

40. *Resafa, Martyrium.* The second of the three churches which it is proposed should be restored with wooden domes, the martyrium (Fig. 184), assigned by Sarre and Herzfeld and Spanner and Guyer to the late sixth or early seventh century, was a further development of the four-lobed plan of the Antiochene church at Seleucia Pieria.[112] The remains of this sanctuary on the eastern border of Syria have been misinterpreted, first, because in its ruined condition so many essential features of its plan were concealed in the debris and, second, because of the prevailing misconcep-

[109] See p. 150.
[110] Crowfoot, *Churches at Bosra and Samaria-Sebaste*, and *Early Churches in Palestine*, 94ff.
[111] M. Golding, "The Cathedral at Bosra,"

Archaeology, I, 1948, 151-157.
[112] Sarre and Herzfeld, *Archäologische Reise*, II, 28-39; Spanner and Guyer, *Rusafa*, 35-38, 56-62, Taf. 25.

tion regarding the importance of the domical church in Syria. Although Sarre and Herzfeld considered its plan to be a combination of a trichora with a basilica, Spanner and Guyer restored it, without regard for its apsidal exedrae, as a basilica. Later Guyer modified the restoration so that the church had a square tower covered with a gable roof.[113] The ruined and buried condition of the interior may make it uncertain whether the central square with flanking apses had L-shaped piers, like those at Seleucia Pieria and Bosra, or detached columns, as at Kal'at Sim'ân, to carry the transverse arches making it a central church. The dimensions of what remains, however, establish its central character and show how it was a modification of the four-lobed cruciform plan.

By taking the existing width of the northwest pier with its responds at *a* and applying that dimension on either side of the lateral apses at *b*, *c*, *d* and *e*, a central square is formed with a span of 10.50 m., while the doorways into the ambulatory become proportionate on both sides of the nave. Also it will be noted that the central square and lateral apses about 7.50 m. in width are approximately the same as those of Seleucia Pieria. Hence the resultant plan reveals a conscious and purposeful modification of the plan at Seleucia Pieria. Instead of having the eastern sanctuary tacked onto the central martyrium, the east and west exedrae of the original, four-lobed plan were pulled out, thereby keeping the domical and cruciform character of the memorial elements, but subordinating the Cult of Martyrs and Relics to the Eucharistic cult. These essential modifications in the plan, creating a kind of domed basilica (Fig. 183) were the result of the growing desire of the Church, whose power in Syria was in the hands of the Patriarch of Antioch, to establish a more orthodox liturgy and a more uniform type of church which preserved the popular symbolic features of the traditional martyrium with its heavenly dome and at the same time centered the service in the eastern apse, where the one altar of the church was the tomb, communion table and throne of Christ.[114]

Resafa, at the time when this martyrium was built, had an earlier martyrium of S. Sergius, its patron saint, which will be taken up as a domed basilica.[115] Why then should it have had two martyria, in addition to the "Grave Church" outside the walls? The most reasonable explanation is that sometime after Sergiopolis had been made a metropole, and, perhaps, at the time when the "Place of Commemoration" in the center of the early martyrium of S. Sergius was no longer considered orthodox, the old martyrium was turned into a regular basilica church by the introduction of columns between the piers of the nave (Fig. 198) and a new martyrium of S. Sergius was erected, conforming to the ceremonial requirements after the Great Entrance and the service in the prothesis chapel to the north of the apse had been accepted by the Church at Antioch.

41. *Amida, Church of the Virgin.* It is not surprising to find even in Mesopotamia a church of the Virgin, presumably dating from the end of the sixth or the

[113] S. Guyer, "Vom Wesen der byzantinischen Kunst," *Münchner Jahrbuch*, VIII, 1931, 104, Abb. 3.

[114] Grabar, *Martyrium*, I, 335-357.

[115] See p. 126.

beginning of the seventh century, which was essentially the same as the martyria at Resafa and Seleucia Pieria, because the diocese of Amida was under the religious jurisdiction of Antioch. After the Council of Ephesus had recognized the Virgin in her capacity as the Mother of God and her domical tomb was erected at Jerusalem, her cult became very popular in the sixth century and many churches of the domical, martyrium type were dedicated to her in the Patriarchate of Antioch.[116] The plan of this church (Fig. 185), which Miss Bell and then Guyer reconstructed from the scanty evidence in the midst of centuries of Islamic rebuilding, is little more than an indication of its general outlines.[117] In republishing Guyer's hypothetical plan I have made the same addition which was made to the plan of the martyrium at Resafa, in order to show that the center of its traditional, lobed design was a square, covered by a dome. With the addition of this transverse arch, carried on columns, which repeats a similar arch at the beginning of the apsidal sanctuary, it is seen how this church fits into the development of Syrian architecture, emanating from Antioch, and is not, in any sense, an indication that the dome and tri-lobed plan were Iranian elements here being introduced into the Christian East, as Strzygowski asserted in his *Amida*.

G. Tri-lobed

The trefoil plan, usually surmounted by a dome, was taken over by the Christians from the sepulchral architecture of the Romans and at first used for small mortuary chapels, then enlarged into more monumental martyria and finally combined with the basilica to produce a new type of church with a memorial chevet. In Roman architecture, where it originated, Strzygowski to the contrary, the domical *cella trichora* presumably had a cosmic and celestial symbolism as a sepulchral shelter and imperial audience hall, while the tri-apsidal plan when used for nymphaea, baths, palaces and other public monuments must have had comparable divine and royal connotations. During the proto-Christian period it was the Roman sepulchral use of *cellae trichorae* (Fig. 186), as Grabar has pointed out,[118] which led to their adoption for small martyria, but, by the end of the fifth and during the sixth century, when the tri-lobed chevet began to be popular in the Near East, the Christians were undoubtedly influenced by the royal implications of the trichora as it was used as an audience hall and triclinium in the imperial palaces.[119]

[116] See Chap. v n. 33.

[117] M. van Berchem and Strzygowski, *Amida*, 1910, 187-207; Sarre and Herzfeld, *Archäologische Reise*, II, 32 (plan of Guyer), Abb. 149; Lassus, *Sanctuaires*, 154, fig. 70.

[118] Grabar, *Martyrium*, I, 102-119; the mortuary use of the tri-lobed plan was not peculiar to Rome, for it occurs in a hypogeum of 108 A.D. at Palmyra (R. Amy and H. Seyrig, "Recherches dans la nécropole de Palmyre," *Syria*, XVII, 1936, 229ff., pl. XXXI).

[119] A summary of Strzygowski's theory of the Eastern origin of the trefoil plan in "Der Ursprung des trikonchen Kirchenbaues," *Zeitschrift für christliche Kunst*, XXVIII, 1915. The refutation of this assumption and proof of classical origin in the following: E. Weigand, "Das Theodosioskloster," *Byz. Zeit.*, XXIII, 1914-19, 167-216; A. Blanchet, "Les Origines antiques du plan tréflé," *Bull. Mon.*, 1909, 450ff.; Vincent, "Le Plan tréflé dans l'architecture byzantine," *Rev. archéol.*, series 5, XI, 1920, 82-111; E. H. Freshfield, *Cellae Trichorae*, II, 1918.

The use of the tri-apsidal motif for pagan tombs, while rare in Syria, does occur in a second century hypogeum at Palmyra.[120] In the same century the tri-lobal plan occurs at Kanawat at the end of a rectangular hall, which was, perhaps, dedicated to the Cult of the Caesars as part of a palace complex and later was incorporated into a Christian basilica.[121] By the sixth century it must have been common in Syria because it was used as an audience hall in the episcopal palace at Bosra[122] and in the imperial palace at Kasr ibn-Wardān.[123]

The adoption of the trefoil plan by the Christians appears to have taken place at Rome where there were four *cellae trichorae*, used as oratories and martyria-mausolea, of which the two in connection with the catacombs of S. Callixtus may date from the third century.[124] It has been suggested that these early oratories were originally open on the sides, like a sepulchral ciborium.[125] By the fourth century the tri-apsidal martyrium had begun to spread to Pannonia, Gaul and North Africa.[126] Unfortunately for the purposes of this study there is no evidence to prove that the earliest examples were domical, and in North Africa it is known that they were frequently covered with groin vaults which may, or may not, have been decorated in the Roman fashion with domical motifs. Nevertheless, the whole history of domical symbolism, the Roman use of the domical *cella trichora* for tombs, audience halls, state dining rooms and public baths, and the spread after the fifth century of domical, tri-lobed churches in the Near East all combine to sustain the assumption that the symbolic dome was usually an essential feature of this type of martyrium.

Outside of Syria and Palestine there are a number of Eastern churches which show that the dome was commonly associated with the tri-lobed memorial. Among these are the remarkable little sanctuary discovered by Howard Butler in the ruins of the great temple at Sardis,[127] the martyrium attached to the south side of the early church at Corinth,[128] the mortuary chapel on the north side of the apse at Tolemaide (Fig. 214), and the Coptic churches at Sohag, Dendera and Nagada with their tri-apsidal chevets.[129] The evidence in Syria and Palestine that the dome went with this type of plan is unsatisfactory, largely because of the ruined, or rebuilt, condition of the churches. Although the famous reliquary of Aachen (Fig. 188), is late, having been made for a *stratigos* of Antioch between 969 and 1080 A.D.,[130] it is an indication of the early existence of this type of domical martyrium, because no such elaborate architectural receptacle for relics would have been made, even in the eleventh century, unless there had been a long-established and well-recognized precedent. It is, there-

[120] Amy and Seyrig, *Syria*, XVII, 1936, 229ff.; Grabar, *Martyrium*, I, 116.

[121] De Vogüé, *Syrie centrale*, pls. 19, 20; Butler, *Architecture and Other Arts*, 357-361; 402-405; fig. 126.

[122] Butler, *Syria*, II, A, 288, ill. 248.

[123] Butler, *Syria*, II, B, 34-40, pl. IV.

[124] Grabar, *Martyrium*, I, 102-109.

[125] F. X. Kraus, *Gesch. d. christl. Kunst*, I,

1896, 264; Grabar, *Martyrium*, I, 105.

[126] Grabar, *Martyrium*, I, 106ff.

[127] Butler, *Sardis*, I, 1922, 170-174, fig. 189.

[128] Sotiriou, 'Αρχ. 'Εφ., 1919, 1-31; 1931, 208-210; Grabar, *Martyrium*, I, 336ff., fig. 44.

[129] Grabar, *Martyrium*, I, 384.

[130] G. Schlumberger, "L'Inscription du reliquaire . . . ," *Mon. Piot*, XII, 1905, 201-205, pl. XIV.

fore, probable that the reliquary preserves the shape of some renowned martyrium church at Antioch.

The peculiar non-masonry dome on the Aachen reliquary was not, as many have thought, a creation of Arab fancy, because this melon-like shape occurs during the Early Christian period in specific relation to both regular and theophanic martyria. In the Codex Rossanensis it is depicted in the scene of the Entry into Jerusalem (Fig. 16) upon a building which was probably the Holy Sepulchre, while in the scene of the translation of relics on an Early Christian ivory of Trier Cathedral (Fig. 152) a melon dome covers the tomblike martyrium. It also occurs on the martyrium of the Holy Athenogenes (Fig. 153) and appears in the Syrian landscape on the mosaics at Damascus (Fig. 41). Presumably this kind of cupola, which must have taken shape in wood carpentry, went back in origin to the idea of the petal rosette, which had for centuries been common upon the lotus cups of Egypt where it had a life-giving symbolism. By the time when the heavenly dome was beginning to acquire so much significance in Christian imagery there was a linguistic, and probably a symbolic, relation between the petal motif and the word κιβώριον, which meant cup, lotus, and a domical ritualistic covering with mortuary implications, while for centuries in India it had been customary to combine the lotus flower with the celestial dome (Fig. 139). Hence, the appearance of the petal motif, or lotus rosette, on the domical ceiling of a pagan tomb at Tall Hinnom (Fig. 77) and on the apsidal half-dome of the martyrium of S. Sergius at Resafa (Fig. 183) is evidence as to the symbolic origin of the melon-shaped dome and how it came to take shape in wood carpentry.

42. *Siyagha, Mt. Nebo, Memorial of Moses.* A *cella trichora* (Fig. 187) which was an early memorial to Moses was uncovered on Mt. Nebo.[131] The intrusion of five tombs before the fifth century place the date of this memorial in the fourth century, or earlier, and make it the earliest known oratory of its kind in Palestine. During the fifth century, when the site was visited by pilgrims, the tri-apsidal sanctuary was incorporated into a basilica which was destroyed and replaced late in the sixth century by a second basilica. Although no indications were found as to the covering over the ancient sanctuary, I have presented the plan with a suggested dome, which not only fits the space but would have preserved the heavenly significance of the original tomb shelter of Moses. In the early seventh century chapel on the south side of the nave, which was both a martyrium and chapel of the Theotokos, the mosaic shows two bulls, or a bull and a lion, on either side of a domical ciborium which has been called the tabernacle of Yahweh, such as was represented on Hebrew coins (Fig. 151).[132]

43. *Jerusalem, Church of S. John the Baptist.* It is generally believed that the martyrium of John the Baptist with its tri-apsidal east end (Fig. 189) always had a

---

[131] S. J. Saller, *The Memorial of Moses on Mount Nebo*, 1941; P. B. Bagatti, "Edifici cristiani nella regione nel Nebo," *Riv. di arch. crist.*, XIII, 1936, 101ff., pls. II, III.

[132] Saller, *op.cit.* (I, 233ff., fig. 30; II, pl. 109), merely refers to the domical tabernacle as an arched gateway.

dome of masonry over the central square with its span of 5.15 m.[133] Although the church is not mentioned before the beginning of the sixth century, it is thought to have been erected around the middle of the fifth century and to be the earliest Palestinian church of its type. Nothing is known about the shape of the earlier memorials of the Baptist at Sebaste (before 362), Constantinople (394), Alexandria (396), Damascus (c. 400) and Emesa (453), except that the one at Alexandria replaced the domical Serapeion and is depicted upon the mosaics at Gerasa with a dome (Fig. 30).

44. *Der Dosi, Theodosios Church.* The tri-apsidal and domical church of the Theodosios cloister (Fig. 190), with its span of 5.10 m., was similar to the martyrium of John the Baptist. It was probably built in the second half of the fifth century and the early part of the sixth.[134]

45. *Gerasa, cella trichora.* On the south side of the church of S. Theodore (494-496 A.D.) was discovered an early *cella trichora*, probably a martyrium, which, when it was rebuilt as the baptistery of the fifth century church, had its side niches concealed.[135]

46. *Mt. Admirable, S. Simeon Stylites the Younger.* On the south side of the eastern arm of the main church was a large three-aisled chapel which had a *cella trichora* in place of an apse (Fig. 173). This exceptional sanctuary, which looks as if it may have been added after the chapel was built, was probably a martyrium and, as such, should have been covered with a small dome.

47. *Madaba, Church of the Theotokos.* The plan of this church, dedicated to the "Sovereign Mother of God" is only known from a rough sketch (Fig. 191) of its outlines which were seen imbedded in modern houses.[136] Although usually described as if it had been a rotunda with a large apse, the sketch published in 1892 indicates that it might have been tri-apsidal.[137]

48. *Gaza, Church of S. Stephen.* The account of Choricius, which describes the sixth century church as a basilica with a tri-apsidal east end covered with a wooden dome, has already been discussed.[138]

49. *Sinai.* A church at Sinai, purporting to have been built over the grave of Aaron, had lateral apses in the exterior walls, while on the interior four columns supported a small dome on a low drum.[139] The building, which presumably dates from the sixth century and was later incorporated into an Islamic weli, may have been the church dedicated to the Mother of God that Procopius (Bldgs., v, 8, 4) says

[133] Vincent and Abel, *Jérusalem,* II, 642-668, pl. LXV; Watzinger, *Denk. Paläs.,* II, 137f.

[134] E. Weigand, "Das Theodosioskloster," *Byz. Zeit.,* XXIII, 1914-19, 167-216, Abb. 2.

[135] Crowfoot, "The Christian Churches," *Gerasa* (ed. Kraeling), 224.

[136] D. G. Manfredi, "Piano generale delle antichità di Madaba," *Nuovo bolletino di archeologia cristiana,* series 6, v, 1889, 152ff.;

Cabrol, *Dict.,* "Madaba," col. 862, fig. 7421; Grabar, *Martyrium,* I, 325.

[137] P. M. Séjourné, "Médeba," *Rev. bibl.,* I, 1892, 638ff., fig. 6.

[138] See p. 38.

[139] T. Wiegand, *Sinai (Wissenschaftliche Veröffentlichung des deutsch-türkischen Denkmalschultz-Kommandos,* 1), 1920, 136ff.

Justinian built for the monks at the place where Moses received the Tables of the Law.

50. *Ed-dschunêne.* This grave memorial, built, according to Schneider, during the early Byzantine period in connection with a ruined Greek monastery, is of such massive construction as to indicate that its central square (Fig. 192), with a span of 6.51 m., carried a masonry dome.[140]

51. *Antioch, Church of S. Martha.* Nothing is known about this church, which was presumably a martyrium, except that it had a tri-apsidal plan.[141]

Doubtful Examples. The churches at *et-Taijibe*[142] and *Rouhaibed*,[143] which have been cited as having a tri-apsidal plan, are not listed as presumably domical structures because of the uncertainty of their date and the fact that their lateral apses were so much smaller than the eastern apse as to make it unlikely that they had a square crossing, necessary for domical construction.

H. Rectangular

Grabar recognized the ideological significance of the domed basilica as a form of martyrium[144] when he challenged Strzygowski's theory as to its origin, and called attention to the dome in front of the apse on the fifth century, three-aisled church at Ilissos,[145] near Athens, and over the center of the nave at Tsaritchin Grad in Serbia, dating from about 500 A.D.[146] He did not, however, raise the question of how and where the type originated, except to imply that it would not have appeared during the fifth century in such widely separate places as Serbia and Greece unless it had already been an established and venerated type of sanctuary. Although there were rectangular and gable-roofed oratories and mortuary chapels among the early martyria, which were taken over from the sepulchral architecture of the late antique period,[147] it was probably not this type of rectangular chapel which was transformed into a domed martyrium church because of the growing tendency during the fourth and fifth centuries to associate the symbolic dome with all martyria. Instead, there are reasons to assume that at this time, when the popularity of the Cult of Martyrs was enlarging the domical martyria into monumental places of worship and the eastern churches were endeavoring to adapt such structures to the eucharistic service, the basilica was given the distinction of a martyrium church by, at first, substituting a wooden dome for the gable roof. The process, which was all part of the growing importance of the symbolic dome in the Near East, produced several variants by introducing the dome in front of the sanctuary, by raising a single dome over the center of the nave, and by covering the whole nave with one or more domes.

[140] A. M. Schneider, *Oriens Christianus*, series 3, V, 1930, 236-239.

[141] Cabrol, *Dict.*, I, 2379; *Acta Sanct.*, "May," V, 421; *Mart.*, II, 421.

[142] A. M. Schneider, "Die Kirche von et-taijibe," *Oriens Christianus*, series 3, VI, 1931, 15ff.

[143] Vincent and Abel, *Bethléem*, 30, fig. 6.

[144] Grabar, *Martyrium*, I, 393-399.

[145] Sotiriou, 'Αρχ. 'Εφ., 1919, 1-31; 1931, 208-210; Grabar, *Martyrium*, I, 336, 394, fig. 43.

[146] Grabar, *Martyrium*, I, 180, 394, fig. 57; only briefly published since excavations in *Starinar*, XII, 1937, 81-92; XIII, 1938, 179-196.

[147] Grabar, *Martyrium*, 87-102.

Where, then, did this form of domical church develop? As long as the domed basilica was thought of in the structural terms of a masonry dome and only in relation to those churches of Asia Minor whose ruins chanced to preserve the pier construction which was considered necessary for domical vaulting, it was impossible to trace the type back to its ideological origins. Strzygowski, before he became involved with his theory of Armenian and Iranian origins for Byzantine architecture, came very near to the truth when he suggested that the domed basilica was a late Hellenistic type of building, originating perhaps in Antioch.[148] There were two reasons why this possibility was not given more careful consideration: one was the prevailing misconceptions regarding the absence of the dome and the uniform gable-roof tradition in Syria which led scholars to overlook the evidence for the domical basilica in the Antiochene sphere of influence; and the other was the tendency to identify the earliest known examples of the type, which were discovered in Isauria and Cilicia, with Asia Minor rather than with Antioch. In endeavoring to trace the domed basilica back to its origins, it is necessary to keep in mind the early use of the wooden dome, which did not require massive supports. Also, in considering the importance of the churches at Koja Kalessi and Meriamlik, it should be recalled that Isauria and Cilicia, while geographically in Asia Minor, were under the religious domination of Antioch. This meant that the development of religious architecture in these regions was strongly influenced by the architects and workmen of Antioch, as well as by its powerful Patriarch. In fact, Koja Kalessi should be considered an Antiochene church, which helps to explain the plan and construction of a number of churches in Syria.

In the monastic church at Koja Kalessi (Fig. 195) there are two cruciform piers with columns to carry the transverse arches over the nave.[149] The use of columns for the support of arches resembles Kal'at Sim'ân, Amida (Fig. 185) and the proposed restoration for the martyrium at Resafa (Fig. 183), while the introduction of columns between the piers of the nave arcade recalls the martyrium of S. Sergius at Resafa (Fig. 198). The transverse arches divide the nave, leaving a large, rectangular bay in front of the sanctuary. The walls of this one bay were not only carried up higher than the bays on either side (Fig. 194), but had at the corners niche squinches on colonnettes, like those in the octagon at Kal'at Sim'ân (Fig. 36) and in the north tower of the Sergius martyrium at Resafa (Fig. 197). The presence of these squinches, as Headlam recognized, was to bring the rectangle to an octagon and provide the necessary imposts for a dome. The absence of any vaulting debris in the nave, and the fact that this dome had to be made of wood, has troubled scholars who were accustomed to think of domes in terms of masonry construction.[150] The date of this church, whose sculptural details and construction show the influence of North Syrian architecture,

[148] Strzygowski, *Kleinasien*, 131.

[149] A. C. Headlam, *Ecclesiastical Sites in Isauria* (*Journal of Hellenic Studies*, Suppl. Papers, 1), 1893; Strzygowski, *Kleinasien*, 109-115; figs. 78-80; O. Wulff, *Altchristliche und byzantinische Kunst*, I, 255; Creswell, *Early Muslim Architecture*, II, 109f.

[150] Although Strzygowski assumed that it must have had a masonry dome, Headlam carefully emphasized that "there is no sign of débris in the church sufficient to have formed a dome."

was placed by Headlam sometime before 461 A.D. Strzygowski endeavored to push the date back to the fourth century, while Wulff favored the second half of the fifth century. It is, therefore, safe to assume that it was built sometime around the time when the great monastic church at Kal'at Sim'ân was constructed, and, what is more important, that it preserved in all probability an Antiochene type of domed basilica.

The second domed basilica that may have some bearing upon reconstructing certain churches of Syria is at Meriamlik.[151] It was published by Herzfeld and Guyer, who dated it around 470 A.D. and suggested that it might have been erected by the Emperor Zeno. The massiveness of the piers (Fig. 193) is a clear indication that it had a masonry dome over the nave. Here, however, as at Koja Kalessi, the piers formed a square and domical bay in front of the sanctuary, while columns were used between the piers in the nave arcades. It is true that all the evidence from as early as the fourth century, when Gregory was building his cruciform and domical martyrium at Nyssa,[152] implies that the growing shortage of building lumber for domical and gable roofing in Asia Minor had led to the early development of masonry vaulting. Nevertheless, it seems more likely that this church at Meriamlik (Seleucia), which could easily have imported lumber from Syria, was built in the sixth century, at the time when masonry domes were becoming more common in North Syria. It should be noted for later reference that on the south side of this church is a partially excavated structure which may have been a tomb.

Before leaving these two churches in the northern part of the Patriarchate of Antioch and turning to similar Syrian churches, which I propose to restore with transverse arches and wooden domes, it is fair to point out that although the restoration of these Syrian churches with domes is hypothetical, their previous restorations with gable roofs was also hypothetical. In every example where a domical restoration is suggested there are either cruciform or T-shaped piers to show that the nave was, or could have been, divided into square bays. The argument that these piers with transverse arches were developed to save roofing timber does not seem valid, because the construction of heavy stone arches would have required more timber, as centering, than would have been saved in the gable roof. Furthermore, it will be noted that in every church where such piers were used, the builders went to some trouble to place the piers in such a way as to get one, or more, square bays. This would not have been necessary, especially as a means of saving roofing timbers, if the arches were merely intended to carry a gable roof. The basic reason, however, for insisting upon a domical restoration for many of these churches is an ideological one, for the churches at Ruweha (Fig. 199) and il-Anderin (Fig. 200) had tomb buildings adjacent to them, as did the similar domed basilicas at Ilissos, Tsaritchin Grad and, perhaps, Meriamlik.

52. *Resafa, Martyrium of S. Sergius.* The first church (Fig. 198) at Resafa, the city of the martyred S. Sergius, could date from about 434 A.D., when the city was made

---

[151] E. Herzfeld and S. Guyer, *Monumenta Asiae Minoris Antiqua*, II, *Meriamlik und* Korikos, 1930, 46-74, figs. 45-46.
[152] See p. 32.

an episcopal seat, its first bishop was appointed by John of Antioch, and it was probably renamed Sergiopolis.[153] There was a church to S. Sergius at Eitha around 353 A.D., indicating that the saint must have already been recognized in the city where he was buried. Early in the fifth century the Bishop of Hierapolis, in whose diocese Resafa was then located, consecrated three hundred pounds of gold to erect a church over his tomb. His church grew rich. Therefore, in view of the new importance of Resafa, or now Sergiopolis, as a metropole in 434 A.D., and the close similarity of its martyrium to the early church at Koja Kalessi, it is difficult to believe, on stylistic comparisons, that the church was not finished at about this time.

Sarre and Herzfeld, followed by Spanner and Guyer, nevertheless, dated the church for stylistic reasons around 500 A.D.[154] Both groups agreed that the building had been both altered and rebuilt in what they believed to be the ninth and eleventh centuries, although they admitted that the first alterations made use of old materials. It is not clear why no importance was attached to the period of Justinian, who, we know from Procopius, rebuilt the defenses of the city, because Herzfeld saw what he considered to be an inscription and work of Justinian. No one, of course, questions the existence of the church at this time, because Procopius says that the Emperor surrounded the "old church" of the saint with a remarkable wall.[155] At the same time that the date of the church has been brought into line with certain preconceptions of architectural chronology in the Near East, authorities have uniformly restored the building as a basilica whose gable roof was carried by transverse stone arches.

Inasmuch as the church was an early martyrium, similar to Koja Kalessi (Fig. 195), and had in the middle of it a great bema, like the bemas found in the martyria of S. Babylas and at Seleucia Pieria, it is proposed to restore it as a domical structure. The nave (Fig. 198) is divided into three bays by cruciform piers whose lateral sections correspond to the responds along the side-aisle walls. These piers, which originally carried transverse arches across the nave, recall the church at Koja Kalessi, while the other details of the building are so closely related to the architecture of North Syria as to leave no doubt that the martyrium was built by Syrian workmen, presumably under the direction of Antioch. The placing of the piers with evident care for the resultant dimensions is significant. Although their longitudinal responds are much wider than the lateral ones they are so located that the central bay is a square of 12.60 m., while the two end bays are somewhat shorter. On the grounds, then, that the dome was an essential symbolic feature of a real martyrium, that the church is essentially identical to Koja Kalessi (Fig. 194), and that there was no justification for this careful placing of the piers if the roof had a continuous gable, I have restored it (Fig. 197) with the central bay raised and covered with a wooden dome. The necessity of assuming that the church had a heavenly dome over the

[153] E. Lucius, *Les Origines du culte des saints dans l'église chrétienne*, 1908, 315.

[154] Sarre and Herzfeld, *Archäologische Reise*, II, 3-16; Spanner and Guyer, *Rusafa*, 22-34, 52-

55, Taf. 13 (plan), 14 (side elevation), 15 (sections) and 18 (squinch).

[155] Procopius, *Buildings*, II, ix, 3-9.

memorial bay in the center was recognized by Grabar when he was discussing the purpose of its central bema.[156]

One reason why the church has always been treated as an ordinary basilica is that part of its intact clerestory has on it the Antiochene type of colonnette on corbels, such as was found at Kal'at Sim'ân and Kalb Lauzeh as a means of supporting the roofing timbers. Although the existing piers on the interior of the nave carry meaningless pilasters up to the top of the clerestory, Herzfeld recognized that their capitals indicated the original presence of transverse arches. It has, therefore, been assumed that the rebuilding, which removed these arches and introduced the columns between the piers, took place in the ninth century and left the clerestory the way it was, although it was admitted that this rebuilding made use of old materials.[157] The rebuilding of the piers without the original transverse arches proves that at least the clerestory wall of the central bay was drastically changed at some period. When that change took place is of architectural and, perhaps, liturgical, importance.

In view of the resemblance of this church, as restored (Fig. 197), to Koja Kalessi, and the presumption that Resafa must have had its first church at least shortly after it became an episcopal seat in 434 A.D., there seem to be strong reasons for dating it around the middle of the fifth century, at the time when Koja Kalessi was built and when the martyrium at Seleucia Pieria had a central platform of liturgical importance beneath a celestial dome. Once this earlier date for the original church is considered possible, the subsequent rebuilding and the presence of another martyrium at Resafa become much more comprehensible. Sometime towards the end of the fifth century, a hundred years or more after the martyrium was first built, the church was either badly injured or for other reasons, perhaps liturgical, it was decided to build a new martyrium for the city's saint (Fig. 184). At that time the original martyrium was rebuilt as a regular basilica with a gable roof by removing the transverse arches, carrying up the pier responds as pilasters and reconstructing the clerestory of the central bay so that it would be the same as the clerestory walls of the two end bays.

The means by which the wooden dome was adjusted to the square bay of the original martyrium is clearly shown by the arch squinches on colonnettes which were found in the corners of the square tower of the northeast side-chamber, which resemble the squinches found in the octagon at Kal'at Sim'ân (Fig. 36) and in the church at Koja Kalessi (Fig. 194). It has already been pointed out that there was no reason for the use of these squinches except to bring a square to an octagon and provide a continuous impost for a circular dome. The presence of domes over the towers flanking the east end of Resafa will be taken up in the next chapter with the other evidence which shows that the domical symbolism was extended, probably in the sixth century, from the mortuary martyrium proper to the side-chamber, where the relics were kept and where there were not infrequently oratories in the upper chambers. The justification for restoring the fragmentary remains of the southeast

[156] Grabar, *Martyrium*, I, 346.
[157] Restoration of original church as a basil- ica (Sarre and Herzfeld, *op.cit.*, 4, fig. 133).

128

tower with an opening from the second-story chapel into the side aisle is the *Coenaculum* of Sion Church at Jerusalem, which was the renowned chapel where Christ performed the first communion as a symbolic Last Supper and martyr's feast. This chapel was in the second story to the south of the apse and had an opening into the aisle, or transept, beneath, so that the people could indirectly take part in the hidden mystery.

53. *Ruweha, Martyrium Church of Bizzos.* The presence of the domical tomb of Bizzos (Fig. 59) just beyond the southeast corner of the church and of another tomb structure on the north side are strong indications that the church, which Butler dated in the last quarter of the fifth century, was a martyrium, and as such should have been domical.[158] At the time when it was visited and drawn by De Vogüé the upper part of its façade and the whole clerestory had fallen, and there is nothing in either De Vogüé's or Butler's study of it to show that they found any evidence of its having had a triangular gable, or anything else to indicate a gable roof. The plan (Fig. 199), on the contrary, has its T-shaped piers placed in such a manner as to produce three square bays. The only satisfactory explanation for the elaborate construction of the piers and their careful division of the nave into square bays by means of transverse arches is the assumption that there were wooden domes over one or more of the bays. As a domical structure the church becomes comparable to the martyrium at Resafa, the cathedral at Aleppo, and the church at Koja Kalessi, while the fact that it was built in relation to tomb buildings relates it to the domed basilica of the fifth century at Ilissos and the Serbian church at Tsaritchin Grad (c. 500 A.D.).

54. *Aleppo, Cathedral.* The Cathedral of Aleppo, which was incorporated into the mosque of the Madrasa al-Halawiyyah, was possibly a domical basilica with either one or three domes.[159] Although the present dome is presumably of Moslem construction and our available plan (Fig. 196) is unreliable, the architectural details, such as the wind-blown capitals and the use of columns to carry transverse arches, have been compared to Kal'at Sim'ân. It still seems possible that it was built at the end of the fifth century in spite of the fact that recent opinions have dated it as late as the second half of the sixth century.[160]

55. *Mt. Admirable, S. Simeon Stylites the Younger.* On the north side of the eastern arm of this church (Fig. 166), which has never been adequately published, is a large, three-aisled chapel with piers that is reported to have been a domical basilica.[161]

[158] De Vogüé, *Syrie centrale*, pls. 68, 69; Butler, *Architecture and Other Arts*, 225ff., fig. 90; *Syria*, II, B, 3, 142-148, pls. XV-XVIII; *Early Churches*, 145-148.

[159] S. Guyer, "La Madrasa al-Halâwiyya à Alep," *Bulletin de l'Institut français d'archéologie orientale du Caire*, XI, 1914, 217-231; Lassus, *Sanctuaires chrétiens de Syrie*, 153, fig.

69; Butler, *Early Churches in Syria*, 170f.; Van Berchem and Strzygowski, *Amida*, 199f.

[160] J. Sauvaget, *Alep.*, 1914, 59, fig. 16. A study by M. Écochard, comparing the church to the cathedral of Bosra, is announced.

[161] See Chap. V n. 76, and Lassus, *Sanctuaires*, pp. 134-135.

56. *il Anderin, South Church, No. 6.* The church (Fig. 200), found on the south side of the city and dated by Howard Butler in 528 A.D. on the basis of an inscription found among its ruins, was a martyrium, as indicated by the tomb attached to its northeast corner and by its location within a walled enclosure outside the city.[162] Butler found a pair of T-shaped piers, like those at Ruweha, near the west end, but restored the interior with the rectangular piers of a continuous arcade. It is not only unlikely that the builders would have used two kinds of piers of such a different structural character, but also surprising that they made such an unnecessarily short bay at the west end. The reason for the short western bay becomes apparent when another pair of T-shaped piers is introduced and it is found that the space was exactly long enough for two square bays, 8.53 m. wide. The resultant relation, then, of this building, as a martyrium, to Koja Kalessi, Resafa and Ruweha justifies its restoration with either one, or two, domes.

57. *il-Anderin, Church No. 7.* The liturgical provisions of this church (Fig. 201), with passages from both side-chambers into the apse, seem to indicate a late date, and while there is no more reason to consider it a martyrium than the chapel customarily restored with a dome (Fig. 47), the proportions of its plan strongly suggest that a single dome was over the bay in front of the apse.[163]

58. *il-Anderin, Church No. 8.* Church No. 8 is restored with either one or two domes (Fig. 196), not because there are any indications that it was a martyrium but because it is similar to the previous church and again raises the issue of whether we have been justified in thinking of all rectangular churches in Syria as having a gable roof.[164]

59. *Bosra, Church No. 1.* An even stronger presumption in favor of a domed basilica is raised by the plan of the church (Fig. 203) which Butler found in the southeast quarter of the city.[165] Having discovered *in situ* one cruciform pier, indicating a square bay, 6 m. wide, in front of the apse, and column bases down the remainder of the nave, Butler's church, when restored with a wooden dome in front of the apse, becomes comparable to the fifth century church at Ilissos and a possible precursor of similar domical basilicas. Unfortunately nothing was found to indicate whether it was earlier or later than the martyrium cathedral.

60. *Jericho, Cloister Church.* Although the church (Fig. 198) with a single dome over the central bay of the nave, which is 22 m. wide, was rebuilt as a vaulted structure in the mediaeval period, Schneider believes that it stood on an older foundation which was a basilica.[166] In view now of the presumption that there was no sharp change in the development of domical architecture between the Early Christian and the mediaeval period, it is possible that the existing church at Jericho preserved the

---

[162] Butler, *Syria*, II, B, 2, 58-61, ill. 54; *Early Churches*, 80, ill. 209.

[163] Butler, *Syria*, II, B, 61, ill. 57; *Early Churches*, 82, ill. 88.

[164] Butler, *Syria*, II, B, 62, ill. 60; *Early Churches*, 80, ill. 87.

[165] Butler, *Syria*, II, A, 4, 279f., ill. 246; *Early Churches*, 118f., ill. 117.

[166] A. M. Schneider, "Das Kalamon-Kloster in der Jerichoebene," *Oriens Christianus*, series 3, XIII, 1938, 39-43, Abb. 1.

essential domical form of the earlier basilica that might have had a wooden dome.

61. *Jerusalem, New Church of the Virgin.* It is not clear from the accounts whether the Nea, begun in 513 and dedicated in 543 A.D., after much of its construction had been completed by the builders of Justinian, was an ordinary basilica, or a domed martyrium, as it should have been. The detailed description by Procopius of the great care taken by the builders in finding the proper timbers for its roof implies more than a customary gable construction[167] and suggested to Crowfoot that the Nea had a wooden dome.[168] Vincent and Abel, on the other hand, believe it to have been a basilica, even though its proportions, 48 by 58, which they worked out from the dimensions given in the *Commemoratorium,* seem to be those of a central-type martyrium.[169]

62. *Jerusalem.* While there are no longer any justifiable historical and archaeological reasons for believing that the Aksa mosque was a rebuilding of a domed basilica of Justinian, any more than there is for assuming that the great mosque at Damascus made use of the domical transept of a Christian church, it is still necessary to assume that both these early Islamic buildings, with their wooden domes at what would have been the crossing of a Christian basilica, must have been modeled after well-known and common types of Christian sanctuaries in the region.[170]

Summary

Without attempting to labor the conclusions, it appears from this review that there are between fifty and sixty known churches in Syria and Palestine which were, or should have been, domical. When these examples are compared with the lists of recorded martyria in all the cities of this region, of which we know little more than their names, it becomes apparent why we have to give more consideration to the domical traditions of Syria and the Holy Land. This available evidence, which is still inadequate for historical purposes, appears more convincing when it is realized that among all the other churches not included in this list there is no central-type martyrium which is known not to have been domical. At the same time the basilicas with gable roofs, which might be called "martyrium basilicas" because of their oratories, appear to have had these reliquary chapels added on or built into them, because the popularity of the Cult of Martyrs had impelled every church to enjoy the sanctity of possessing sacred relics.

[167] *Buildings* (Loeb), v, vi, 15.
[168] Crowfoot, *Churches at Bosra and Samaria-Sebaste,* 13.
[169] Vincent and Abel, *Jérusalem,* II, 914-919;
Cabrol, *Dict.,* VII, 2337.
[170] Creswell, *Early Muslim Architecture,* I, 110ff. (Damascus), 21-26 (Aksa).

VI · THE PLACE OF COMMEMORATION

A. The Problem

THE problem of explaining the liturgical purpose of the large platform, or bema, discovered in the middle of the fourth century cruciform church of S. Babylas (Fig. 170) at Antioch and of the fifth century four-lobed cruciform martyrium at Seleucia Pieria (Fig. 182) involves many controversial issues regarding the ceremonies which took place in the martyria of this period. It is further complicated by the apparent relation of these large bemas in the martyria to the "exedras," or enclosures, which have been discovered in the center of a number of basilica churches of northern Syria. The purpose of this chapter is to present the reasons which show why these bemas were at first associated with the Cult of Martyrs and had their origin in the domical martyria before they became a "Place of Commemoration" when the cults of martyrs and relics were introduced into many of the regular basilica churches during the fifth and early sixth centuries.

In advancing a new explanation it is with great reluctance that I differ with the explanations of scholars such as Grabar and Lassus. It is to be hoped that a new theory will contribute as much as their studies to an eventual solution of the problem. While it is dangerous for an architectural historian to raise liturgical questions and attempt to answer them without help of clergy, it has become evident that the liturgical specialists will not attempt to deal with the architectural evidence until someone takes the initiative and presents an explanation that can be criticized. Already, I believe, Syrian architecture of the fourth to the seventh centuries has shown that there was not the widespread uniformity of religious usage which has often been assumed. In fact, the architectural evidence makes one suspect that many of the efforts to deal with the problems of this transitional period, such as the architectural provisions for the ceremonies of the Martyrs' Cult and the veneration of relics, the tradition of a single altar in the east, and the liturgical antecedents of the table of oblations, the prothesis chapel and Great Entrance, have been unduly influenced by the later, established usage of the orthodox Greek church.

There are other reasons, besides the conviction that the bemas in question were connected with the veneration of martyrs, which make it necessary to challenge the accepted doctrine of continuity. During the fourth and fifth centuries, when the popular enthusiasm for the martyrs was presenting the Church with many serious problems, certain radical changes must have taken place in the ceremonial provisions for this cult before the Eastern churches were able to standardize the liturgy and shift the whole emphasis to the worship of God. That there were special ceremonies which took place in the "Churches of Martyrs" is indicated by the efforts of the Church to correct their abuses and to subordinate everything connected with the saints to the one service of Christ.[1] Two of the clearest indications of these changes seem to be, first,

[1] E. Lucius, *Les Origines du culte des saints*, 1908, 432-451.

132

the gradual transformation of the central and domical martyrium into a regular church, and, second, the sudden disappearance of the bemas and exedras under discussion, probably before the end of the seventh century.

Histories of the cult do not attempt to reconstruct the ceremonies which took place in the great Eastern martyria of the fourth and fifth centuries. They emphasize the importance of all-night vigils, of prayers, offerings and hymns sung in honor of the martyrs. They do not, however, make it clear under what conditions the early practice of making all kinds of gifts to the martyr was continued and how long it was before readings on the life of the saint, eulogistic sermons, poems and addresses were entirely discontinued. It would seem as if some special provisions would have been necessary for the great feasts which, before they were abolished because of the abuses, were the most popular communal feature of the cult.[2] During the fourth and fifth centuries in Syria, when the mounting fervor of the people was carrying over into Christianity so much of the pagan cult of heroes, one wonders whether the vast crowds which gathered on the saint's feast day and on other days usually connected with some great act in his life would have been satisfied with the orthodox arrangements and liturgy as they are now known. There must, in fact, have been special provisions at this time so that the emotional crowds, who desired to press around the tomb or relics while awaiting a miracle, could present their gifts, take part in the communal meal and make their prayers of intercession as if the martyr were in their midst.[3] At this time when the popular enthusiasm was at its height, and the churchmen themselves were split into opposing factions, it is inconceivable that the whole service was focussed upon the apsidal altar of Christ and that everything connected with the cult of relics was relegated to small chapels and oratories. It was not until the close of the sixth century that one would expect that such conditions could have been imposed with any uniformity.

The Church Fathers were apparently in complete agreement in differentiating very clearly between "sacrifice to the martyrs," which could have developed into a new form of polytheism, and "sacrificing to God in memory of the martyrs, as we do constantly" (Augustine). Nevertheless, it does not follow that, after the Recognition when the Cult of Martyrs began to have such tremendous appeal to the masses with their pagan heritage, the Church in Syria and in other parts of the Empire did not

[2] Lucius (*ibid.*, 416) emphasizes that during the fourth and fifth centuries the martyrs' feasts were more communal than ecclesiastic and that it was some time before they were fully controlled by the Church. Although both the Council of Laodicea and the Rule of S. Basil forbade the holding of agapes and the eating of banquets in the House of God, it was necessary for the Synod of Trulles in 692 to prohibit agapes and the cooking of food at the altar (*ibid.*, 434).

[3] *Ibid.*, 377 n. 4; 385ff. Some of the evidence

to show that the Cult of Martyrs during the fourth century was becoming a new form of hero worship and was "by way of degenerating into a refined polytheism and idolatry" has been presented by P. Schaff (*History of the Christian*, 1891, III, 432-436), who cites the opposition of the Spanish presbyter, Virgilanius, in the fifth century and the description by Theodoret of how "the feasts of the gods are now replaced by the festivals of Peter, Paul, etc." (*Graec. affect. curatio. Disp.*, VIII).

countenance ceremonial customs, presumably influenced by the pagan Cult of Heroes, and hence did not find it necessary, as S. Augustine wrote, to "bear for a time with some things that are not according to our teaching" (*Contra Faustum*, xx, 21). This conclusion is forced upon us when we endeavor to find some basis of fact for the ceremonies which took place in the "Churches of Martyrs" during the fourth century and for the origin of the table of prothesis and the Great Entrance, which does not appear in the actual liturgies until so much later. Also it is further indicated by the many architectural differences in the liturgical arrangements of the Syrian churches that suggest regional variations in the service. In fact, one suspects that the church historians of the period deliberately ignored these variations as long as they did not involve fundamental issues of the creed. The repeated prohibition by the councils of the unorthodox preparation of communal meals in the churches and even the emphatic insistence of the churchmen that altars and offerings were not for the martyrs, but for the "God who gave the crown of martyrdom," imply that during the transitional period, when the Church was endeavoring to resolve the more fundamental problems of the heresies that flourished in the Patriarchate of Antioch, the Church was unable to attain the desired uniformity.

Now that it is generally recognized that the services in the early Syrian churches must have varied very markedly from the developed liturgy of the Greek Church, it is difficult to understand why it is necessary to assume that at no time in the East was there ever more than the one altar, dedicated to Christ. Instead, it is reasonable to believe that for some time the popular feeling, as Lucius has pointed out, would have considered an altar indispensable to the veneration of martyrs, because, as a place of distinction, it gave a sense of immediate presence when prayers and invocations were addressed to a saint.[4] If there was a special place for the location of the martyr's service, which was in the midst of the congregation, it could have been con-

---

[4] Lucius, *op.cit.*, 375-377. At the same time that it is generally recognized that there was only the one altar in the Eastern churches, there was not only the later tradition of the "little altars" in both the prothesis and diaconicon (Papàs Marco Mandala, *La Protesi della liturgia nel rito Bizantino-Greco*, Grottaferrata, 1935, 41), but also the early custom of having altars in oratories, such as the *Coenaculum* at Sion. Apart from Lassus' discovery of a small altar in the prothesis chapel which was built onto the cathedral of Brad at the close of the sixth century, there is no specific evidence of a prothesis altar before the eighth and ninth centuries when it is regularly referred to in the orthodox liturgy (Mandala, *op.cit.*, 60; Petrouskj, *Histoire de la rédaction slave de la liturgie de S. Jean Crystome*; P. P. de Meester, *Les Origines et les développements du texte grec de la liturgie de S. Jean Chrysostome*, 245-357). Inasmuch, however, as the preparation of the offertory at a table was an early Syrian custom of symbolic implications which developed into the elaborate ritual of the Great Entrance and was finally introduced into the liturgy, it follows that there must have been a table of oblations, located in either the diaconicon or the nave of the Syrian churches, which from an early date served an important role in the ritual (Dom G. Dix, *The Shape of the Liturgy*, Westminster, 1945, 290ff.). Also in the Syrian churches, where the relics were seldom placed under the altar but were usually kept in a small chamber or chapel at one side of the apse, there is the possibility, amounting almost to probability, that on feast days, when the crowds would have been too great to approach the relics in a small chapel, the relic, or something intimately connected with it, like the oil, was brought out to a centrally located altar, or "table," in the midst of the people.

sidered a "table" and hence not recognized as an altar.[5] Later, after reviewing the evidence of the Antiochene churches and the *Testamentum*, the question will arise whether such a *mensa*, at first located in the midst of the people, in addition to serving for some special ceremony in connection with the Cult of Martyrs, may not have been used as a kind of prototype for the "table of oblations" and eventually transferred into the prothesis chapel alongside the sanctuary. Since it is now generally agreed that there was no prothesis chapel in the Syrian churches until after the introduction, or development, of what was to be the orthodox liturgy with its Little and Great Entrances, probably towards the close of the sixth century, it is necessary to discover the precedent for both the "table of oblations" and the transmission of the Sacred Elements through the congregation to the high altar, for it is also agreed that the altar of prothesis and the Great Entrance were originally part of the Syrian service.

B. The Monuments

1. DOMED MARTYRIA

The architectural evidence for liturgical provisions in the center of a Syrian church falls into two groups: first, those churches which were primarily martyria and presumably domical; and, second, those churches which were ordinary basilicas.

1. The earliest known bema in what is now to be considered a domical martyrium is the one discovered in the martyrium of S. Babylas (Fig. 170) at Antioch-Kaoussie, which was built about 381 A.D.[6] Its rectangular portion is 8.42 m. long by 7.15 m. wide, while its semicircular projection at the west end was originally about 3.57 m. deep, or one-half the width of the platform, although with its outer course of masonry removed its actual imprint is only 2.82 m. deep.

This platform, whose rectangular portion alone was 27′ 6″ long by 23′ 6″ wide, could not have been merely the provisions for an ambon (although it will be seen that it presumably had a lectern for readings), first, because it was far too large and, second, because it was the *only place* in the church for the altar and its service. The central square where this bema was located was the actual tomblike sanctuary, itself a kind of monumental, sepulchral ciborium, like the original square martyrium of S. John at Ephesus (Fig. 83) and the square church at Edessa with its cosmic dome. This is proved by the absence of any provisions for the services in the eastern arm of the cross, by the lower levels of the four naves, and by the references to them in the inscriptions as exedrae. Therefore, the four naves, which lay "outside" the crossing, were enclosed spaces for the throngs of faithful who gathered for the festival and services of the saint and also, as the interments show, for those desiring burial *ad sanctos*. The remains of S. Babylas were not deposited beneath the altar, as was the custom in the West, but were interred along with the body of Bishop Meletius in a double sarcophagus at the northwest corner—that is, at one side of the actual sanctuary. In view of these facts any explanation of the Syrian bema must recognize that

---

[5] Lucius, *op.cit.*, 453.   [6] See p. 109.

here in Antioch, towards the close of the fourth century, our earliest known plat-form was in the center of a real martyrium, presumably under a memorial and celestial dome, and was the place where the altar stood beneath its own domical ciborium.

2. At Seleucia Pieria (Fig. 182) a second bema, undoubtedly belonging to the original fifth century structure, was found in the middle of the martyrium.[7] In the sixth century, when the church was restored and enlarged, this platform was redeco-rated and repaired. Larger than the sanctuary of many Syrian churches, this bema has a rectangular section 10.5 m. long by 5.6 m. wide, while its semicircular west end is 3.5 m. deep. The church itself, although still a cruciform and domical martyrium, is radically different from the martyrium of S. Babylas because of its eastern and apsidal sanctuary, which architecturally appears to be an appendage to the martyrium.

In view of the size and importance of this bema in the main body of the church and its similarity to the fourth century bema in S. Babylas, which had to be the loca-tion of the main altar, we are apparently confronted with provisions for two altars. Compared to S. Babylas, this central-type building with its eastern sanctuary for the altar of Christ shows a transitional stage in the development of the martyrium, and, perhaps, of the liturgy. The question, therefore, arises whether there was at this time, when the Church of Antioch was torn by so many controversies, the usage of only the one altar which was to prevail in the East. That some development was taking place in the form and use of the central-type martyrium is further shown by the baptistery and side-chambers which were added on either side of the eastern sanctuary in the sixth century. If there were provisions in the fifth century upon the great platform in the martyrium for services of the saint in the midst of the congregation, then what use was made of this bema in the sixth century after the whole emphasis was shifted to the altar of Christ in the eastern sanctuary?

3. A third bema was discovered by Spanner and Guyer in the middle of the nave

[7] See p. 116. The conclusion of the excavator, W. A. Campbell (*Antioch-on-the-Orontes*, III, 1941, 51), that the central platform was built in the sixth century at the time when the church was rebuilt after an earthquake, was based upon the appearance of the pavement around it which belonged to the original con-struction in the fifth century. Because its edges, where they came up against the founda-tions of the bema, were irregular, he con-cluded that the pavement had been removed in the rebuilding to make a place for the plat-form. Actually, the one place where the pave-ment had an unnaturally irregular and broken edge (*ibid.*, fig. 63) was where a semicircular pilaster, or base, was added to the existing bema. Otherwise the pavement edge next to the platform, where it was preserved (*ibid.*, pl. x), showed an edge no more irregular than might be expected, since it would have been originally covered by the marble revetment of the bema which had largely disappeared ex-cept for a few sculptured fragments. Quite apart from the excavation data, it is impossible to believe that such an important liturgical structure would have been introduced into an existing church in the sixth century, if it had not already been there in the fifth century when the church was first built. The excava-tions showed, as Campbell has recorded, that both the church and the platform underwent two periods of construction. Therefore, in ad-dition to the fact that a similar bema existed in the near-by fourth century martyrium at Antioch, one would expect the building and rebuilding of the platform to conform to the two building periods of the church, which would place the original construction of the platform in the fifth century, where it belongs in the development of church architecture.

of the martyrium of S. Sergius (Fig. 198) at Resafa.[8] The reasons for dating this church, built over the grave of the martyr, around the middle of the fifth century and for restoring the superstructure with a dome over the square bay where the bema was located have already been presented.[9] Here in a martyrium of Sergiopolis, where John of Antioch was appointed bishop in 437 A.D., the platform, which was better preserved than the other examples, consisted of a rectangular section surrounded by eight colonnettes and a semicircular exedra with concentric banks of seats. Later, when Jean Lassus reexamined the platform he found that the measurements given by Spanner, for what he called "the tribune," were inaccurate.[10] According to Lassus' description and drawing (Fig. 216) the rectangular portion, 7.5 m. long, consisted of a platform 6 m. square and a vestibule at the east end, while on its raised portion were the moulded outlines of what appeared to be an altar set within the four bases of ciborium columns.

After these discoveries at Resafa it seemed to Lassus and others that the bema must have been a kind of chapel, like an oratory, situated in the midst of the congregation and that it had hangings to conceal the clergy seated in the exedra and to veil the high-place with its altar under a ciborium. If it is possible to prove that these bemas were developed in the Antiochene martyria and used in connection with martyrs' ceremonies which were eventually abolished, we may have an explanation for the later transformation of this particular domed martyrium into a gable-roofed church. The reasons have already been discussed why I believe that it was around the end of the sixth century that the transverse arches of the nave were removed and columns added in the nave arcades. The architectural changes in S. Sergius suggest a parallel with the martyrium at Seleucia Pieria and again raise the questions of how such a bema was used first in the fifth century and then later, after the martyrium had been made into a regular church of Christ.

4. At Edessa, in the church of Hagia Sophia, rebuilt in 539 A.D., the Syrian hymn describes a structure in the center, beneath the cosmic dome, which it calls a bema and says it was *of the type of the Coenaculum at Sion.*[11] Furthermore, it goes on to describe it: "Et, au-dessous d'elle (se trouvent) onze colonnes, les onze Apôtres qui s'étaient cachés (au Cénacle à Sion)." The symbolism of this comparison with Sion will be discussed later, but it should be kept in mind that any explanation of these bemas should take into consideration this very specific reference to the domical oratory at Sion where Christ with his Apostles performed his own martyr's feast, the double communion, for this chamber, which was a kind of domical martyrium, had its own altar.[12]

Limited as our knowledge is, the presence of large bemas in four central-type and presumably domical churches suggests several conclusions regarding their purpose and origin for which there is other evidence. The first is that all these central bemas

[8] H. Spanner and S. Guyer, *Rusafa*, 1926, 23. fig. 32.
[9] See p. 127.
[10] J. Lassus, *Antioch-on-the-Orontes*, II, 36,
[11] See pp. 36, 143.
[12] See p. 36.

were peculiar to Syrian churches of the martyrium type during the fourth and fifth centuries, if it is assumed that the sixth century rebuilding of the church at Edessa continued the architectural forms and interior arrangements of the fourth century edifice. The second is that these bemas originated as a platform for an altar, because it was customary during the fourth century to have the altar located in the middle of the domical "Churches of Martyrs" and because in S. Babylas there were no other provisions for an altar. And finally there is the probability that this custom of having a central altar under a heavenly dome was taken over from a pagan Syrian tradition.

That the altar was commonly located in the center of the domical martyria is indicated by a number of early churches. At Jerusalem the sepulchral chapel over the empty tomb of Christ, with an altar in front of it, was in the middle of the Holy Sepulchre. At Constantinople in the fourth century martyrium of the Holy Apostles the altar and semicircular bank of seats for the clergy were both located in the center of the crossing under the *domation*, which was presumably a wooden dome,[13] while at Ephesus in the original martyrium of S. John (Fig. 63) the ciborium columns indicate that there was an altar over the relics in the center of the square memorial. Even more significant is the square, pagan kalubé at Shakka (Fig. 122) which became a martyrium of S. George in either 323 or 368 A.D. and in which De Vogüé said that the altar stood under the center of the pagan dome.

The probability that the Christians took over from the pagan memorials and temples this custom of locating the shrine in the midst of the worshippers and beneath a symbolic dome is further strengthened by the provisions in the polygonal, Syrian sanctuary of the Janiculum at Rome, for in the center of this structure, which was presumably domical like a kalubé, there was either a tomb or a triangular altar.[14] Also it is beginning to be evident that the many square temples in Syria, such as the fire temple at Sî' (Figs. 123, 124) which had a baldachin in the middle, must have been covered with either a domical canopy or wooden dome. It is difficult to understand why the Christians in the fourth century should have adopted, without a well-established pagan precedent, a type of martyrium which was so different from the regular churches. However, once the centrally located altar and the symbolic dome are recognized as part of a Syrian tradition and in the fourth century as essential distinctions between the two types of sanctuary, many of the difficulties of explaining the beginnings of Christian architecture disappear. For example, there is nothing inconsistent in Eusebius' account of the fourth century church at Tyre, where he describes the altar as in the midst of the people, because everything in his panygeric is consistent with what he calls the "royal house" having been a domical and cruciform martyrium instead of a basilica, which it is usually thought to have been.[15] Furthermore, the reference of Aetheria to the church on Mount Nebo, written between 393 and 396 A.D., implies that it was not uncommon in the early memorial churches to have a raised place, like an oratory, in the middle of a sanctuary where the memory of a sacred person, buried elsewhere, was venerated. In her account she writes, "inside

[13] See p. 33.   [14] See Chap. II n. 33.   [15] Eusebius, *Ecclesiastical History* (Loeb), X, 4, 44.

the church I saw a central place, a little raised, containing about as much space as tombs usually take. I asked the holy men what this was, and they answered, 'Here was the Holy Moses laid by the angels, for as it was written, no man knoweth of his burial.' "[16]

2. BASILICAS

The second group consists of those basilicas in which have been found an enclosure, similar in shape to the bema in the martyria, located in the middle of the nave. Seven of these enclosures, with their semicircular west end, were discovered by Howard Butler, while eight others have been reported by Lassus and Tchalenko. All were found in churches of North Syria. Since most of the examples were found accidentally without excavating, we do not know how common the enclosure was in the Syrian basilicas. The available information on each example will be reviewed in an approximately chronological order, it being understood, however, that with the exception of a few dated churches, the chronology of Syrian churches is more a matter of opinion than fact.

Three examples occur in churches which can be dated either towards the close of the fourth century or at the beginning of the fifth. In the cathedral at Brad (Fig. 205), dated 395-402 A.D., Lassus discovered an enclosure in the nave and also uncovered evidence of an altar in the apse.[17] At the same time he found that the martyrium chapel opening off from the northern side aisle was built in the fifth century, and that a small and crudely constructed chapel containing the table of prothesis was added in the sixth century to the east end of the northern side-chamber. In the West Church at Burdj Hêdar, which is assigned to the fourth century, Lassus reports the discovery of another apsidal enclosure in the nave and points out that sometime after the fourth century the southeastern side-chamber was enlarged into a martyrium chapel with an apse.[18] He also reports the finding of a third enclosure in the East Church at Bābiskā, which is dated 390-401 A.D.[19] It is presumed that the reliquaries which he discovered in this church were in the large chapel at the southeast corner that was built about 480 A.D. Unfortunately his report makes no reference to the size of these enclosures.

At Kharâb Shems (Figs. 209-211), in a church dated by Butler in the fourth century but assigned by Lassus to the fifth century, Butler found a typical enclosure, 3.50 m. wide and something less than 6 m. long.[20] The example that he discovered

[16] P. Geyer, *Itinera hierosolymitana*, 53-55; Cabrol, *Dict.*, XII, col. 1069; Grabar, *Martyrium*, I, 68; M. L. McClure and C. L. Feltoe, *The Pilgrimage of Etheria*, 22.

[17] Lassus, *Sanctuaires chrétiens de Syrie*, 168-173, fig. 77. The plan (Fig. 205) is Butler's to which have been added the results of Lassus' excavations except on the south side where he shows a trapezoidal court and three doors into the south aisle.

[18] *Ibid.*, 175, 208 n. 4, fig. 81.

[19] *Ibid.*, 176, 188, 208 n. 4, fig. 24. He does give his reasons for dating the martyrium chapel in the sixth century and later than the inscription which Butler found on it.

[20] Butler, *Syria, Princeton University Archaeological Expedition to Syria in 1904/5 and 1909*, II, B, 322-325; *Early Churches in Syria*, 32f., ill. 31; Lassus, *Sanctuaires*, 208, fig. 90.

at Mir'âyeh (Fig. 208), which was certainly later than the fourth century, was 4.47 m. wide and something over 6 m. long; furthermore, it consisted of a single course of masonry, .55 m. high and with dowel holes in the top of each stone, indicating that it had a superstructure of wood, or metal, which carried curtains, as did the colonnettes around the bema at Resafa.[21] At Kalôta, in the East Church (Fig. 207) which is dated 492 A.D., the enclosure was only 4.5 m. long.[22] Without publishing any plans or dimensions Butler mentions finding a similar structure in churches at Dehes and Djeradeh.[23]

In buildings dating from either the fifth or sixth century Lassus reports the discovery of enclosures in the nave of churches at Bettir, Berich, Kfer and Behyō.[24] Again no dimensions are given, but the one in the West Church at Behyō appears to be most important because it is reported to have a well-preserved semicircular exedra with seats for the clergy, the four columns of a ciborium and a raised "throne," richly sculptured, in the middle of the enclosure. One of the best preserved examples was found at Kirkbizé in a private house which had been turned into a chapel; here again stone reliquaries were found and there was the remains of what Lassus calls an ambon in the enclosure.[25]

From the sixth century an example is reported having been found in one of the churches at Bakirhā.[26] The enclosure must be late because the West Church is dated 501 A.D. and the East Church 546 A.D. The outlines of a semicircular enclosure were discovered by Butler at il-Firdeh (Fig. 206) in the exceptional church with the elongated sanctuary.[27] At Kalb Lauzeh (Fig. 212) in the church dated by De Vogüé in the sixth century, but which he attributed to the end of the fifth century, Butler found the outline of a semicircular enclosure cut in the pavement.[28] The way in which this imprint had been worn down by the scraping of feet suggests that the liturgical use of the structure had been discontinued, perhaps as early as the first half of the seventh century.

Although none of the examples in the basilicas were raised platforms, like the bemas in the martyria, they were located in the middle of the nave, were entered at the east end, had semicircular terminations at their west end, were presumably veiled and, on the evidence of Lassus, had in them an ambon and ciborium. No examples have been found in the excavated churches of Gerasa and Palestine and it is quite certain that they were not in all the North Syrian churches. The finding of stone reliquaries in so many of the Syrian churches with enclosures and the fact that at Brad, Burdj-Hêdar and Bābiskā martyrium chapels were added to the churches in the fifth century raises the important question of whether or not these nave enclosures

[21] Butler, *Syria*, II, B, 68-69, ill. 74; *Early Churches*, 215, ill. 216.

[22] Butler, *Syria*, II, B, 315-317, ill. 349; *Early Churches*, 67, ill. 68; Lassus (*Sanctuaires*, 175, fig. 85) reports finding fragments of reliquaries in the southeast chamber.

[23] Butler, *Early Churches*, 215.

[24] Lassus, *Sanctuaires*, 208 n. 4, 210.

[25] *Ibid.*, 210.

[26] *Ibid.*, 208 n. 4; he does not specify whether it was the East or West Church.

[27] Butler, *Syria*, II, B, 70-71, ill. 77; *Early Churches*, 161, ill. 173.

[28] De Vogüé, *Syrie centrale*, 135ff., pls. 122-129; Butler, *Architecture and Other Arts*, 221-225, fig. 89.

were connected with the Cult of Martyrs and built into the churches at the time when special relics were acquired and martyrium chapels were constructed. If they were primarily associated with the ceremonies in honor of martyrs and had been taken over at a smaller scale from the bemas in the fourth century martyria, it is readily understood why their use was discontinued at the end of the sixth century. On the other hand, if they were essential to the regular liturgy during the fifth and sixth centuries, it becomes very difficult to explain why their use was discontinued without any survivals in a later period.

C. Theories

None of the theories as to the use of the Syrian bema and enclosure has proved entirely satisfactory because they have not answered all the questions raised by all the evidence. At first, when it was thought that the enclosures were only in the basilicas, it was believed that they must have been choirs. Although Spanner accepted this explanation for the platform in the martyrium of S. Sergius at Resafa, he advanced the impossible suggestion that the semicircular exedra might have been a platform on which stood a statue of the saint.[29] Another unsupported hypothesis was that the enclosures were for the Syrian deaconesses.[30]

1. PROVISIONS FOR AN ALTAR?

Shortly after he had studied the remains of the "tribunes" in the martyria of S. Sergius at Resafa and Antioch-Kaoussie, Lassus advanced the theory that the high altar was located on these platforms in the middle of the nave in much the same way that it was placed in the nave of many North African churches.[31] After his excavations in the cathedral at Brad (Fig. 205), where he found a typical Syrian enclosure in the center of the nave and evidence of an altar in the apse, he discarded this theory. The only reason for now referring to it is because at the time there was enough evidence to persuade a competent excavator that there may have been altars in connection with these bemas and enclosures.

2. AN AMBON?

Grabar's theory, based upon Lassus' dissertation and the evidence of Tchalenko from Behyō and Kirbizé and developed as part of his study of the church at Edessa, presented the Syrian platform in the martyria and the enclosure in the basilicas as a

---

[29] Spanner and Guyer, *Rusafa*, 33f.

[30] J. Mattern, *À Travers les villes mortes de Haute Syrie*, 1933, 116. Eusebius, *Ecclesiastical History* (Loeb), VII, xxx, 10, relates how Paul of Samosata, when he became head of the Church at Antioch about 264 A.D., introduced among his other heretical practices which were condemned, the novel idea of training "women to sing hymns to himself in the middle of the church on the great day of Pascha, which would make one shudder." Although this prac-

tice suggests that singing in the middle of the church was customary in the veneration of a saint, it had nothing to do with the deaconesses, for the *Testamentum* says, "And let the deaconesses remain by the door of the Lord's House."

[31] Lassus, "Remarques sur l'adoption en Syrie de la forme basilicale pour les églises chrétiennes," *Atti del IV Congresso internazionale di archeologia christiana*, 1940, 351.

pulpitum, or ambon.[32] Inasmuch as the evidence from Resafa and Behyō had already proved that the semicircular exedra was a place for the clergy, Grabar assumed that the rectangular portion was a spacious ambon where the reader of the scriptures stood beneath a ciborium with the Sacred Books laid upon the "throne" in front of him, while the clergy sat in the apselike *synthronos*. He believed that this Syrian type of ambon went back in origin to the reading tribunes of the Hellenistic synagogues, as described by Esdras, which were likewise located in the midst of the congregation.[33] It was also part of his theory that the central space in both the martyria and the naves of the basilica churches, where the enclosures were located, was reserved for the ceremonial use of the clergy and that only the side aisles and arms of the church were for the people.

In developing the history of the place of reading, which was variously designated during the Early Christian period as *pulpitum, bema, tribune* and *ambon*,[34] Grabar does not compare these particular churches, where he believes that the ambon was in the center of the nave, with the other Syrian and Palestinian churches in which the pulpit has usually been found at the eastern end of the church, off center, and just in front of the sanctuary, and the three churches where it was on axis, but near the east end.[35] In fact, none of the examples cited in support of a centrally located ambon are Syrian. He attaches the greatest importance to the account of Hagia Sophia at Constantinople by Paul the Silentiary who says the ambon was connected by a solea to the sanctuary and was located "in the central space of the wide church, yet tending rather to the East."[36] Hence, instead of being in the center, this ambon was merely in front of the bema as later Greek writers described it.[37] The other examples of a centrally located ambon, which he cites, are the sixth century church of S. Nicolas at Myra, S. Croix at Mizhet and the tenth century cathedral at Preslov.

The fact that in many Italian and North African churches the ambon was located at or near the center of the nave is no indication of the practice in Syria. On the other hand he might well have referred to the Ursiana at Ravenna where there was a large Syrian colony and close contacts with the East. In the ancient *cattolica*, erected by Bishop Ursus between 379-396 A.D., Agnellus (553-568 A.D.) built an elaborate ambon

---

[32] Grabar, "Les Ambons syriens et la fonction liturgique de la nef dans les églises antiques," *Cahiers archéologiques*, I, 1945, 129ff.

[33] II Esdras, 8, 4; III, 9, 42.

[34] Cabrol, *Dict.*, I, cols. 1330ff.; Grabar, *Cahiers archéologiques*, I, 1945, 130.

[35] At Dair Solaib, Mattern ("Les Deux églises," *Mélanges de l'Université Saint-Joseph*, XXII, 1939, 6ff.) found in the middle of the nave, just in front of the eastern sanctuary, an octagonal stone with projections to the east and west, which he called the base of an altar, but which from its shape was clearly an ambon; at Ma'in (*Rev. bibl.*, XLVII, 1938, 231) De Vaux discovered a similarly located stone

which he called the base of an ambon; the excavations in the church of S. Simeon Stylites at Kal'at Sim'ân uncovered the foundations of a pulpit, located exactly in the middle of the eastern nave, which were quite different from those of the Syrian enclosures under discussion; and, furthermore, at Kal'at Sim'ân it should be noted that the actual center of this martyrium church was in the octagon where the column of the Stylites stood under a heavenly dome (Lassus, *Sanctuaires*, 132, fig. 54).

[36] W. R. Lethaby and H. Swainson, *The Church of Sancta Sophia Constantinople*, 1894, 54.

[37] Cabrol, *Dict.*, I, col. 1338.

in the middle of the nave.[38] At the same time that this ambon is taken into consideration as evidence of a Syrian usage, it should be noted that there is evidence of there
having been two altars in the Ursiana. As yet it is not clear from the sources that I
find available whether the main altar was located in the center of the nave, as the
plan published by Ricci shows,[39] or whether there were always two altars, one of
S. Anastasia and the other the "great altar" dedicated to "Holy Resurrection."[40] In
either event the Ursiana appears to have been another fourth century church with
an altar in the middle of the nave.

The reason for finding Grabar's solution unsatisfactory is not that he says the
bemas and enclosures had lecterns. All the evidence shows that they were used, among
other things, for some kind of reading. The question is whether this was their sole
function and whether they existed *in addition* to a regular ambon. The most serious
objections to his explanation are that he does not account for the differently located
ambons in other Syrian churches, that he does not explain in his theory the comparison of the bema at Edessa to the Coenaculum at Sion, that his theory disregards one
possible interpretation of the evidence in the Testamentum, and that he does not
give any reason for the sudden disappearance of these centrally located bemas, or
"ambons."

His reconstruction of the bema in the domical martyrium of Hagia Sophia at
Edessa is based upon his interpretation of the French translation of the account of
it in the Syrian hymn, which reads, "Et, au dessous d'elle (se trouvent) onze colonnes,
comme les onze Apôtres qui s'étaient cachés (au Cénacle)."[41] Having taken the
French word "estrade" (Syriac for *bema*), which is used to designate this structure,
to mean *pulpitum*, Grabar assumes that the eleven columns, symbolizing the Apostles,
were literally "under" in the sense of being supports, or a first story, of a raised ambon.
Since the *Sougitha* also says that the bema at Edessa was "of the type of the Coenaculum at Sion," it is to be noted that there is nothing in the tradition of Christ and
the Apostles having concealed themselves in the "high-place" at Sion for the performance of the sacred feast to imply a public pulpit. Instead, the emphatic reference
to the Coenaculum suggests that "under it were eleven columns" meant, in a purely
symbolic sense, that the columns surrounding the bema were concealed within, or
"under," the veil, just as the Apostles were hidden in the little oratory at Sion when
they received from Christ the mystical Last Supper. Furthermore, if the bema at
Edessa was supported like a great ambon on eleven columns, then it was in no way
similar to the large bemas in the martyria of Antioch-Kaoussie and Seleucia Pieria and
was entirely different from the one in the martyrium at Resafa which we know was

[38] C. Ricci, *Guida di Ravenna*, 1923, 37;
Cabrol, *Dict.*, I, col. 1339.

[39] Ricci, "L'Antico duomo di Ravenna,"
Felix Ravenna, XXXVII, 1931, 14, taken from
G. F. Buonamici, *La Metropolitana di Ra-
venna*, 1748.

[40] Ricci, *Guida*, 1923, 37-41; G. Berti, *Sull'*

antico Duomo di Ravenna, 1880, 15; G. Rossi,
"Chiesa del Duomo," *Felix Ravenna*, XXXVII,
1931, 29ff.

[41] A. Dupont-Sommer, "Une Hymne syri-
aque sur la cathédrale d'Édesse" (Codex Vaticanus Syriacus, 95, fols. 49-50), *Cahiers archéologiques*, II, 1947, 31, verse xv.

surrounded by small colonnettes. Later a restoration of these bemas (Fig. 217) will be proposed which will not only link them all together but will attempt to explain the references in the *Sougitha* to the symbolic columns and the *Coenaculum*.

3. AMBON, CHOIR AND MASS OF CATECHUMENS?

Lassus, who first advanced the explanation that these enclosures were ambons, has developed a more elaborate liturgical explanation for their use, which includes, in addition to the regular readings of the service, antiphonal or responsive singing and the performance there of the mass of the catechumens.[42] His reasons for placing the reading of the scriptures at these bemas and enclosures are: the discovery of a sculptured *siège* at Behyō and Kirkbizé, and the somewhat ambiguous reference to the ambon in the *Apostolic Constitutions*.[43] Although recognizing that no such ambons have been discovered at Gerasa and that the Syrian ambon was usually just outside the sanctuary, he stresses the importance of the ambons found in the naves of the churches at Kal'at Sim'ân, Dair Solaib and Ma'in which have been discussed in note 33. The evidence in the *Testamentum* where I believe these enclosures are referred to as a "Place of Commemoration" quite distinct from the ambon, which is specifically located near the altar at the east end, will be discussed in the next section.

Lassus' belief that the choir was also located in these enclosures, situated in the middle of the church, is based upon the importance which was given to antiphonal singing in the Church of Antioch.[44] Although he notes that responsive singing was customary at Antioch from the time when the remains of S. Babylas were transferred from Daphne to Antioch in 363, he does not attach any significance to the fact that antiphonal singing was at first peculiar to the Cult of Martyrs at Antioch. Theodoret tells us that under Bishop Leontius (348-357 A.D.) two orthodox deacons, Flavianus and Diodorus "were the first to divide choirs into two parts, and to teach them to sing the psalms of David antiphonally." He then goes on to say that "its originators now collected the lovers of the divine word and work into the *Churches of the Martyrs*, and with them spent the night in singing psalms to God." Perhaps more significant for our purposes is the next paragraph which tells how Leontius, "who favored the Arian error," not daring to stop this popular practice, but wishing to discredit it, asked the two deacons to perform this act of worship in the churches, and so "they summoned their choir to the Church."[45] In fact, all the references to antiphonal singing at An-

[42] Lassus, *Sanctuaires chrétiens de Syrie*, 207-216; the first suggestion that the bema in the church at Edessa and the enclosures in the Syrian basilicas were ambons was made in 1929 by I. E. Rahmani, *Les Liturgies orientales et occidentales*, 43ff.

[43] Although Rahmani (*op.cit.*, 43) says that "in the middle of the nave, facing the sanctuary, is the ambon, that is to say the tribune, supported on four columns" as is prescribed in the *Apostolic Constitutions*, it is not at all clear from the very abbreviated directions in the *Constitutions*, II, sect. 28 (Brightman,

Eastern and Western Liturgies, 1896, I, 29, line 15) that Rahmani and Lassus (*ibid.*, 211 n. 3) are justified in this assumption. As to Lassus' statement (*ibid.*, 211 n. 3, 213) that the same source refers to the ambon as a place large enough, like the Syrian enclosure under discussion, to hold the bishop, priests and other clergy, the *Constitutions*, sec. 28, make it clear from the context that the place where the clergy take their seats is the regular bema at the east end of the church.

[44] Lassus, *op.cit.*, 211 n. 4.

[45] In addition to this reference (*Ecclesias-*

tioch and Theodoret's specific distinction between "the Churches of Martyrs" and "The Church" strengthen the probability that, if the Syrian bemas and enclosures were used as choirs, this usage in the fourth and fifth centuries was associated with the Cult of Martyrs.

In addition to serving as an ambon and choir the Syrian enclosures, according to the theory of Lassus, were used for the Mass of the Catechumens. Presumably, he says the readers and the clergy, during the singing of the *trisagion*, went from the sanctuary to the place in the middle of the nave, and then, after the sacred readings and the sermon, they returned to the apse.[46] When this part of the ceremony was concluded the catechumens were led out, the doors were closed and the Mass of the Faithful followed. Even if Lassus is correct in believing that the liturgical evidence allows of his theory, it is difficult to understand how an architectural variable can be explained by a liturgical invariable. What then was the ceremonial procedure in the many churches that did not have these enclosures? Also, it seems surprising that such elaborate architectural provisions, taking up so much space in the nave, should have originated for a minor part of the service and have had no lasting influence. The major weaknesses, however, of Lassus' theory are that it does not attempt to explain all the evidence, such as: (1) the relation between the enclosures in the basilicas and the bemas in the martyria; (2) the reference in the *Sougitha* to the *Coenaculum* at Sion; (3) the Antiochene use of antiphonal singing in the ceremonies of the "Churches of Martyrs"; (4) his own evidence that the enclosures appear to occur in basilicas which had introduced reliquaries and the Cult of Martyrs; (5) the sudden disappearance of these enclosures; and (6) the possible evidence in the *Testamentum*.

D. The Evidence of the *Testamentum*

The *Testamentum Domini Nostri Jesu Christi* is a compilation of canonical information, written in Syriac, but, according to a colophon, translated from the Greek

---

tical History, II, xix, *Nicene and Post-Nicene Fathers*, III, 1892, 85) to the choir having been divided by Flavianus and Diodorus between 348 and 357 A.D., Theodoret tells how Ephraim, the Syrian, composed songs which "are still used to enliven the festivals of our victorious martyrs" (*ibid.*, IV, 26). Socrates (*Eccl. Hist.*, VI, viii, *M.P.L.* LXVII, 689-692) describes how the Arians during the night chanted songs, "which they call responsive," and credits Ignatius with having introduced at Antioch the custom of singing "responsive hymns," while Sozomenus (*Eccl. Hist.*, VIII, viii, *M.P.L.* LXVII, 1536-1537) tells how the remains of Meletius, when they were being conveyed to Antioch to be "deposited near the tomb of Babylas the martyr, . . . were honored with singing of psalms antiphonally." There is also the refer-

ence in Eusebius (Chap. VI n. 30) to indicate that in the third century at Antioch singing "in the middle of the church" was customary in a service of veneration for a saint. Further evidence that singing continued to be associated with the Cult of Martyrs and that as late as 537 A.D. there were still marked differences of opinion between the orthodox and Arians regarding the services which should take place in the martyria, are indicated by a letter of Severus, Patriarch of Antioch, who wrote, "Where the bones of holy martyrs have previously been laid, it is right to pray, especially when the place is in silence, and the heretics are not unlawfully conducting services or singing inside" (E. W. Brooks, *Select Letters of Severus*, II, trans., part II, 1904, 271).

[46] Lassus, *Sanctuaires*, 212-216.

by James of Edessa in 687 A.D.[47] Puzzling as the history of the manuscript has proved to be, it is considered a reliable source of testimony on Syrian usage during the period of the sixth and seventh centuries, and probably during the preceding century. Conservative scholarship, instead of agreeing with the efforts to trace it back to before the Peace of the Church, places its origin in a monophysite milieu of Syria, at least as early as the time of Severus of Antioch, who at the end of the fifth century quotes some of its passages.[48] Therefore, it belongs to the period and general region that made use of the central bema in the churches.

In the section entitled "How to Build a Church" the *Testamentum* starts with the east end of the church, describing the episcopal throne as *versus orientum*, and says, "Let this place of the throne be raised three steps up, for the *Altar* also ought to be there. Now let this house [church] have two porticoes to right and left, for men and women."[49] Regarding the altar it reads, "Let the Altar have a veil of pure linen because it is without spot." Then in the next and most important paragraph it goes on, "And for the Commemoration let a place be *built* so that a priest may sit, and the archdeacon with readers, and write the names of those who are offering oblations, or of those on whose behalf they offer, so that when the Holy Things are being offered by the bishop, a reader or the archdeacon may name them in this commemoration which priests and people offer with supplication."[50] The paragraph ends, *Talus est enim et typus in coelo*, which has been translated, "For this type is also like heaven," meaning, perhaps, that this place symbolizes heaven.

That this heavenly place was like the bema in the martyria at Antioch, Seleucia Pieria and Resafa is clearly indicated by the next sentence which reads, "And let the place of priests be within a veil near the Place of Commemoration." Since the synthronus with the bishop's throne has already been described, this "place of priests" must be the apselike exedra with its bank of seats which has been seen at the west end of the Syrian bema. Furthermore the *Testamentum* makes it certain that the Place of Commemoration could not be an ambon, although it must have had a lectern for the transcription and reading of names, because in a later sentence it says, "And let the Place of Reading be a little outside the altar," which we have already been told was located with the cathedra in the apse.

The *Testamentum* shows that the enclosures in question were not ambons but presumably a "Place of Commemoration," which by its name and the account of the offering of supplications may have been devoted to the Cult of Martyrs and Relics. It also implies that some early form of the office of oblations took place at it. Moreover, its injunction that the "place of priests be within a veil" suggests that the whole Place of Commemoration, to which the place of priests was connected, was a kind of veiled chapel, such as the evidence from Resafa and Mirayeh has already indicated.

[47] I. H. Rahmani, *Testamentum Domini Nostri Jesu Christi*, 1899; Leclercq in Cabrol, *Dict.*, III, col. 2782; C. M. Kaufmann, *Handbuch der Christlichen Archäologie*, 1913, 175; D. J. Chitty, *Gerasa* (ed. Kraeling), 175.

[48] *Dictionnaire de théologie catholique*, XV, 1943, 194ff.
[49] *Gerasa* (trans. Chitty), 175, pars. 4-5.
[50] *Ibid.*, 176, par. 9.

It has not, however, answered the important question of whether the enclosure in the basilicas was derived from the bema in the domed martyria, and also whether both were provisions for the veneration of martyrs. Since the *Testamentum* specified where the offerings for the regular service were to be made when it says, "and let the *Diaconicon* be to the right of the right-hand entrance (i.e. the southeast side-chamber) to the purpose that the Eucharists, or offerings that are placed there may be seen," it would seem to follow that the oblations offered and recorded at the Place of Commemoration were of a different nature, perhaps having been the special gifts which went with the supplications to the saint.[51] It is tempting to go a step further and ask if the "Holy Things," which the *Testamentum* says were "offered by the bishop," were the elements of the Eucharist, as in the later service of the prothesis, or relics. In either event, would it not have been necessary during a lengthy ceremony which involved naming them "in this commemoration which *priests and people offer with supplication*" to have a "table" for the proper presentation of Holy Things? At this point one comes back to the earlier question of whether at any time this "table" under its ciborium could have been used like the "table of prothesis" in the developed liturgy?

E. The Place of Commemoration

Further excavations and liturgical studies will be necessary before any certain solution can be found for the ceremonial use and historical development of both bemas and enclosures. If the proposed explanation, which is an endeavor to include all the evidence and satisfy all the conditions, proves helpful to others in arriving at a more correct solution, there is no necessity to emphasize its tentative character and to apologize for its unorthodox suggestions. The study started only with the intention of accounting for the bema in the two martyria of Antioch and Seleucia Pieria and of seeing if there was a relation between the centrally located bema and the domical martyrium.

There can be no question but what the large platform with its semicircular west end in the center of the cruciform church of S. Babylas was the actual sanctuary on which was the altar. Some intimation of its appearance may perhaps be derived from Eusebius' account of the dedication of the fourth century church at Tyre, for he writes, "and finally placed in the middle the holy of holies, the altar, and, that it may be *inaccessible to the multitude*, enclosed it with wooden lattice-work, accurately wrought with artistic carving."[52] The fact that there were centrally located altars, partially or wholly veiled by hangings and lattice-work, may help to explain the veiled Place of Commemoration in later Syrian churches.

[51] This specific reference in the *Testamentum* to the offerings in the diaconicon makes it evident that the Place of Commemoration could not have been in the side-chamber. In discussing the *Testamentum*, Mandalà (*La Protesi della liturgie nel rito Bizantino-Greco,*

37-38) says, "locus commemorationes (anche mobile) come sarebbe per alcuni il παρατράπεσον farebbe pensare ad una relazione con l'altarino del nostra protesi actuale."

[52] Eusebius, *Eccl. Hist.* (Loeb), x, 4, 44.

In accounting for the development of the centrally located bema such as we have at Antioch, a distinction must be made between the two types of churches which were quite distinct during the fourth and fifth centuries in Syria. One was the ordinary basilica, "long and with its head to the east" as the *Apostolic Constitutions* describe it, and the other was the so-called "Churches of Martyrs," which was usually domical and had the altar in the center. That the altar during the fourth century was frequently located in the midst of the congregation, especially in the "Churches of Martyrs," is proved by the martyrium of the Holy Apostles, S. Babylas at Antioch, S. John at Ephesus, the martyrium of S. George at Shakka and perhaps by the church at Tyre and the Ursiana at Ravenna where Syrian prestige was strong.[53] Regardless of the apparent conspiracy of silence on the part of both Church Fathers and later historians regarding so many aspects of the Cult of Martyrs, there must have been marked differences between the services in the two types of church, as is clearly indicated by Theodoret's references to antiphonal singing at Antioch. Therefore, it follows, that before everything pertaining to the popular Cult of Martyrs could be gradually subordinated to the regular service of Christ, there were ceremonies at the central altar of the martyria which, even though they were not approved of by the more orthodox clergy, did include special provisions for offerings and prayers. That some survival of these early ceremonies is preserved in the references of the *Testamentum* to the "Place of Commemoration" is a possibility which should be more fully investigated.

By the fifth century when the martyrium at Seleucia Pieria (Fig. 182) was built, the intent of the Church, which eventually was to turn the domical and central-type martyrium into a regular church devoted to the cult of Christ, is apparent in the way the traditional type of martyrium has an eastern sanctuary. At the same time, however, the prominent position in the church was still given to the great bema in the midst of the congregation where, at S. Babylas in the fourth century, the altar had been located. Therefore, in spite of the subsequent history of the Eastern Churches, it seems necessary to assume that in this transitional and controversial period of religious history in the Church of Antioch there were two altars, one for the service of Christ in the apse, and another devoted to the cult of the martyr in the midst of the congregation. This transitional phase of liturgical and architectural development in Syria may then account for the two altars which were probably in the fourth century Ursiana at Ravenna[54] and the church of S. Apollinare in Classe, with its two side-chambers of Eastern origin, which was dedicated in 549 A.D. and presumably had an altar in both apse and nave.[55]

[53] Mattern (*Mélanges de l'Université Saint-Joseph*, XXII, 1939, 12ff.) believes that the stone found in the nave of Dair Solaib was the base of an altar instead of an ambon, and the stone found by De Vaux at Ma'in (*Rev. bibl.*, XLVII, 1938, 231) was also an altar. Mattern cites also the article of P. Batiffol ("De la dédicace des églises," *Revue des sciences phil. et théol.*, XXVIII, 1939, 58ff.) to show the use of altars in the nave.

[54] See p. 142.

[55] C. Ricci, *Guida da Ravenna*, 1923, 192-194. Here the altar in the nave is thought to have been set up in honor of the Virgin by Bishop Maximianus.

By the sixth century the addition of a baptistery and side-chambers in the rebuilding of the martyrium at Seleucia Pieria indicates the triumph of the orthodox desire to focus all the emphasis upon a single altar of Christ in its traditional sanctuary. If so, then what was done with the central bema, which according to the archaeological evidence was rebuilt in the sixth century? In answering this question I am suggesting that by this time there was no longer an "altar" on the bema, only a "table," and that the fourth century bema had already been transformed, as in the basilica churches, into a "Place of Commemoration," which was still used for special ceremonies connected with the cult of a martyr. In the regular service, however, it was entirely subordinated to the altar of Christ in the apse. Also, with some hesitation, I am suggesting that the bema, which had now become a kind of veiled oratory, like a chapel, may for a time have been used for some early form of the office of oblations, which were later to take place at the "table of oblations" in the prothesis chapel. If this were so, then the transference of "Holy Things" from the veiled chapel in the midst of the faithful might have been a forerunner of the Great Entrance.

Around the middle of the fifth century when the martyrium at Resafa (Fig. 198) was built over the tomb of S. Sergius there may have still been two altars. It seems more likely, however, from the plan of the church that the emphasis was on the altar in the apse, and that the indications of an altar beneath a ciborium on the bema only mean that there was a "table" there for use in the ceremonies of the saint and, perhaps, for the oblations. Here at Resafa the bank of seats for clergy and the evidence of colonnettes to veil both priests and "table" show the nature of this Place of Commemoration as a special oratory. By the sixth century it is the memorial character of a veiled place in the center of a church which explains the reference in the *Sougitha* to the bema at Edessa as *"of the type of the Coenaculum at Sion,"* for the "high-place" in the Sion church, it has been seen, was a hidden oratory, a memorial chapel and small domical martyrium. Eusebius tells us that "the martyrs of Palestine were interred in the churches, their tombs being placed in oratories."[56] While in Syria tombs and relics were not placed under the altar or in the Place of Commemoration, the comparison of the Edessa bema to the Sion chapel suggests that these Places of Commemoration were actual oratories. Certainly Aetheria's account of the pulpitum in the fourth century church on Mount Nebo supports this interpretation.

In order to help visualize the scale of these bemas in the martyria and to help explain the description in the *Sougitha* of the one at Edessa, I have attempted to restore the one at Resafa (Fig. 217) using Lassus' plan (Fig. 216) but making certain adjustments. Eleven columns are placed on the two sides of the rectangular platform, as the plan at Resafa allows, in order to show what the *Sougitha* meant. In this way it becomes apparent how the columns, which symbolized the Apostles, were not "under" the bema in the sense of supporting it like an ambon. By restoring the columns around the "place of priests" outside the veil, I have accentuated the symbolic significance of the other columns being "hidden" in the way the Apostles were

---

[56] Eusebius, *De martyr. palest.*, XI, 28.

hidden in the Coenaculum at Sion. The restoration, however, is not intended to give more than a general indication of how such bemas might have looked, because some of them must have had screens of wood and metal.

Before turning from the original bema type in the domical martyria, it should be noted that excavations have shown that there were no such provisions in the sixth century martyrium at Bosra where the whole emphasis had been shifted to the apse with its flanking chambers. At the same time, however, that the central-type martyrium was being adapted to the regular liturgy, many communities were moved, because of the growing popularity of the martyrs, to introduce into the naves of their basilicas a smaller and modified version of the martyrium bemas. It was this simplification of the original provisions for the Cult of Martyrs that the *Testamentum* describes as a "Place of Commemoration." The conclusion that these places in the basilicas were introduced in the fifth century and were connected with special ceremonies in honor of the martyrs is supported by the fact that the three fourth-century basilicas of Brad, Burdj-Hêdar and Babiskā all show the later addition of large martyrium chapels. Furthermore, it is strengthened by the fact that so many of the later basilicas with a Place of Commemoration have been found to have stone reliquaries in one of their chapels.

As yet no place of commemoration in a basilica has been reported to be more than 6 m. long, including the semicircular end for the clergy. On the basis of Butler's evidence from Mir'âyeh, where he found a dowel hole in the top of each stone around the enclosure, these special oratories were veiled as had been the large bemas in the domical martyria. Little else can be added to the present description because no specific information as yet has been published on the ciborium found in the one at Behyō and no picture of the so-called "throne" found at both Behyō and Kirkbizé which Lassus and Grabar said was a place where the reader laid the sacred books. While the reading of names took place in the Place of Commemoration, the *Testamentum* makes it clear that they were not ambons. My only strong reason for questioning Lassus' suggestion that the mass of the catechumens also took place here is, first, the apparently limited use of the Place of Commemoration even in North Syria, and, second, its complete disappearance from the interior of all Eastern churches.

Actually one of the strongest reasons, apart from the evidence of the *Testamentum*, for believing that the Place of Commemoration was essentially devoted to the Cult of Martyrs and Relics is its sudden disappearance and the fact that it seems to have left no survivals in the later churches of the East. It has already been pointed out that the worn pavement with the outline of a Place of Commemoration in the church of Kalb Lauzeh suggests its removal in the seventh century, while the probable transformation at the end of the sixth century of the domical martyrium of S. Sergius at Resafa into a regular basilica implies a liturgical reason, perhaps connected with the great bema in the nave. By the end of the sixth century, when it becomes apparent that the orthodox liturgy with the prothesis chapel and Great Entrance was being adopted in Syria, the Eastern Church had triumphed in its long effort to subordinate everything in the popular Cult of Martyrs to the glory of God and the service of Christ. Hence the transformation of the domical martyrium into an apsidal church with the one altar and the abolishment of the Place of Commemoration.

F. Domical Chapels

In order to strengthen the relation between the original type of central bema and the domed martyrium, it is necessary to see how this association of the mortuary and symbolic dome with the tomb memorial of a martyr was transferred from the "Churches of Martyrs" to the mortuary chapels of the basilicas. In the fourth century the ordinary churches had no relics and the martyrs were honored in independent and tomblike structures. At this time the two small side-chambers flanking the apse in the basilica churches, which had been taken over from pagan temples, were used as vestries and for the reception of offerings from the congregation.[57] Hence these *pastophoria* were not only small, but they were of little significance in the liturgy. At Brad (Fig. 205) it was not until late in the sixth century that the actual prothesis chapel with its table was added to the northeast side-chamber; and in the sequence of churches at Gerasa, Crowfoot found no indication that the pastophoria were considered a part of the sanctuary, by being cut off from the side aisles by a chancel, until after the introduction of the orthodox liturgy.[58]

During the fifth and sixth centuries many basilicas acquired relics and sometimes either built special martyrium chapels, as at Brad and Bābiskā, or enlarged one of the side-chambers into a mortuary chapel.[59] For the most part, however, they deposited their relics in one of the pastophoria, usually the one on the south side,[60] which also

[57] I cannot agree with Crowfoot's conclusions that the Syrian side-chambers came "into existence by a sort of structural necessity to fill in the dead space at the end of the aisles on either side of an internal apse" and that "not one of these chambers was built for liturgical purposes" (*Gerasa*, 181). Crowfoot uncovered several churches at Gerasa which had a large lateral chapel opening off a *western* forecourt, one of which was designated as a *diaconia* in an inscription (*Gerasa*, 178, 228, plan, xxxv), but I cannot agree with his interpretation of the *Testamentum* and his belief that the churches at Gerasa, which obviously combine Syrian features with the Palestinian custom of having a western atrium, follow the usage in the *Testamentum* and so prove the liturgical unimportance of the North Syrian side-chambers. When the *Testamentum* says, "And let the Diaconicon be to the right of the right-hand entry, to the purpose that the Eucharists, or offerings that are offered, may be seen," and "Let there be a Forecourt, with a portico running round, to this Diaconicon" (*Gerasa*, 175, par. 2), it does not mean, as Crowfoot says,

that the "Diaconicon" was meant to be at the right-hand corner of the west façade. All the North Syrian churches have the forecourt, or atrium, on the south side with the two entrances into the south aisle and usually the prescribed portico, showing that the *Testamentum* refers to the southeastern side-chamber which was "to the right of the right-hand entry," where the clergy entered. Furthermore, it is this chamber in most North Syrian churches that had an arched opening into the side aisle and was the place where most reliquaries have been found.

[58] It is Crowfoot's opinion (*Gerasa*, 182) that there is no evidence at Gerasa of a prothesis chapel before 611 A.D. when the church of Bishop Genesius was built, although in both the church of Procopius (526/27 A.D.) and the church of SS. Peter and Paul (c. 540 A.D.) the chancel was found to extend across the side aisles in front of both side-chambers (*Gerasa*, plans XLIII and XXXIX).

[59] Lassus, *Sanctuaires*, 162.

[60] Churches with a martyrium chapel on the north side were usually early: the fourth cen-

served as the "Diaconicon" in the sense that it is described in the *Testamentum*. In spite of this growing popularity of martyrs the strong determination on the part of the Eastern churches both to subordinate the Cult of Relics and separate it from the Eucharistic cult prevented that union of altar and martyrium which became the rule in the West where relics were placed under an altar.[61] Therefore, by making use of their traditional side-chambers for relics the Syrian churches were able to keep the Eucharistic sanctuary and the martyrium chapel under one roof without abandoning the basilica type of church. This means that there were two related tendencies going on in the development of religious architecture; at the same time that the independent and domical martyrium was being adjusted to the regular service of Christ, by the addition of apse and side-chambers, the elongation of its central axis to focus upon the one altar, and the shifting of the relics to the pastophoria, the martyrium concept was also moving into the basilicas.

It is impossible to say at exactly what time this combination of martyr's chapel with the regular basilica resulted in the adoption of the domical symbolism. At first the side-chambers of the basilicas were usually one-story chambers either under the ordinary side aisle roof or with their own pent house roofs. By the fifth century we do know that the Sion church had two domical side-chambers at the south side of the apse, on the second story, which were famous oratories.[62] If for no other reason, the sanctity and prestige of the domical *Coenaculum* at Sion would have resulted in the spread of similar domical oratories. Although it is impossible to tell from the ruined condition of Syrian churches when the pastophoria were built-up into flanking towers to provide second-story oratories, or if the chambers that began to appear at the west end flanking the entrance were also used as chapels, we do have evidence that some such development was taking place. At Resafa, for example, Spanner and Guyer

---

tury church of S. Euphemius in Chalcedon had a domical oratory to the north of the apse (Evagrius, *Hist. Eccl.*, II, 3; Grabar, *Martyrium*, I, 336); the fifth century church of Ilissos had a cruciform and domical martyrium on the north side (Sotiriou, 'Αρχ. 'Εφ., 1919, 1-31, 208-210; Grabar, *Martyrium*, I, 336); the south church, il-Anderin, had a cruciform tomb at the northeast corner (Butler, *Syria*, II, B, 59, ill. 54); the separate martyrium chapel of 525 A.D. at Kefrnabū (Butler, *Syria*, II, B, 295); Brad (Lassus, *Sanctuaires*, 168, fig. 77); perhaps at Palmyra (*ibid.*, 168, fig. 76); and at Mar Saba in Palestine the relics of the Sabaite martyrs are recorded as having been in the northwest corner of the church (*Gerasa*, 178 n. 9; Cyril of Scythopolis, *Eccl. Gr. Mon.*, III, 243).

Reliquaries have been found in the southeast chambers in Syria at Sokani, Taklé, Kal'at Kalôtā and several other places recorded by

Lassus (*Sanctuaires*, 167-176); at Gerasa in the fourth century cathedral (*Gerasa*, 183); at Apamea (Lassus, *Sanctuaires*, 166); in S. Nicholas at Myra in Lycia (Grabar, *Martyrium*, I, 343), and in S. Barnabas at Salamis in Cyprus (*ibid.*, 342-343).

[61] Grabar, *Martyrium*, I, 349-356; F. Wieland, *Altar u. Altargrab der christlichen Kirchen im 4 Jahr.*, 1912, 98-105. At the same time it should be noted that at Gerasa in the church of SS. Peter and Paul (*Gerasa*, 183, 253) and at S. George (*ibid.*, 183, 245) stone reliquaries were found in the floor of the apse behind, or beneath, the probable location of the altar; Grabar (*Martyrium*, I, 352 n. 3) says the bishop of Maïouma in Palestine deposited the relics of three martyrs beneath the altar; and other similar examples are also cited by Grabar (*ibid.*, n. 6).

[62] See p. 36.

discovered in corners of the square north tower of S. Sergius (Fig. 198) arched squinches supported upon columnar corbels, which were the same as those in the corners of the octagon at Kal'at Sim'ân (Fig. 35) and in the domical tower over the nave at Koja Kalessi (Fig. 194). While they correctly interpreted the purpose of these squinches as a means of fitting a dome onto a square impost, they restored both flanking towers with masonry domes concealed beneath gabled roofs of wood and tile. For reasons that should now be apparent, and because of certain specific evidence, I have restored these towers with domes of wood on the exterior as a traditional manifestation of the celestial and mortuary nature of the symbolic tomb chambers beneath them.

This insistence that the towers at Resafa had visible, gilded domes does not mean that all the reliquary chapels in the basilicas were domical. It does, however, signify a tendency in this direction. The Syrian landscape preserved in the mosaic of the mosque at Damascus shows domical towers (Figs. 41, 42), while the mosaic from Khirbit Mukhayyat (Fig. 44) has domical towers flanking the façade of a church. Moreover, the ampulla of the Holy Athenogenes (Fig. 153) indicates that a domical tower was a symbol of a saint's martyrium. Add to this evidence the prestige of the domical oratories in the basilica church at Sion and we have strong proof that the domical symbolism originally associated with the independent martyrium had penetrated the basilica.

In fact, it is the transference of the dome from the martyrium to the oratory which, when taken in combination with the growing popularity of domical mysticism that was gradually transforming the domical martyrium into a regular type of church, explains the appearance of the dome over the side chapels of the Coptic churches and, perhaps, the use of corner domes in connection with the central dome on later Byzantine churches. Furthermore, it accounts for the effort to construct masonry domes over the elongated side chapels of the "Grave church" at Resafa (Fig. 176) and over the square chambers at the east end of the North African basilica (Fig. 213) at Tolemaide.[63] In this relatively late basilica, where the character of the stonework (Figs. 214, 215) recalls the small domes in the corners of the church at Resafa, it will be noted that the tri-lobed plan of the north chamber and the cruciform plan of the south chamber continue the same early tomb-types which the Christians took over from the Romans for their martyria.

It is because of this evidence and the general pattern of ideas which was involved that I have restored the two martyria at Resafa with domical towers and have shown the martyrium of the Prophets, Apostles and Martyrs at Gerasa (Fig. 175) with similar wooden domes at the four corners. It was the Syrian tradition of subordinating the importance of the relics to the Eucharistic cult by enshrining them in subsidiary

[63] P. Romanelli, "La Basilica cristiana nell' Africa settentrionale italiana," *Atti del IV Congresso internazionale di archeologia cristiana*, 1940, 279-286, figs. 28 (plan), 30, 31. Although the author suggests a fourth or fifth century date, the tunnel vault over the side aisles, the presence of *matronei* and the stone-cutting of the vaults all indicate a late sixth century date after this region came under Syrian and Palestinian influences.

chapels which leads to the presumption that the four corner chambers at Gerasa were small oratories and that other Syrian churches may have had domical towers at the four corners. It is only by means of such a restoration that we obtain an explanation for the recently discovered church at Dair Solaib where, in addition to an independent tomb building as at Ruweha, the church has four square chambers, one at each corner and with columnar porches between them on the north, south and west façades.[64] If anyone desires to change the shape of the domes which I have restored on the Syrian churches, because they seem too prominent, or too Islamic, that is immaterial to the basic thesis that the dome had great significance in Syria and was closely associated with the martyrium as a spiritual and eternal Domus.

[64] Mattern, R. Mouterde and A. Beaulieu, "Dair Solaib," *Mélanges de l'Université Saint-Joseph*, XXII, 1936, 6ff., pl. 1. The tomb, which is free standing at the southwest corner, has a cruciform plan and appears to have a "cloister" dome over the crossing. The second half of the fifth century is suggested for the date.

APPENDIX

DESCRIPTION OF THE CHURCH OF S. STEPHEN AT GAZA
BY CHORICIUS, SECTIONS 37-46[1]

TRANSLATION AND NOTES BY G. DOWNEY

(37) But the eastern end, and its varied craftsmanship, has drawn me to it so quickly that I cannot bear to linger further on the details of the outside [of the church], and it has rightly compelled me to come to it before I have gone through the other features [of the building]. Beginning on the pavement itself, a well-executed concavity[2] distinguishes[3] the wall, the lower part of which maintains a constant width[4] as far as the arch[5] which stands upon the corners; and the remainder is gradually drawn together in breadth, harmoniously with the arch. (38) On either side there is a pair of holy men, each of them bearing the appropriate marks of distinction; the one on the right of the spectators holds the church in his hand, and on the left you see the Forerunner. (39) The lower part [of the wall] gleams with marbles of all kinds. Among these, one particular stone, of one kind by nature but made by skill into many forms, surrounds the window, which is both broad and tall in proportion, which lies in the middle [of the lower part of the wall]; this [stone] alone supplies the facings on either side along the edges of the window which it entirely surrounds, and, adorning the two walls on either side, it does not stop until it has mounted up on both sides and has reached the band[6] resting on the window, which is itself of the same stone.[7] (40) For in this way bands of marbles conceal the wall in well-joined fashion, and are so well fitted that you would suppose that they were the work of nature, and they are so variegated by their natural colors that they do not fall short

---

[1] *Laud. Marc.*, II, 37-46, in *Choricii Gazaei opera*, ed. Förster-Richtsteig, Leipzig, 1929, 37-39. Words enclosed in square brackets in the present version have been added by the translator. There are translations by R. W. Hamilton, "Two Churches at Gaza, As Described by Choricius of Gaza," *Pal. Expl. Fund, Quart. St.*, 1930, 178-191, and by F.-M. Abel, "Gaza au VIe siècle, d'après le rhéteur Choricius," *Rev. bibl.*, XL, 1931, 5-31, neither of which is wholly satisfactory in the rendition of certain details.

[2] κοιλότης: a literary circumlocution describing the semicircular plan of the apse; cf. κοιλότησις in Procopius of Gaza, *Ekphrasis*, III, ed. P. Friedländer, *Spätantike Gemäldezyklus in Gaza* (Vatican City, 1939; Studi e Testi, 89), 5, 23, also Procopius of Caesarea's description of the apse of St. Sophia, *De aed.*, I, i, 32.

[3] I.e. beautifies.

[4] Abel mistranslates εὐρυνομένου as "se dilate."

[5] ἁψίς means "arch," not "apse"; cf. below, sec. 45, and *Laud. Marc.*, I, 34.

[6] Or "girdle." ζώνη is used by Constantine of

Rhodes to describe leveling or crowning courses which ran around the interior walls of the church of the Holy Apostles at Constantinople (v. 677, ed. E. Legrand, *R.E.G.*, IX, 1896, p. 56); see also Theophanes Continuatus, ed. Bonn, p. 326, 18. Paulus Silentiarius (*Ambon*, 63, 201) and Nikolaos Mesarites, in his description of the church of the Holy Apostles at Constantinople (XXXVII, ed. A. Heisenberg, *Grabeskirche u. Apostelkirche*, II, p. 79, 3), speak of such a course as ζωστήρ, which Hesychius (s.v. ζωστήρ) gives as the equivalent of ζώνη; and Paulus Silentiarius uses the verb ζώννυμι in equivalent contexts (*St. Sophia*, 362; *Ambon*, 122). Constantine of Rhodes (vv. 678, 747) and Mesarites (XXXVII, 79, 5) also speak of a certain type of course as κοσμήτης, which Mesarites gives as the equivalent of ζώνη. On ζώνη see also Sotiriou, 'Αρχ. Δελτ., VII, 1921-22, 107, and Birnbaum "Die Oktogone von Antiochia, Nazianz u. Nyssa," *Rep. f. Kunstwiss.*, XXXVI, 1913, 199-200, with n. 20 and text on 192.

[7] Literally, "of no other stone."

155

of human painting. Indeed, if the painters' students, whose task it is to choose and copy the fairest things in existence, should be in need of columns to reproduce, or lovely stones—and I have seen many such things painted—they will find many fine models here.

(41) On one band—the highest, I mean—there rests a novel shape.[8] Geometrical terminology,[9] I understand, calls this a half cone,[10] the term receiving its origin as follows. (42) You have perhaps seen in your country the pine tree, and if this was originally a maiden—for there are some who tell this story, how Boreas, smitten with amorous jealousy, was about to slay her, when Earth, deeply pitying her plight, sent up a tree of the same name as the maiden.[11] I neither believe the people who tell this nor is it my intention to relate it, but only to say that it bears a fruit which is called the cone. This is the origin of the term applied to the form.[12] This much I can describe to you by a graphic image. But if you wish to hear a full description, it is like this. (43) A carpenter, cutting circles,[13] five in number, from the material which his craft furnishes him,[14] and cutting each of them equally in two, and joining nine of the slices[15] to each other by their tips,[16] and also joining them by their middles[17] to

---

[8] Or, "architectural element." σχῆμα is wrongly translated "ornament" by Hamilton, while Abel's rendering of "élément" is inappropriate. The word ordinarily means "shape," "figure," or "form," and is employed in Greek quite as loosely as these words are in English. Choricius uses it to mean both "decorative pattern" (*Laud. Marc.*, I, 18) and "architectural element" (*ibid.*, 38). Previous translators supposed that the whole of secs. 37-45 refers to the eastern apse of the church; but there are plain indications to the contrary. Choricius makes it plain that he has changed his subject, emphasizing that he is now writing about an architectural element which rests upon the highest of the "bands" of stone. There are several of these (sec. 40), of which he has previously described only one, that which rests upon the window of the apse (sec. 39). Choricius is clear that the one he is now describing is different, being the highest in the church. The references to the "bands" are a literary device by which the transition from one subject to another may be made. The remark about the students of painting (sec. 40) also indicates a change of topic.

[9] Literally, "geometry." Choricius is fond of displaying his technical knowledge. Describing the apse of the church of St. Sergius, he states (*Laud. Marc.*, I, 27) that he writes in the technical language of the μηχανοποιοί, the architects (on their use of geometric methods and terminology, see G. Downey, "Byzantine Architects," *Byzantion*, XVIII, 1946-48, 99-118). Choricius is also more exact than many writers in his references to spherical domes. A central

dome is called "a hollow sphere divided equally" (*Laud. Marc.*, I, 19), and an apsidal semi-dome is "the fourth part of a hollow sphere" (*ibid.*, 27). Choricius likewise gives a very precise description of the springing of the central dome in the same church (*ibid.*, 38). Most writers, when calling a dome a "sphere" (which is the commonest term) do not trouble to note that it is a hollow sphere, nor do they, like Choricius, call a dome a "half-sphere" and a semi-dome a "quarter-sphere"; see G. Downey, "On Some Post-Classical Greek Architectural Terms," *Trans. of the Amer. Philol. Assoc.*, LXXVII, 1946, 22-34.

[10] Hamilton renders "half cone," and Abel "demi-cône." That Choricius means a truncated cone rather than a vertical section of a cone is shown by his description of the apse of the church of St. Sergius, which he calls an "upright section of a cylinder" (*Laud. Marc.*, I, 27). Had he employed corresponding phraseology in the present passage, he would have written "upright section of a cone."

[11] The grammatical structure of the sentence is deliberately distorted for literary effect.

[12] I.e. to the geometrical form.

[13] Hamilton's and Abel's translation of κύκλοι by "discs," "disques," is unwarranted; cf. *Laud. Marc.*, I, 18.

[14] I.e. wood.

[15] Or "sectors" or "segments." In geometrical terminology, a τμῆμα is a sector of a circle or a segment of a circle.

[16] At the summit of the dome.

[17] I.e. at their middle parts. These must be the points which had been the middles of the

the band which I just now mentioned was the highest one, sets upon them pieces of wood,[18] which he makes concave,[19] equal in number to these,[20] which begin in broad fashion from below and gradually become narrower and rise up to a sharp point, so as to fit the concavity of the wall; and drawing together all the tips[21] into one, and bending them gently, he produced a most pleasing spectacle. (44) But while I have cut five circles in half I have described the function of only nine of the sectors, and I realize that you are probably seeking the remaining part[22] of the circle. (45) This part, then, is itself divided equally and part of it being placed on one side of the nine, and part on the other, an arch of the same material rests over each of the two,[23] hollowed out in front, contributing an increase to the beauty of the image which is depicted there,[24] in the middle, of the Ruler of all things. And gold and colors make the whole work brilliant.

(46) So these things are constructed in this fashion. And since it is necessary for each of the colonnades [stoas] to have some kind of distinction at the eastern end, and at the same time necessary that they should not have so much [distinction] as the middle,[25] they are adorned with other forms, but without the variety given by the cones[26] which I have described.

---

circles before they were cut, and now form the lower end of each half-circle.

[18] The half-circles formed the ribs of the dome. On these were laid planks, tapering upward to a point, which formed gores between the ribs.

[19] Choricius employs the same usage as that in sec. 37, where he describes the apse, in plan, as a "concavity."

[20] ἰσάριθμα does not necessarily mean that the planks laid upon the ribs were nine in number, for in that case they would be very broad, whether laid vertically or horizontally. Wishing to make his picture as accurate as possible, Choricius means that there was one gore (i.e. one set of planks) to each rib; ξύλα are the gores, not the individual planks of which they were composed.

[21] The tips of the ribs and the tips of the gores.

[22] Or, "the remainder." μέρος is used here as a neutral, non-graphic term.

[23] Choricius introduces the idea of quarter-circles in order to indicate the profile of the supporting semi-domes. His purpose is not to describe the construction of the supporting semi-domes, but to relate their configuration to the central dome. The tenth semi-circle is introduced, not as an actual structural element of the supporting semi-domes, but in order that it may be cut in two so as to illustrate their profile. The metaphorical employment of each of these semi-circles is illustrated by the way in which an arch is said to rest upon them.

[24] I.e. in the main element which he has just described.

[25] The middle of the church, i.e. the central dome.

[26] The "cones" are, loosely, the central dome, a half-cone, plus the supporting semi-domes, which had similar profiles. The description of the semi-domes is to be inferred from that of the central dome.

INDEX

ILLUSTRATIONS

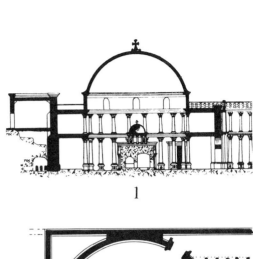

1

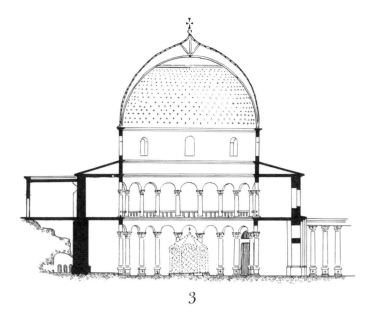

2

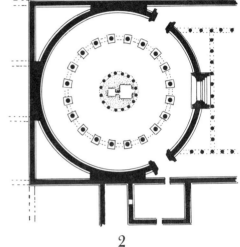

3

4

5

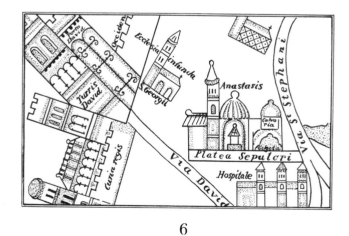

6

1. Holy Sepulchre, section, fourth century, restoration (Vincent and Abel, II, pl. XXXIII)
2. Holy Sepulchre, plan (Vincent and Abel)
3. Holy Sepulchre, section (restoration by author)
4. Holy Sepulchre, interior, seventeenth century (after drawing by de Bruyn)
5. Holy Sepulchre, c. 1400, Greek manuscript (Vincent and Abel, II, fig. 136)
6. Holy Sepulchre, c. 1150, plan of Cambrai (ibid., II, figs. 317, 387)

7. Women at the Tomb, sarcophagus, Basilica Vaticana, Rome (Garrucci, pl. 350/4)
8. Women at the Tomb, ivory book cover, National Gallery, Munich
9. Tomb of Christ, ivory book cover, Trivulzio Collection, Milan
10. Women at the Tomb, Rabula Gospels
11. Holy Sepulchre, mosaic, Madaba
12. Women at the Tomb, mosaic S. Apollinare Nuovo, Ravenna
13. "De Sepulchris," Agrimensorum Romanorum, Wolfenbüttel
14. Women at the Tomb, reliquary box, Museo Sacro, Rome
15. "City of Jerusalem," miniature (Grabar, *Les Miniatures du Grégoire de Nazianze de l'Ambrosienne*, I, pl. LII/1)

16

17

18

19

20

21

22

23

16. Entry into Jerusalem, Codex Rossanensis
17. Memorial, coin of Maximianus (Maurice, *Numismatique Constantinienne*, pl. XIX/10)
18. Memorial, coin of Maxentius struck in honor of Constantius Chlorus (*op.cit.*, pl. VII/5)
19. Memorial, coin of Divus Romulus struck after death in 309 (*op.cit.*, pl. VII/10)

20. "Tomb" of Maximianus, coin of Maxentius (*op.cit.*, pl. XIX/1, 2, 9)
21. Memorial, coin of Maxentius (*Die Antike*, XII, Abb. 25/d)
22. Shrine of Melicertes at Corinth, coin of 161-169 A.D., British Museum (Donaldson, *Architettura Numismatica*, no. 16)
23. Raising of Lazarus, gold-glass (G. Ferretto, *Note storico-bibliografiche di archeologia cristiana*, 236, fig. 401)

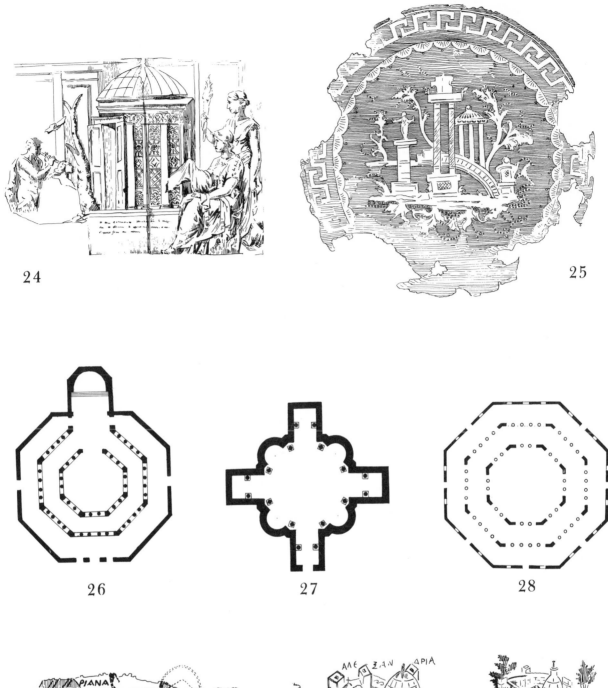

24
25

26
27
28

29

30
31

24. Symbolic tegurium, Roman relief drawn by Fra Giocondo
    (*Mél. d'archéol. et l'hist.*, XI, 1891, 136, fig. 1)
25. Funeral box cover from Tresilico, Museo di **Reggio** (Galli,
    Rivista dell' Instituto d'arch. e storico dell' arte, VI, 1937, pl.
    1)
26. *Domus aurea*, plan, Antioch
27. Martyrium, plan, Nyssa (after Keil in Strzygowski, *Klein-
    asien*, Abb. 62)

28. Martyrium, plan, Nazianzus (*op.cit.*, Abb. 63)
29. *Domus aurea* of Antioch, mosaic from Yakto (Levi, *Antioch
    Mosaic Pavements*, pl. LXXX/c)
30. City of Alexandria, mosaic from SS. Peter and Paul, Gerasa
    (*Gerasa*, pl. LXXV/a)
31. City of Alexandria, mosaic from S. John the Baptist
    Gerasa (*op.cit.*, pl. LXVII/c)

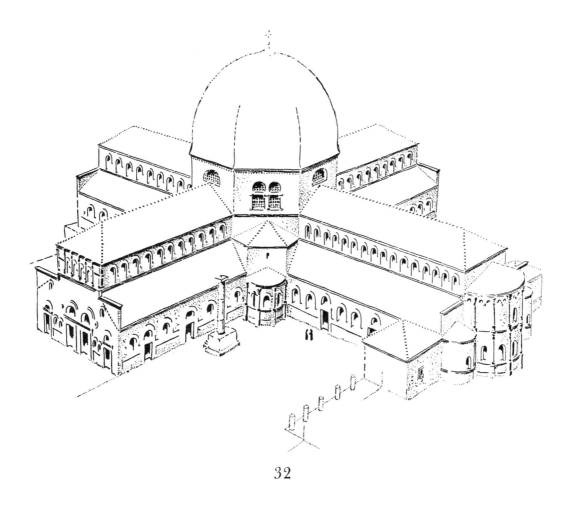

32

33

34

32. S. Simeon Stylites, Kal'at Sim'ân, exterior (after Krencker)
33. Silver paten from Stûmâ, Museum, Istanbul

34. Silver paten from Rîhā, Dumbarton Oaks Collection, Washington, D.C.

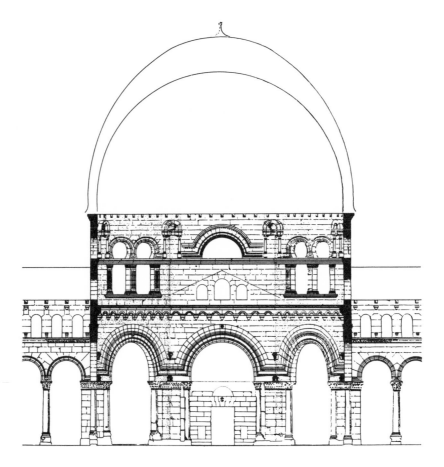

35

36

35. S. Simeon Stylites, Kal'at Sim'ân, section of octagon (after
    Krencker)
36. Church of Mahoymac, mosaic at Ma'in (De Vaux, *Rev.
    bibl.*, XLVII, pl. XIV/4)

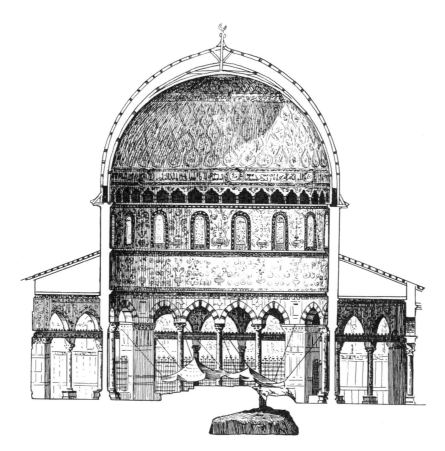

37

38

37. Dome of the Rock, section, Jerusalem (De Vogüé, *Le Temple de Jérusalem*, pl. xix)
38. Dome of the Rock, exterior (De Vogüé, *Les Églises de la Terre Sainte*, pl. xix)

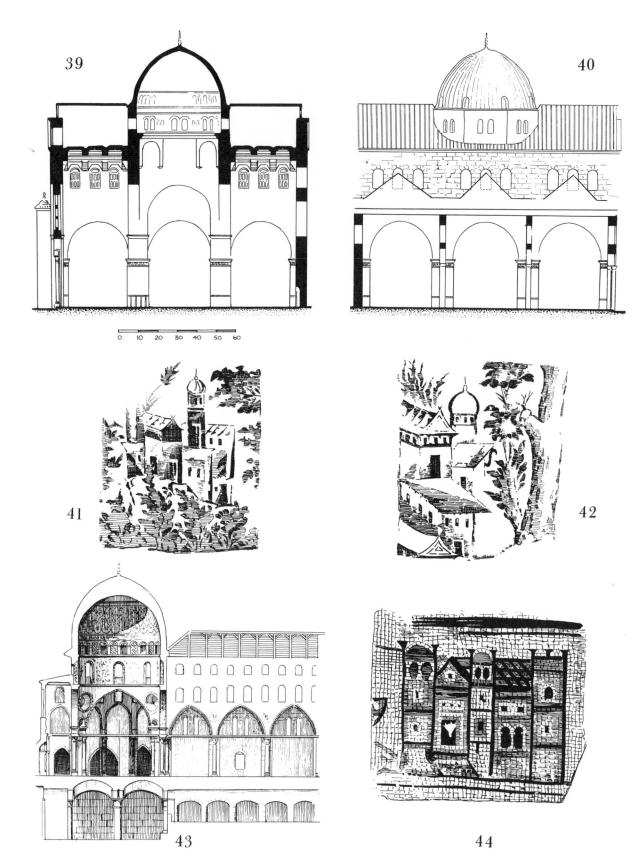

39. Great Mosque, section, Damascus (Creswell, *Early Muslim Architecture*, I, fig. 63)

40. Great Mosque, section through nave, Damascus

41. Syrian landscape, mosaic of Great Mosque, Damascus (Creswell, *op.cit.*, pl. 43/a)

42. Syrian landscape, mosaic of Great Mosque, Damascus (*ibid.*, pl. 43/b)

43. El Aksa Mosque, section, Jerusalem (De Vogüé, *Le Temple de Jérusalem*, pl. XXXI)

44. Church of S. Lot, mosaic from Khirbit Mukhayyat (Lemaire, *Rev. bibl.*, XLIII, pl. XXVI/1)

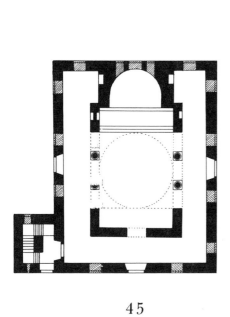

45

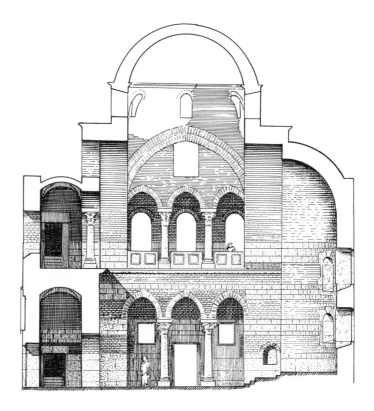

46

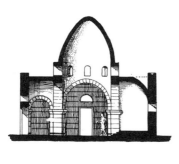
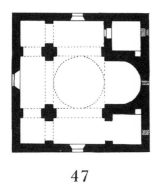

47

48

45. Church, plan, Kasr ibn Wardān (after Butler)
46. Church, section, Kasr ibn Wardān (after Butler)
47. Church No. 3, plan and section, il-Anderīn (after Butler)
48. Round Church, plan, Fa'lul (after Butler)

49a. Cathedral, section, Bosra (restored by author)
49b. Cathedral, plan, Bosra (Crowfoot, *Early Churches in Palestine*, fig. 7)
50. Martyrium of S. George, section, Zorah (De Vogüé, pl. 21/1)
51. S. George, plan, Zorah (pl. 21/2)
52. S. George, exterior in 1900, Zorah (after Butler)
53. S. George, exterior in 1936, Zorah

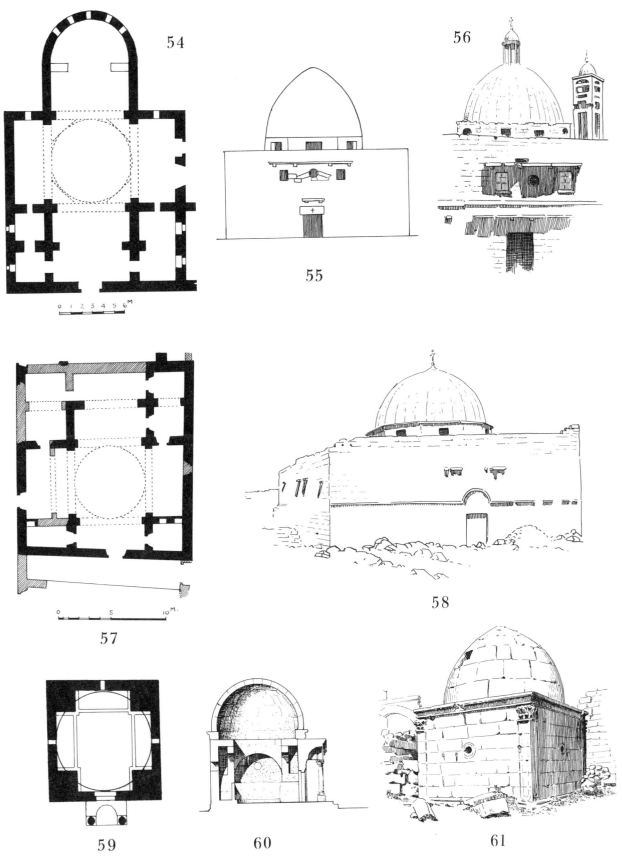

54. Martyrium of S. Elias, plan, Zorah (after Lassus)
55. S. Elias, restored elevation, Zorah (after Lassus)
56. S. Elias, exterior, Zorah (after Lassus)
57. Martyrium, plan, Chagra (after Lassus)

58. Martyrium, exterior, Chagra (after Lassus)
59. Tomb of Bizzos, plan, Ruweha (De Vogüé, pl. 91/1)
60. Tomb of Bizzos, section, Ruweha (De Vogüé, pl. 91/3)
61. Tomb of Bizzos, exterior, Ruweha

62

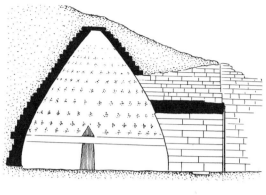

63

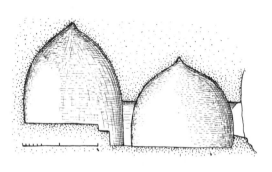

64

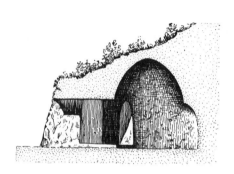

65

66

62. Neolithic tomb, Holland (Van Giffen, *Prae. Zeit.*, XIV, 1922, 52)

63. Tholos tomb of "Atreus," Mycenae

64. Rock-cut tomb, Caltagirone, Sicily (Pace, *Arte e civiltà della Sicilia antica*, I, fig. 129)

65. Etruscan rock-cut tomb, Viterbo (Rivoira, *Architettura romana*, fig. 305)

66. Tholos tomb of third century B.C., Kazanlak, Bulgaria (Verdiani, *A.J.A.*, XLIX, 1945, figs. 1-13)

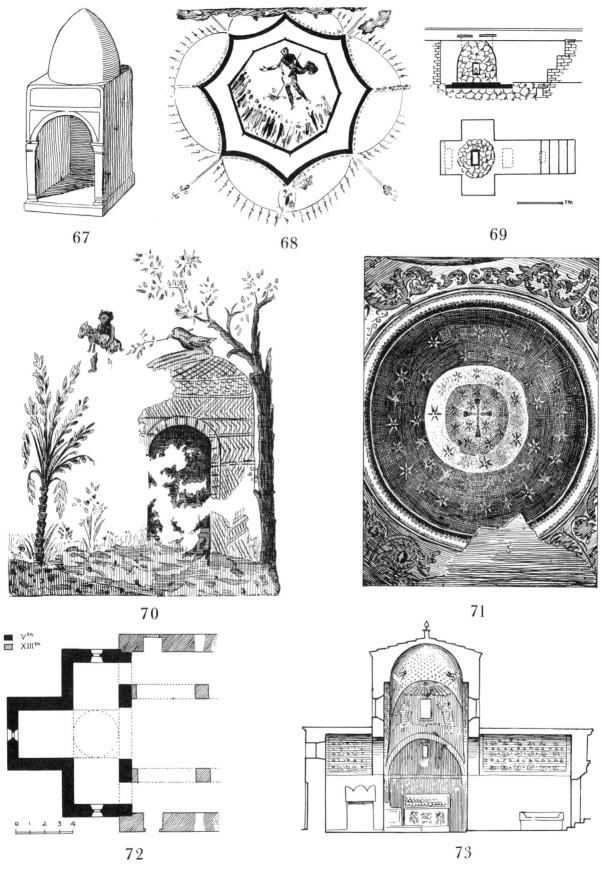

67

68

69

70

71

72

73

67. House grave-stele from La Horgne, Museum, Metz (Linckenheld, *Les Stèles funéraires en forme du maison*, fig. 19)
68. Tomb of M. Clodius Hermes, catacombs of S. Sebastiano,
Rome (Wirth, *Röm. Wandmalerei*, pl. 50)
69. Stone reliquary in crypt of S. Demetrios, Saloniki (Soteriou,
'Αρχ. 'Εφ., 1929, figs. 72-74)

70. Soul of Jonah carried to celestial tegurium, fresco, Sardinia (De Rossi, *Bull. di arch. crist.*, III, 1892, pl. VI)
71. Dome mosaic of fifth century martyrium, Casaranello, Italy
(Bartoccini, *Felix Ravenna*, 1934, fig. 19)
72. Martyrium, plan, Casaranello (*op.cit.*, fig. 6)
73. Tomb of Galla Placidia, section, Ravenna

74. Tomb stele, 'Amrith
75. Rock-cut tomb, plan, Tall Hinnom, Jerusalem (Macalister, *P.E.F., Quart. St.*, 1901, no. 38)
76. Tomb, 'Amman (Creswell, *Early Muslim Architecture*, fig. 364)

77. Ceiling rosette, Tall Hinnom, Jerusalem (*op.cit.*, no. 60)
78. Tomb, plan, Qusayr an-Nuwayis (Watzinger, *Denk. Paläs.*, Abb. 99)
79. Tomb, section, Sebastya (Creswell, *op.cit.*, fig. 386)
80. Tomb, plan, Kades (Watzinger, *op.cit.*, Abb. 8)

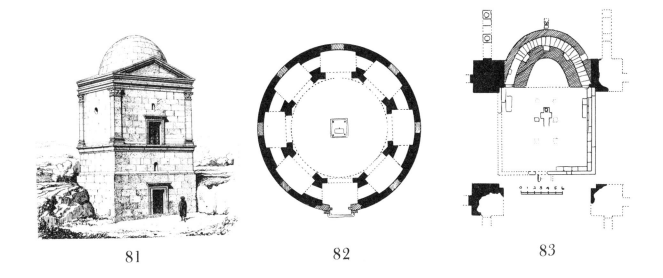

81

82

83

84

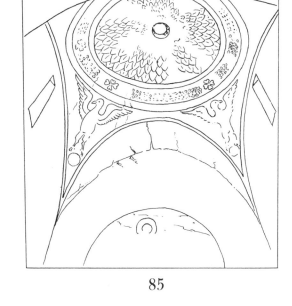

85

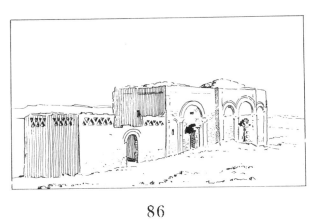

86

87

81. Tomb, Hass (De Vogüe, pl. 72)
82. Martyrium or tomb, plan, Hierapolis (Strzygowski, *Klein-asien*, fig. 293)
83. S. John, plan of original martyrium, Ephesus
84. Islamic weli, "Tomb of Rachel," Hebron

85. Dome decoration, funerary chapel, Bagawat, Egypt (W. de Bock, *Matériaux . . .* , 20, fig. 31)
86. Funerary chapels, Bagawat (Bock, *op.cit.*, 10)
87. Tomb, Kharga, Egypt (Freshfield, *Cellae Trichorae*, II, pl. 50)

88

89

90

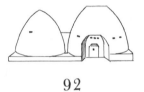

91

92

93

88. Syrian qubâb village
89. Rock-cut house forms near Utch hissar, Cappadocia
90. Rustic cabin and trees, painted sherd of fourth millennium, Arpachiyah (Mollowan and Rose, *Prehistoric Assyria*, fig. 20)

91. Syrian village, relief of Sennacherib's palace, Nineveh
92. Qubâb types (Banse, *Orientalisches Archiv.*, II, Abb. 59, 60)
93. Shrine of Nyakang, Fenikang in Nilotic Sudan

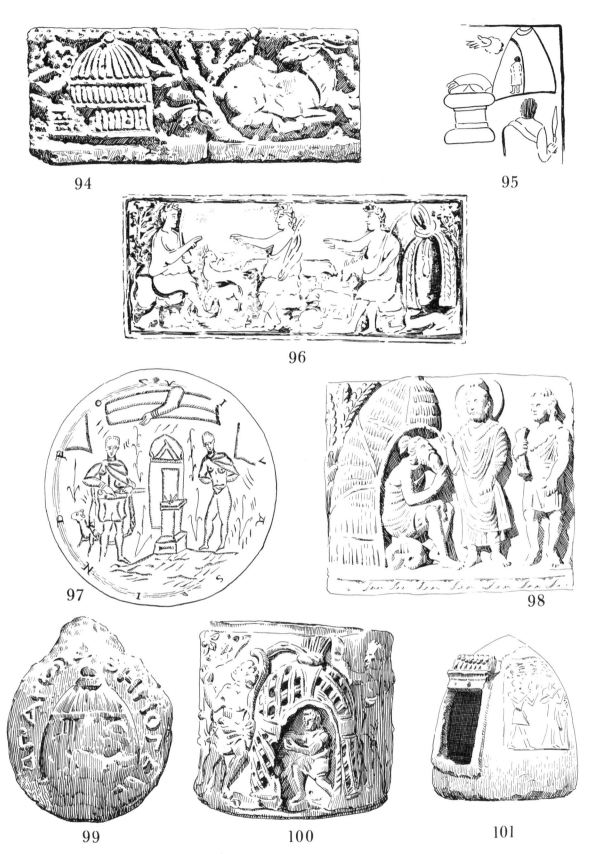

94

95

96

97

98

99

100

101

94. Paradise, relief from martyrium at Seleucia Pieria, Princeton University
95. Sacrifice of Isaac, Jewish Synagogue, Doura Europa
96. Scene from Eclogues of Virgil (*Pictura ornamenta, codicis Vaticani* 3867, Abb. 30)
97. Sacrifice of Isaac, glass medallion from Trier
98. First meeting of Gotama with Brahmanic anchorite, relief, Mardân (Foucher, *L'art gréco-bouddhique*, I, fig. 189)
99. Heavenly abode of S. Athenogenes, ampulla from Egypt, Sieglin Collection, Dresden
100. Shepherd's hut, ivory pyxis
101. Stone "naos of goldsmiths," Dynasty XX, Abydos (Roeder, *Naos,* pl. 45)

102   103   104

105   106   107

108   109   110

102. Eagle in shrine, coin of Laodicea ad mare (*Brit. Mus. Cat. Coins, Galatia, Cappodocea and Syria*, no. 111, pl. XXXI/7)

103. High priest under baldachin, Rossano Gospels (Haseloff, *Codex Rossanensis*, pl. XI)

104. Domical tent shrines over altars of Dioskouroi, coin of Sagalossa, Pisidia (Imhoof-Blumer, *Kleinasiatische Münzen*, II, pl. XIV/11)

105. Domical tent shrine, Canopus, coin of Alexandria (*Coll. Dattari*, pl. XXXIX/1132)

106. Altar of Zeus, Pergamum, coin of Septimius Severus (*Brit. Mus. Cat. Coins, Mysia*, no. 315, pl. XXX/7)

107. Domical tent shrine, Antioch in Pisidia, coin of Gordianus (Imhoof-Blumer, *op.cit.*, no. 25, pl. XII/20)

108. Portable tent shrine of Tyche, Tyre, coin of Trebonianus Gallus (*Brit. Mus. Cat. Coins, Phoenicia*, no. 437, pl. XXXIV/3)

109. Portable shrine of Tyche, Antioch, coin of Trebonianus Gallus and Volusian (*Brit. Mus. Cat. Coins, Galatia*, no. 656, pl. XXVI/5)

110. Shrine of veiled goddess, Caesarea ad Libanum (*Brit. Mus. Cat. Coins, Phoenicia*, no. 6, pl. XIII/7)

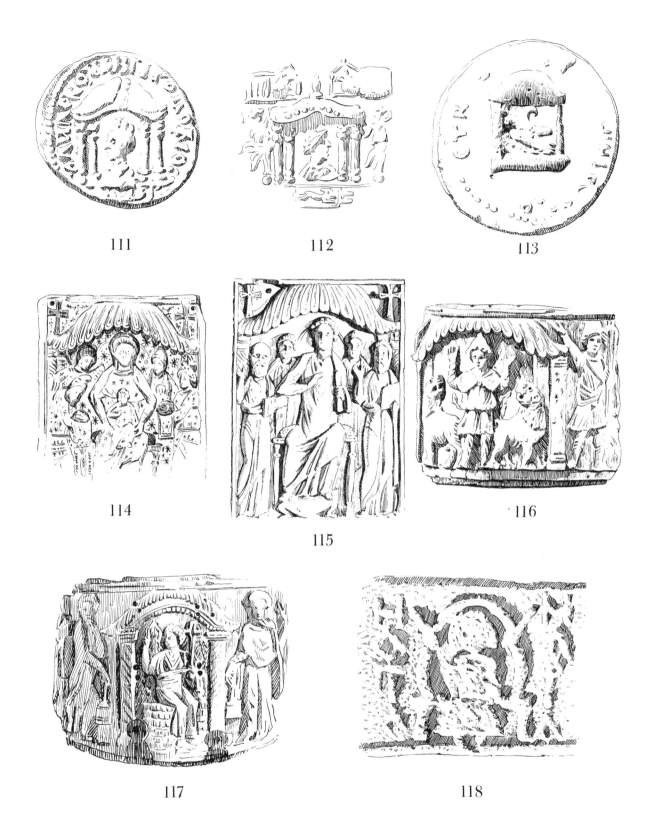

111. Domical shrine of Tyche, Damascus, coin of J. Domna
(*Brit. Mus. Cat. Coins, Galatia*, no. 11, pl. xxxiv/9)

112. Shrine of "Tyche"? Damascus (*op.cit.*, no. 26, pl. xxxv/3)

113. Eagle in domical shrine, Laodicea ad mare, coin of Caracalla and Plautilla (*ibid.*, no. 95, pl. xxx/14)

114. Celestial baldachin over Virgin and Child, ivory, John Rylands Library, Manchester

115. Baldachin over enthroned Christ, Murano book cover, Civic Museum, Ravenna

116. Daniel in lion's den, ivory pyxis, British Museum

117. Women at tomb, ivory pyxis

118. Baldachin over enthroned Virgin and Child, relief, Ruweha (Lassus, *Inventaire archéologique*, pl. xxiii/2)

119

120

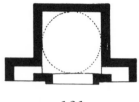

121

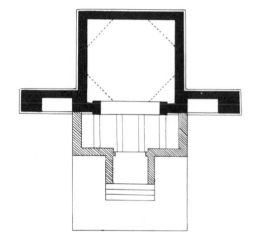

122

123

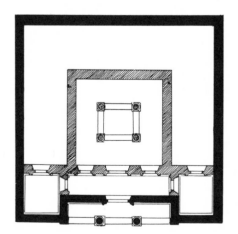

124

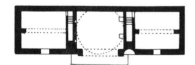

125

119. Heavenly home, basalt lintel, Queraté, Syria (Lassus, *op.cit.*, fig. 18)

120. *Kalubé* of 282 A.D., Umm-iz-Zetum (after De Vogüé with dome altered)

121. *Kalubé*, plan, Umm-iz-Zetum (De Vogüé, *Syrie centrale*, pl. 6)

122. *Kalubé*, plan, Shakka (De Vogüé, pl. 6/1)

123. Temple of Ba'al Shamin, possible restoration, Si'

124. Temple of Ba'al Shamin, plan, Si' (Butler, *Syria*, II, A, 6, ill. 335)

125. *Kalubé*, plan and elevation, il-Haiyât (Butler, *Architecture and Other Arts*, fig. 142)

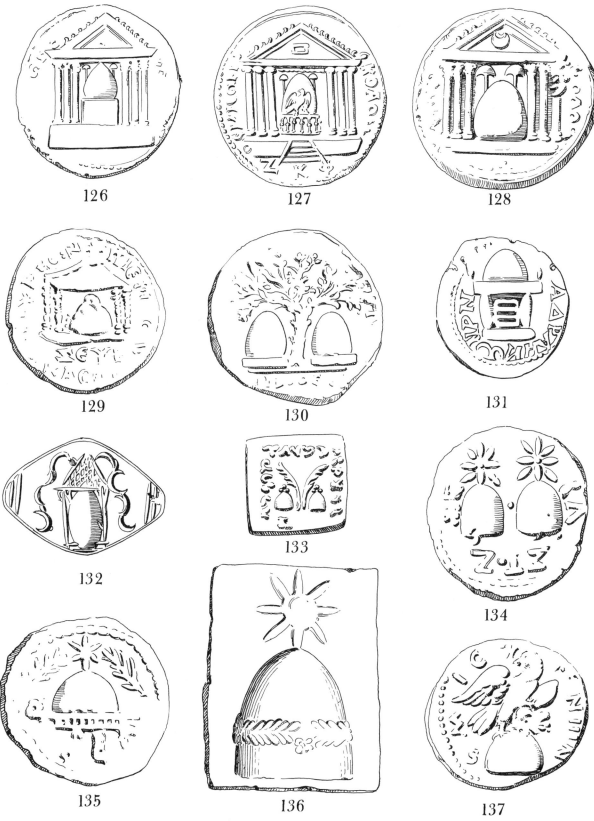

126. El-Gabel in temple, Emesa, coin of Caracalla (*Brit. Mus. Cat. Coins, Galatia,* no. 16, pl. XXVII/13)

127. El-Gabel in temple, Emesa, coin of Caracalla (*ibid.,* no. 15, pl. XXVII/12)

128. El-Gabel in temple, Emesa, coin of Uranius Antoninus *ibid.,* no. 24, pl. XXVIII/2)

129. Baetyl of Zeus Kassius in aedicula, Antioch, coin (S. A. Cook, *The Religion of Ancient Palestine,.etc.,* pl. XXX/1)

130. Conoid baetyls, Tyre, coin of Gordianus (*Brit. Mus. Cat. Coins, Phoenicia,* no. 430, pl. XXXIII/15)

131. The god Dushara, Adraa, coin of Gallienus (*Brit. Mus. Cat. Coins, Arabia,* no. 2, pl. III/5)

132. Ovoid baetyl in rustic shrine, engraved gem from Minoan Crete (Evans, *Palace of Minos,* I, fig. 494)

133. Conoid forms and tree, coin of Eucratides II of 175 B.C., India (Cambridge, *History of India,* I, pl. VIII/44)

134. Piloi of Dioskouroi, coin of Alexandria (*Coll. Dattari,* no. 54, pl. XXVIII)

135. Celestial helmet, coin of Herod I (S. A. Cook, *op.cit.,* pl. XXXIV/38)

136. Pileus of Dioskouroi, relief, Samaria (Vincent, *Rev. bibl.,* XLV, 1936, 221)

137. Eagle on conoid form, Emesa, coin of Antoninus Pius (*Brit. Mus. Cat. Coins, Galatia,* no. 6, pl. XXVII/9)

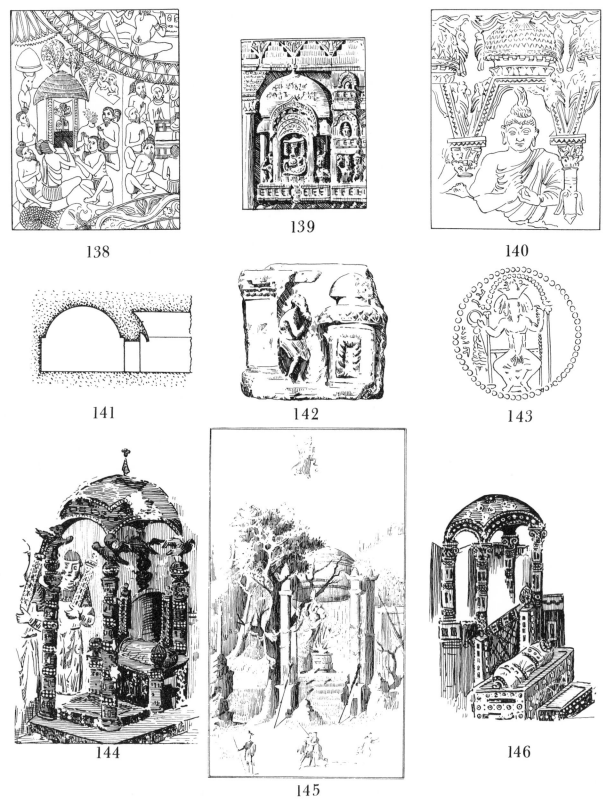

138. Buddhist fire temple, relief of stupa balustrade, Amarāvatī (Foucher, *L'Art gréco-bouddhique*, I, fig. 228)

139. Temple of the gods in the heaven of Indra, relief from Bhārhūt, Museum, Calcutta (Coomaraswamy, *History of Indian and Indonesian Art*, fig. 43)

140. Enthroned Buddha, relief, Art Museum, Seattle

141. Rock-cut sanctuary, section, Sudāma cave near Buddha Gaya (Simpson, *R.I.B.A. Transactions*, VII, fig. 118)

142. Indian fire temple, relief, Lahore Museum (Foucher, *op.cit.*, fig. 44)

143. Sassanian deity under baldachin, coin (Herzfeld, *Iran*, fig. 409)

144. Throne of Theodosius, MS grec., Paris 510, fol. 239 (Omont, *Manuscrits grecs*, pl. XLI)

145. Domical ciborium over fire altar, fresco, Domus Vesonius Primus, Pompeii (Rostowzew, *Röm. Mitt.*, XXVI, fig. 24)

146. Throne of David, MS grec., Paris 510, fol. 143 (Omont, *op.cit.*, pl. XXXIII)

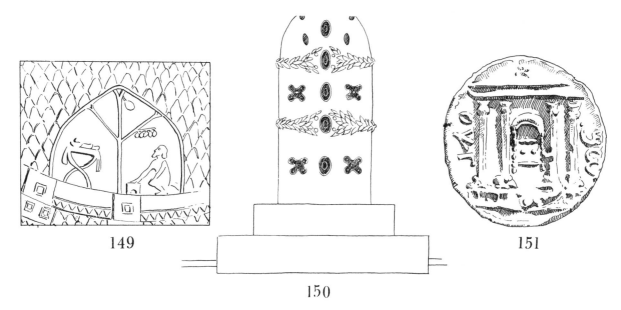

147. Pre-Islamic qobba, relief, temple of Bel, Palmyra (Seyrig, *Syria*, xv, 1934, pl. xix)

148. Audience tent of Emperor Kienling from eighteenth century engraving (Yule edition, *Marco Polo*, 1, 394)

149. "Shepherd Tent of the World"? Assyrian relief, Nineveh

150. Portable Ark, Jewish synagogue, Doura Europa (Du Buisson, *Les Peintures de la Synagogue, etc.*, pl. xxvi/3)

151. Jewish Ark in temple, coin of Second Revolt

152. Martyrium, ivory, cathedral at Trier

153. Martyrium of S. Athenogenes, ampulla from Alexandria, Museum, Berlin (Wulff, *Altchristliche und mittelalterliche Bildwerke*, 1, 1403, pl. lxix)

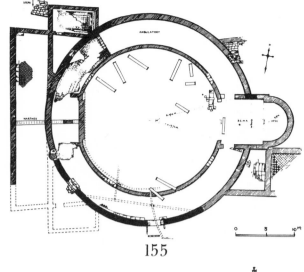

154

155

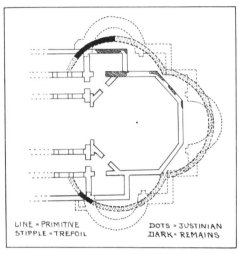

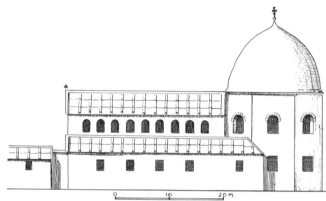

156

157

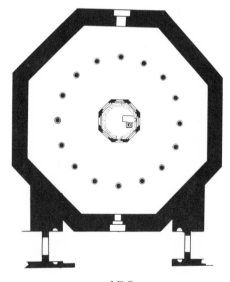

158

159

154. Dome, Hagia Sophia, Istanbul

155. Church, plan, Beisan (Fitzgerald and Nickson, *Penn. Mus. Journal*, XV, 1924)

156. Church of the Nativity, plan of excavations, Bethlehem (Vincent, *Rev. bibl.*, 1936)

157. Church of the Nativity in fourth century, Bethlehem (after Vincent with dome added)

158. Women at tomb, phial, Dumbarton Oaks Collection, Washington, D.C.

159. Church of the Ascension, plan, Jerusalem (Vincent and Abel, II, fig. 155)

160. Church of the Theotokos, plan, Garizim
161. Tomb of the Virgin, plan, Jerusalem
162. Baptistery, plan, Kal'at Sim'ân
163. Baptistery, plan, Der Setā
164. Small church, plan, Midjleyyā
165. Octagonal church, plan, Mir'âyeh
166. Holy Calvary, ampulla, S. Colombo, Bobbio (G. Celli, *Cimelli Bobbiesi*, fig. 9)

167. Martyrium of S. John the Baptist, proposed restoration, Gerasa
168. "Holy Calvary"? sixth century mosaic, Hagia Sophia, Constantinople (E. M. Antoniadi, *Hagia Sophia*, II, p. 17, fig. 201)
169. Martyrium of S. John the Baptist, 531 A.D., Gerasa (Crowfoot, *Early Churches in Palestine*, fig. 19)

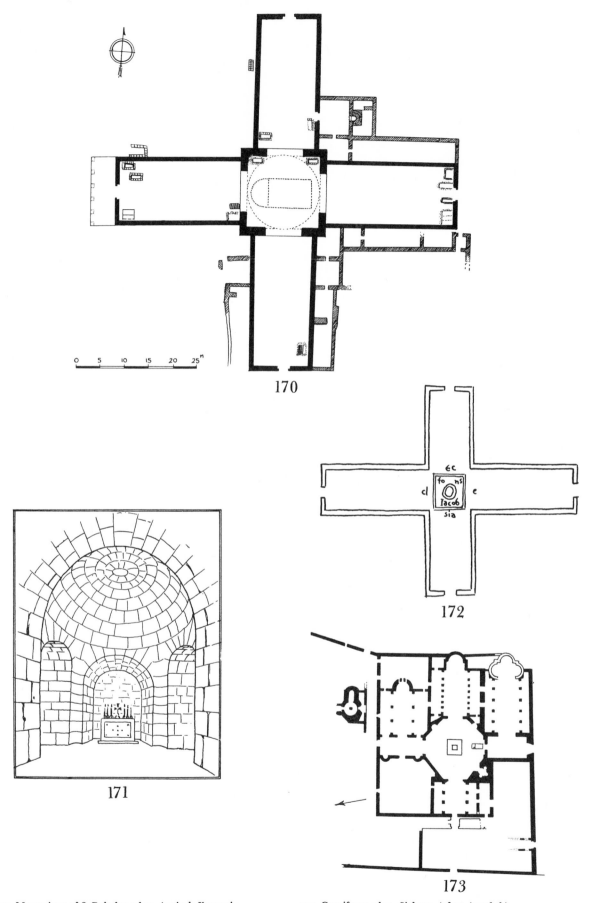

170. Martyrium of S. Babylas, plan, Antioch-Kaoussie
171. Roman cruciform tomb, "Capella del Crocifisso," Cassino

172. Cruciform plan, Sichem (after Arculph)
173. Church of S. Simeon Stylites the Younger, plan, Mt. Admirable

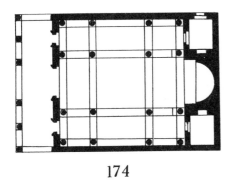

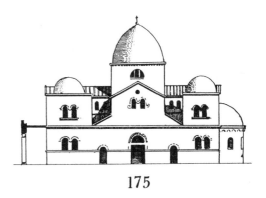

174

175

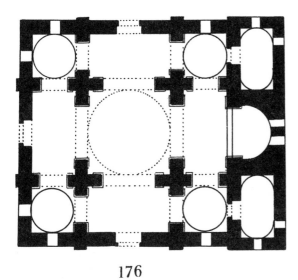

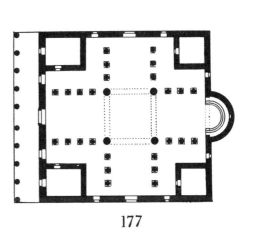

176

177

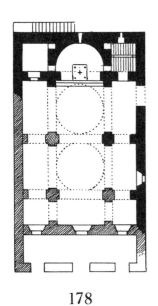

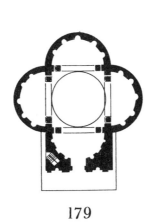

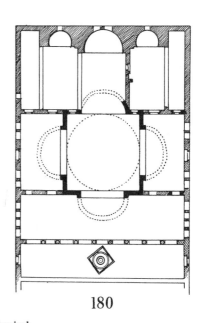

178

179

180

174. Roman Tychaion, second century A.D., Mismiyeh

175. Martyrium of the Prophets, Apostles and Martyrs, proposed restoration, Gerasa

176. "Grave church," plan, Resafa

177. Martyrium of the Prophets, Apostles and Martyrs, plan,
Gerasa (Crowfoot, *op.cit.*, fig. 8)

178. Church of 582/3 A.D., plan, it-Tûba (after Butler with
domes added)

179. Roman mausoleum, after Montano (Grabar, *Martyrium*, I,
fig. 49)

180. Martyrium, plan, Korykos, Cilicia

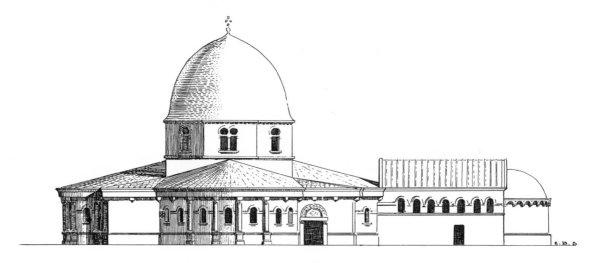

181

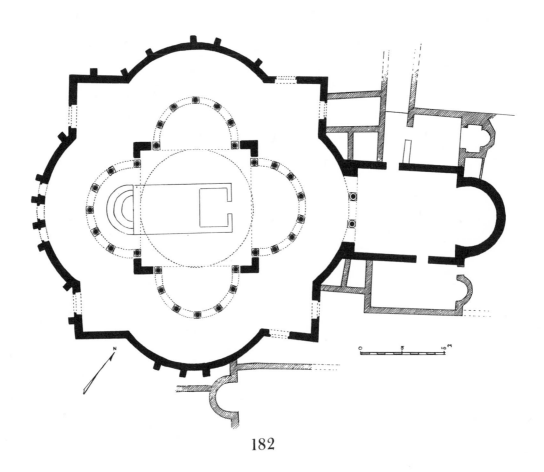

182

181. Martyrium, proposed restoration, Seleucia Pieria
182. Martyrium, plan, Seleucia Pieria

183

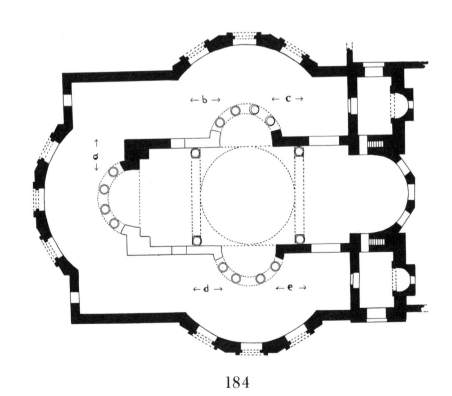

184

183. Martyrium, proposed restoration, Resafa
184. Martyrium, plan, Resafa (after Spanner and Guyer with
    dome added)

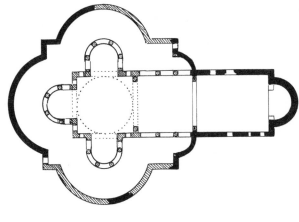

185

186

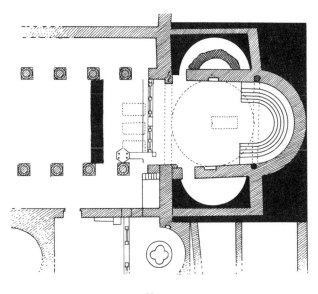

187

188

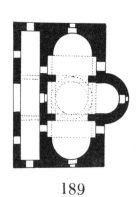

189

190

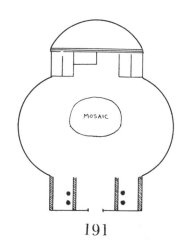

191

185. "Church of the Theotokos," plan, Amida (after Guyer with dome added)
186. Roman mausoleum, after Montano (Grabar, *op.cit.*, fig. 48)
187. Church of Siyagha, "Memorial of Moses," Mt. Nebo (after Saller with dome added)
188. Reliquary of Aachen, from Antioch

189. Martyrium of S. John the Baptist, Jerusalem (Vincent and Abel, II, pl. LXV)
190. Theodosios Church, Der Dossi (E. Weigand, *Byz. Zeit.*, XXIII, 1914-16, Abb. 2)
191. Church of the Theotokos, Madaba (Séjoune, *Rev. bibl.*, I, 1892, fig. 6)

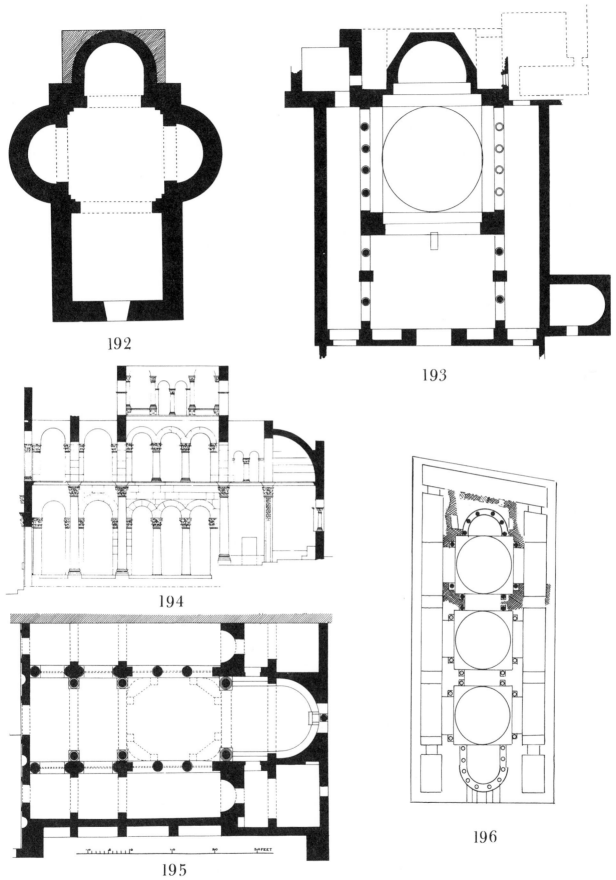

192. "Grave memorial," Ed-dschunêne (Schneider, *Oriens Christianus*, 1930)

193. Martyrium, Meriamlik

194. Church, longitudinal section, Koja Kalessi (after Headlam)

195. Church, plan, Koja Kalessi (after Headlam)

196. "Cathedral," in Madrasa al-Halawiyyah, Aleppo (after Guyer)

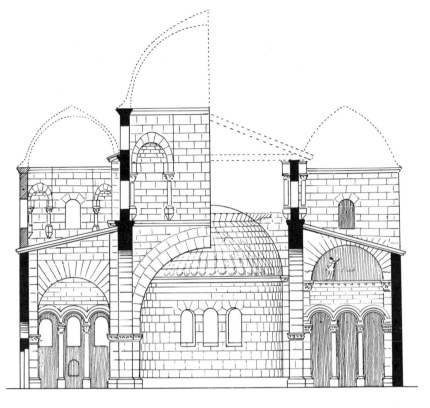

197

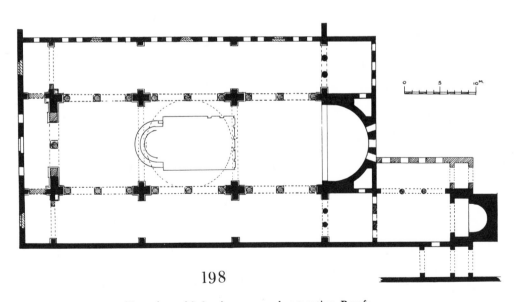

198

197. Martyrium of S. Sergius, proposed restoration, Resafa
198. Martyrium of S. Sergius, plan, Resafa (after Spanner and
Guyer, *Rusafa*, with dome added)

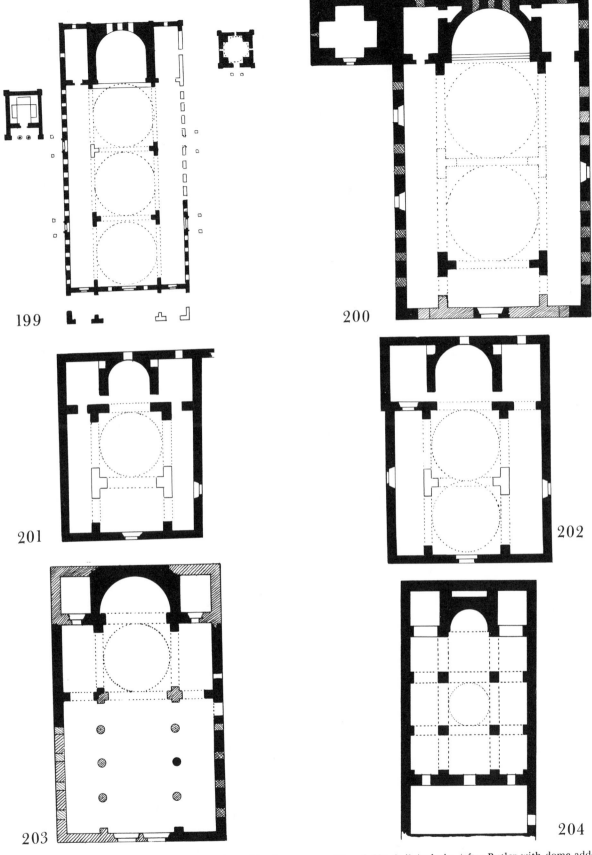

199. Church of Bizzos, Ruweha (after Butler with domes added)

200. Martyrium, or south church, il-Anderin (after Butler with domes added)

201. Church No. 7, il-Anderin (after Butler with dome added)

202. Church No. 8, il-Anderin (after Butler with dome added)

203. Church No. 1, Bosra (after Butler with dome added)

204. Church, Jericho (Schneider, *Oriens Christianus*, xxxv, 1938, Abb. 1)

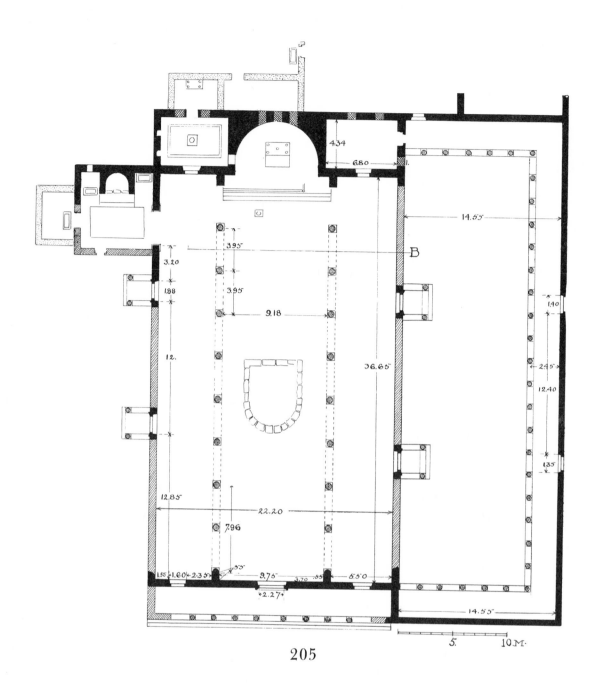

205

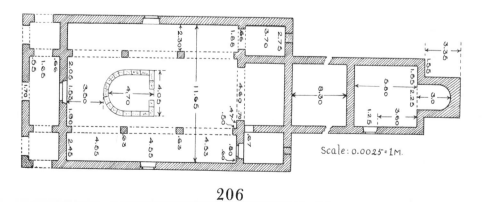

206

205. Cathedral, Brad (plan from Butler with results of Lassus' excavation added)　　206. Church, il-Firdeh (after Butler)

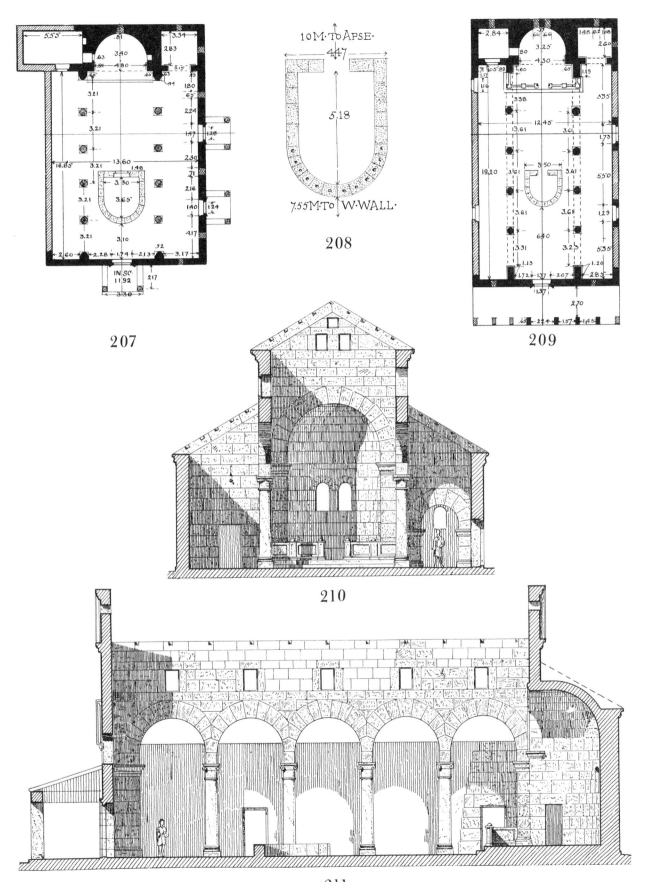

207. East church of 492 A.D., Kalôta

208. "Place of Commemoration," church at Mir'âyeh

209. Church, plan, Kharâb Shems

210. Church, cross section, Kharâb Shems

211. Church, longitudinal section, Kharâb Shems

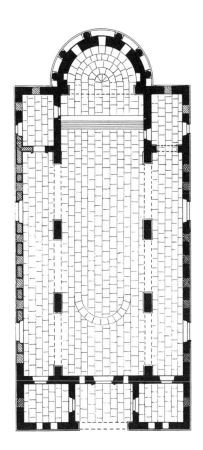

SCALE: 0.0025=1M.

212

METRI 10

213

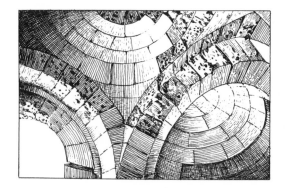

214

215

212. Church, Kalb Lauzeh
213. Church, Tolemaide, North Africa

214. Domical vault, north side-chamber, Tolemaide
215. Domical vault, south side-chamber, Tolemaide

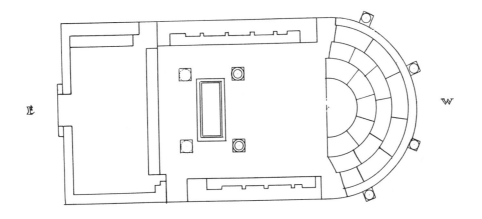

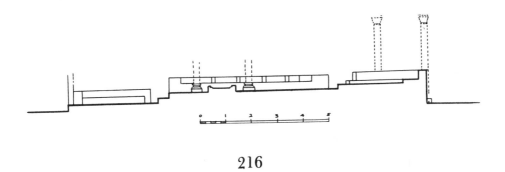

216

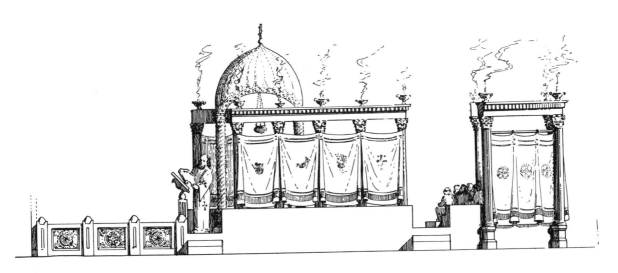

217

216. "Place of Commemoration," plan, S. Sergius, Resafa (after
    Lassus)
217. "Place of Commemoration," tentative restoration

218

219

220

221

222

223

224

225

226

227

228